Hossein Bidgoli

California State University, Bakersfield

Information Systems Literacy

DOS 6.0

Macmillan College Publishing Company
New York

Maxwell Macmillan Canada
Toronto

Maxwell Macmillan International
New York   Oxford   Singapore   Sydney

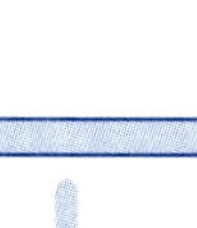

Cover art/photo: Copyright © Douglas E. Walker/Masterfile. Cover photo insets courtesy of International Business Machines Corp.

Editor: Charles Stewart
Production Editor: Louise N. Sette
Photo Editor: Chris Midgol
Art Coordinator: Peter A. Robison
Cover Designer: Russ Maselli
Production Manager: Pamela D. Bennett
Electronic Text Management: Marilyn Wilson Phelps, Matthew Williams, Jane Lopez

This book was set in New Baskerville by Macmillan College Publishing Company and was printed and bound by Von Hoffmann Press, Inc. The cover was printed by Von Hoffmann Press, Inc.

The Publisher offers discounts on this book when ordered in bulk quantities. For more information, write to: Special Sales Department, Macmillan College Publishing Company, 445 Hutchinson Avenue, Columbus, OH 43235, or call 1-800-228-7854

Macmillan College Publishing Company
866 Third Avenue
New York, New York 10022

Macmillan College Publishing Company is part of the
Maxwell Communication Group of Companies.

Maxwell Macmillan Canada, Inc.
1200 Eglinton Avenue East, Suite 200
Don Mills, Ontario M3C 3N1

Library of Congress Cataloging-in-Publication Data
Bidgoli, Hossein.
    Information systems literacy. DOS 6.0 / Hossein Bidgoli.
        p.   cm.
        Includes index.
        ISBN 0-02-309525-3
        1. Operating systems (Computers) 2. MS-DOS (Computer file) 3. PC-DOS
(Computer file) I. Title.
    QA76.76.O63B55   1994
    005.4'469—dc20   93-37705
                                                                    CIP

Printing: 1 2 3 4 5 6 7 8 9   Year: 4 5 6 7

To so many fine memories of my brother, Mohsen,
for his uncompromising belief in the power of education.

Dr. Hossein Bidgoli is professor of management information systems at California State University, Bakersfield. He holds a Ph.D. degree in systems science from Portland State University with a specialization in design and implementation of MIS. His master's degree is in MIS from Colorado State University. Dr. Bidgoli's background includes experience as a systems analyst, information systems consultant, financial analyst, and he was the Director of the Microcomputer Center at Portland State University, where the first PC Lab in the United States was started.

Dr. Bidgoli, a two-time winner of the MPPP (Meritorious Performance and Professional Promise) award for outstanding performance in teaching, research, and university/community service is the author of forty-two texts and numerous professional papers and articles presented and published throughout the United States on the topics of computers and MIS. Dr. Bidgoli has also designed and implemented over twenty executive seminars on all aspects of information systems and decision support systems.

Preface

Information Systems Literacy: DOS 6.0 is a component of a modular series of textbooks developed for use in introductory computing coursework. This DOS 6.0 text is written for first courses in operating systems, or for use in conjunction with texts in any course where an operating system tutorial is required.

Chapter 1, *The World of Microcomputers,* takes a comprehensive look at microcomputer hardware and software and their applications. This chapter offers a thorough discussion of the types of application software used today, and provides the foundation for the hands-on section of the text.

The software tutorials in this book are designed to give the student comprehensive training and reference, all organized into manageably sized chapters. This approach gives the instructor a choice as to which and how many topics to cover, and gives the student a valuable reference to use long after the class is completed. Advanced topics not covered in many texts are included here, as a growing number of students are coming into introductory courses with some software literacy; this book allows students to go further in their studies.

The software chapters are pedagogically designed with the student in mind. Features include:

- Introductory sections that explain, in basic terms, what the software is, why it was developed, and how it is used. Too many books "jump right in" without giving the student a sense of context.
- Frequent use of computer screen illustrations to augment written instruction.
- Each chapter ends with 15 to 25 review questions, 5 to 8 hands-on experience assignments, and 10 multiple choice and 10 true/false questions.
- Each chapter includes a complete summary of key terms and key computer commands.
- When appropriate, chapters include a unique section entitled "Misconceptions and Solutions." Common errors, improper operating procedures, and ways to avoid or solve them are highlighted for the student.

In any hands-on computer lab, having an accurate text makes managing the lab far easier. The best way to make a text accurate is to use it. During the six years I spent developing this text, I have received corrections and suggestions that make this book one you should find both easy to use and reliable.

Appendix A includes command summaries, as well as typical examples of AUTOEXEC.BAT and CONFIG.SYS and the most common error messages. Also, as an aid to students, answers are given to selected end-of-chapter review questions.

Appendix B provides comprehensive information about file transfer: how to export and import data files to and from the most popular software programs.

Appendix C explores Windows 3.1, the most popular graphical environment for personal computers.

Ancillaries available to instructors using this text are

- Instructor's Manual, including Test Bank, Transparency Masters, and data diskettes that enable students to access the programs and exercises included in the text. The manual also has lecture outlines, answers to review questions/exercises, and additional projects.
- Computerized Test Bank.

ACKNOWLEDGMENTS

Several colleagues reviewed different versions of this manuscript and made constructive suggestions. Without their help the manuscript could not have been refined. The help and comments of the following reviewers are greatly appreciated: Kirk Arnett, Mississippi State University; Tom Berliner, University of Texas, Dallas; Glen Boswell, San Antonio College; Michael Davis, Texas Technical University; Steve Deam, Milwaukee Area Technical College; Beth Defoor, Eastern New Mexico University, Clovis; Richard Ernst, Sullivan Junior College; Barbara Felty, Harrisburg Area Community College; Pat Fenton, West Valley College; Phyllis Helms, Randolph Community College; Mehdi Khosrowpour, Pennsylvania State, Harrisburg; Candice Marble, Wentworth Military Academy; John Miller, Williamsport Area Community College; Charles McDonald, East Texas State University; Sylvia Meyer, Community College of Vermont; J. D. Oliver, Prairie View A&M University; Greg Pierce, Penn State University; Eugene Rathswohl, University of San Diego; Herbert Rebhun, University of Houston, Downtown; R. D. Shelton, Loyola College; Sandra Stalker, North Shore Community College; G. W. Willis, Baylor University; and Judy Yeager, Western Michigan University.

I thank Stephen Brown, Gannon University; Jerry Chin, Southwest Missouri State University; Don Harris, Lincoln Land Community College; Ray Knab, Central Connecticut State University; Mable Kung, California State University-Fullerton; and Sam Wiley, LaSalle University, for reviewing the Corepack modules.

Many different groups assisted me in completing this project. I am grateful to over five thousand students who attended executive seminars and various classes in information systems and software productivity tools. They helped me fine-tune the manuscript during its various stages. My friend Bahram Ahanin helped me to improve many concepts of hardware/software and put them in a non-technical and easy-to-understand format. My colleague and friend Dr. Reza Azarmsa provided support and encouragement. I am grateful for all of his encouragement. My colleague Andrew Prestage assisted me in numerous troublespots by running and debugging many of the screens presented in the book.

I am indebted to Jacki Lawson, Denise Candia, Julie Gunn, and Vivian Cochneuer, who typed and retyped various versions of this manuscript. Their thoroughness and patience made it easier to complete this project. They deserve special recognition for all this work.

A team of professionals from Macmillan Publishing Company assisted me from the very beginning of this venture. Charles Stewart had faith in this project's potential from the onset, for which I thank him. Louise Sette, JoEllen Gohr, and Russ Maselli, all from Macmillan, assisted me in completing this project. I am grateful and appreciate their work.

Finally, I want to thank my family for their support and encouragement throughout my life. My two sisters, Azam and Akram, deserve my very special thanks and recognition. My wife, Nooshin, has been very supportive and patient. My little baby, Morvareed, has been very patient throughout this work. I extend my deepest love and appreciation to both.

Contents

C

Appendix C: A Quick Trip Through Microsoft Windows — 173

Information
Systems
Literacy

DOS 6.0

1–1   INTRODUCTION

In this chapter we discuss microcomputer fundamentals. Hardware and software for micros are described. Different classes of application software are introduced. Guidelines for successful selection and maintenance of micros are highlighted. A brief explanation of the advantages of micros compared with mainframes is presented. The chapter also includes a hands-on session with a microcomputer. The chapter concludes by defining these important concepts: computer files; types of data, values, and formulas; and priority of arithmetic operations. The information in this chapter should help you to be a more effective microcomputer user.

1–2   WHAT IS A MICROCOMPUTER?

The terms **personal computer** (PC), **micro**, or **microcomputer** refer to the smallest type of computer when measured by such attributes as memory, cost, size, speed, and sophistication. Although small, these computers are so powerful that sometimes the difference between PCs and larger computers is blurred. The reason for such confusion is the ever-increasing power and capability of PCs.

Since the beginning of the microcomputer era in roughly 1975, the capability of these computers has improved beyond imagination. Still, some experts believe this is only the beginning—there is a lot more to be done by micros.

A microcomputer consists of input, output, and memory devices. Figure 1–1 illustrates a typical microcomputer system. The **input device** is usually a keyboard. A PC keyboard is similar to a typewriter but with some additional keys. Figure 1–2 displays an IBM enhanced keyboard and a standard keyboard. In the future, voice input devices may be part of the system. Other input devices include a mouse, touch technology, light pen, graphics tablet, optical character reader (OCR), magnetic ink character recognition (MICR), camera, sensor, and bar code readers.

The common output devices for microcomputers are a cathode-ray tube (CRT) monitor, sometimes called video display terminal (VDT), and the printer. The

Figure 1–1
Typical microcomputer system (courtesy of Radio Shack, a division of Tandy Corp.).

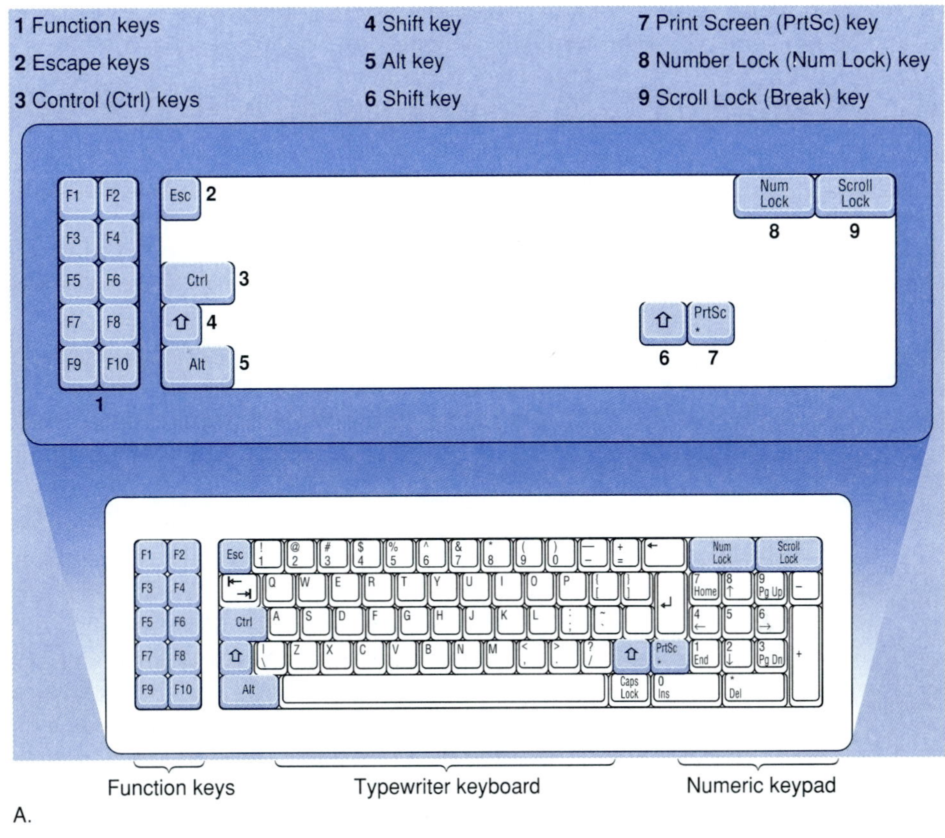

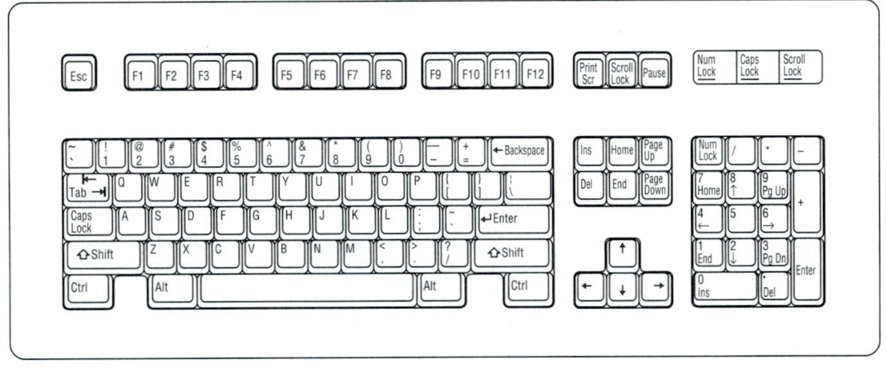

Figure 1–2
A. IBM standard keyboard. B. IBM enhanced keyboard (courtesy of International Business Machines Corp.).

output generated on the monitor is called soft copy and printed output is referred to as hard copy. Other output devices include cameras, floppy disks, and plotters.

Two types of monitors display output. Some microcomputers utilize a monochrome-type screen. As the name indicates, this type of screen generates one color, such as green, although some screens are amber (orange). Either type of monochrome monitor can generate graphic output if accompanied by a graphics card or graphics adapter. The other type of monitor is called a color monitor (sometimes referred to as an **RGB** monitor—red-green-blue monitor). It shows data in a color format.

The sharpness of images on the display monitor is referred to as resolution. The intersection of a row and a column is called a pixel. The higher the number of these pixels, the higher the resolution. Color monitors come in various levels of resolution such as CGA, EGA, VGA, super VGA, and XGA:

- A color graphics adapter (CGA) displays 320-by-200 (pixels) resolution in 4 colors
- An enhanced graphics adapter (EGA) displays 640-by-350 resolution in 16 colors. More advanced versions of EGA display 640-by-480 resolution in 16 colors and 320-by-200 resolution in 256 colors.
- A video graphics array (VGA) displays 640-by-480 resolution in 16 colors and 320-by-200 resolution in 256 colors. Super VGA and XGA monitors display more than 640-by-480 resolution in many different colors. The exact resolution depends on the specific type of the monitor.

The processing part of a microcomputer, that is its **central processing unit** (CPU) or microprocessor, includes three components:

1. **Main memory** stores data, information, and instructions.
2. **Arithmetic logic unit** (ALU) performs arithmetic and logical operations. Arithmetic operations include addition, subtraction, division, and multiplication. Logical operations include any types of comparisons, such as sorting (putting data into a particular order) or searching (choosing a particular data item).
3. **Control unit** serves as the commander of the system. It tells the microcomputer what to do and how to do it.

Figure 1–3 illustrates two different microprocessor chips, or microchips, which contain the electronic components necessary for processing.

Microcomputers are getting smaller but more powerful. Among the various types are portable (laptop) micros and notebook micros (see Figure 1–4).

A.

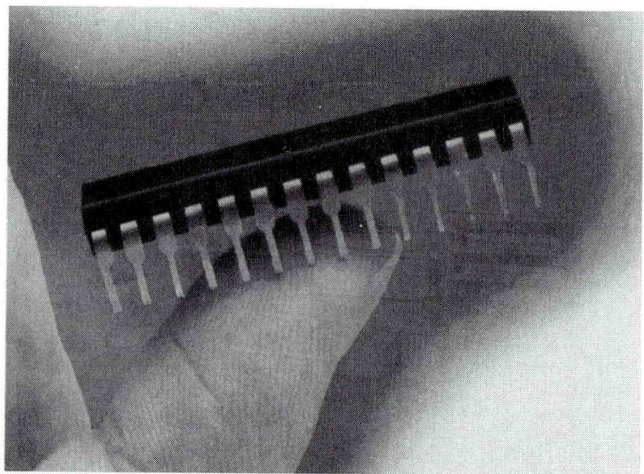

B.

Figure 1–3
A. Motorola MC 68020 microprocessor in its protective ceramic package (courtesy of Motorola, Inc.).
B. AT&T Bell Labs microprocessor (courtesy of Radio Shack, a division of Tandy Corp.).

A.

B.

Figure 1–4
A. The all-in-one design of the Apple Macintosh Portable integrates the CPU, Active Matrix Liquid Crystal Display, keyboard, pointing device, battery and disk storage into a single easy-to-carry package. B. With the Macintosh PowerBook computer, customers can take advantage of notebook convenience and Macintosh power anywhere, whether at home, school or on the road for business (courtesy of Apple Computer, Inc.).

1–3   THE KEYBOARD

As you can see in Figure 1–2B, an enhanced keyboard is divided into three sections. On the top are 12 function keys. In a standard keyboard, there are only 10 function keys. Some keyboards have the function keys on the left (Figure 1–2A). With most application software, these keys perform special functions, or they can be programmed to perform a particular task. For example, Lotus 1-2-3, Quattro Pro, dBASE, and WordPerfect effectively use 12 keys (F1 through F12) for performing different tasks.

The middle part of the keyboard is similar to a typical typewriter. However, notice some special keys that a typewriter does not have (e.g., the Alt key).

The right section has a numeric key pad similar to that of an adding machine. It is used to facilitate numeric data entry (when the Num Lock key is pressed down) or for cursor movement.

The purpose of function keys and some of the special keys varies in different application programs. For example, F1 in WordPerfect 5.1 cancels a selection or performs "undelete" operations. In Lotus 1-2-3, Quattro Pro, or dBASE, it accesses the online help command.

1–4   IMPORTANT AUXILIARY DEVICES

Besides the obvious input/output devices, some additional devices are required for effective utilization of a microcomputer. Disk drives and adapter cards are two of the most important devices.

1–4–1   Disk Drives

Disk drives enable the microcomputer system to retrieve data from a disk into main memory and to store data from main memory to a disk. Disk drives come in various capacities. Your system may have one or more floppy disk drives. It may also have a hard disk drive. As you will see later, **hard disks** are capable of storing masses of information. The capacity of a hard disk is many times greater than that of a **floppy disk** (also called a diskette or just a floppy). A floppy disk can hold from 360 kilobytes (K) to 1.44 megabytes (MB) of data. Some new floppies are capable of storing 2.88 MB. The capacity of a hard disk varies from 5 to 600 MB or more.

The capacity of a storage device is measured in terms of bits or bytes of data stored on that device. Table 1–1 summarizes the memory equivalents.

1–4–2   Adapter Cards

Adapter cards are installed in expansion slots (channels) inside the computer (see Figure 1–5). These cards are used to attach a particular option to the system unit. Table 1–2 summarizes typical adapter cards.

Table 1–1
Memory Equivalents

0 or 1 is equal to one bit

8 bits is equal to one byte

1,024 (2^{10}) bytes is equal to one kilobyte

1,048,576 (2^{20}) bytes is equal to one megabyte

1,073,741,824 (2^{30}) bytes is equal to one gigabyte

10,995,627,776 (2^{40}) bytes is equal to one terabyte

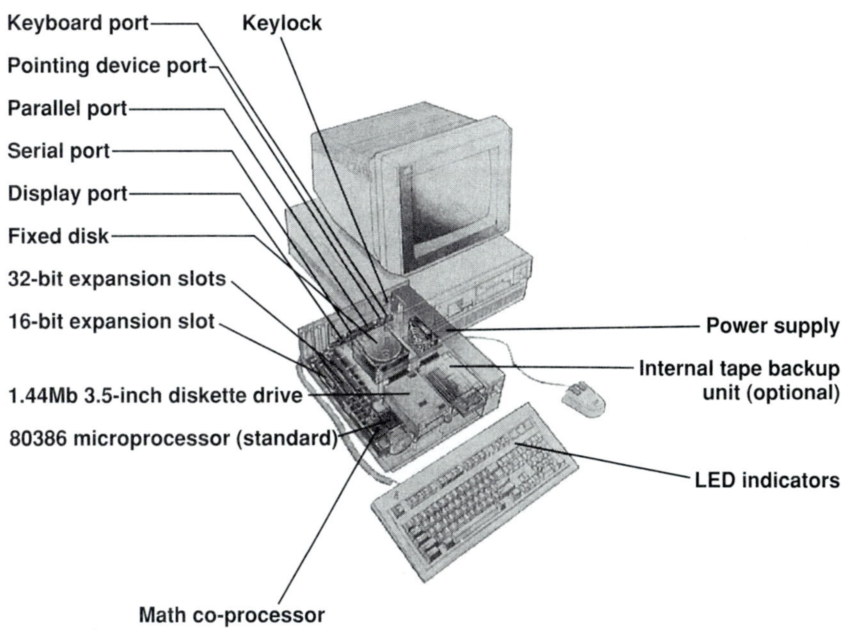

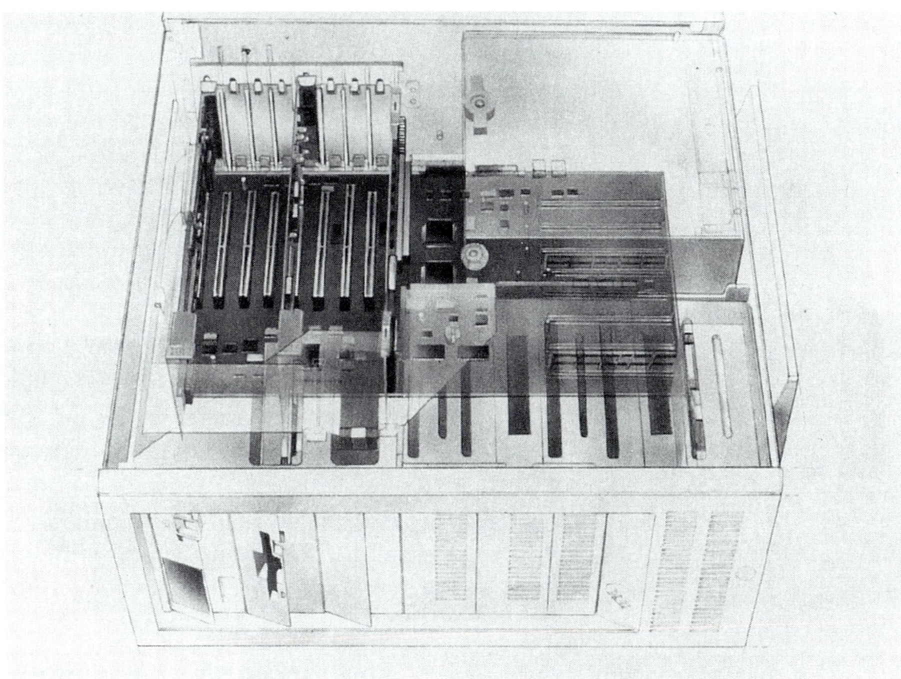

Figure 1–5
Inside your PC. A. Port and expansion slots in a microcomputer (courtesy of International Business Machines Corp.). B. Inside a microcomputer. This model is IBM's PS/2 95XP 486 (courtesy of International Business Machines Corp.).

Table 1–2
Commonly Used Adapter Cards

- Disk drive card for connecting disk drives to the system unit
- Display card for connecting the CRT to the system unit
- Memory card for connecting additional RAM to existing memory
- Clock card for connecting a clock to the system unit
- Modem card for connecting the PC to the outside world
- Printer interface card for connecting a printer to the system unit

The original IBM PC has five expansion slots; the IBM XT and AT have eight slots. Adapter cards usually have outlet ports that are accessed at the back of the system unit. It is important to know that the newer PCs do not require as many adapter cards. Ports, which are either parallel or serial, connect devices to the system unit. You must connect a serial device to a serial port and a parallel device to a parallel port. Serial devices transfer one bit of data at a time; parallel devices transfer a series of bits of data at a time.

1–5 TYPES OF PRIMARY MEMORY

Computers store data in two kinds of memory: main, or primary memory, and auxiliary, or secondary memory. **Primary memory** is the heart of the microcomputer; it is usually referred to as **random-access memory** (RAM). This is a volatile memory. Data stored in RAM will be lost in the event of a power failure. To avoid this type of loss, always save your work on a permanent memory medium (i.e., secondary memory), such as a diskette.

Three other types of memory also can be referred to as main memory, but the user cannot have direct control over them:

1. **Read-only memory** (ROM): A prefabricated ROM chip is supplied by vendors. This memory stores some general-purpose instructions or programs. For example, some commands of the Disk Operating System (DOS) and some versions of the BASIC language are stored on ROM chips. DOS is the operating system for IBM microcomputers and compatible systems.
2. **Programmable read-only memory**: By using a special device, the user can program this memory. However, once programmed, the user cannot erase this type of memory.
3. **Erasable programmable read-only memory**: This type of read-only memory can be programmed by the user and, as the name indicates, erased and programmed again.

1–6 CONVENTIONAL, EXPANDED, AND EXTENDED MEMORIES

With the introduction of 386- and 486-based computers and the Pentium (the new high-powered microprocessor introduced by Intel), two new types of main memory have entered the market and have made the memory discussion even more confusing. The next few paragraphs briefly describe these two new memories and differentiate them from conventional memory.

Conventional memory, or RAM, is the first 640 K of the memory of your computer. The majority of XT-type machines come with 1 MB of memory; however, DOS can only directly reach the first 640 K of this memory. The other 384 K (1024 K–640 K) is used (as shown in Figure 1–6) by ROM BIOS (Basic Input Output System), adapter ROM, video memory, and the EMS (Expanded Memory Specification) window.

Expanded memory is located outside of the conventional memory and works based on a technique called bank switching. Lotus, Intel, and Microsoft (LIM) corporations devised the LIM Expanded Memory Specification (EMS) for expanded memory. This is like a memory storage area on an EMS-compatible expansion card inside your computer. To utilize expanded memory on your computer, you need both an EMS-compatible memory expansion card and a device driver known as Expanded Memory Manager (EMM). The EMM helps the microprocessor find a page(s) of data that your software is looking for and puts the data into a 64-K page frame as four 16-K pages. DOS can then locate the data, and your software program can use it. Expanded memory is useful for designing large spreadsheets.

Extended memory is also outside of conventional memory, but it functions basically as additional RAM and is accessible to your computer directly. No bank switching occurs with extended memory. This means that after DOS addresses the first 640 K of conventional memory, it then automatically accesses the next chunk of the memory, which is the extended memory (see Figure 1–6). A 286-based PC can access up to 16 MB of RAM, and 386- and 486-based PCs can access up to 4,096 MB of RAM.

Which memory should you get, expanded or extended? Well, the software in use dictates the type of memory. Earlier software requested expanded memory. Today's graphical environments, such as Windows, prefer extended memory. In fact, your additional memory can be configured either way using special software.

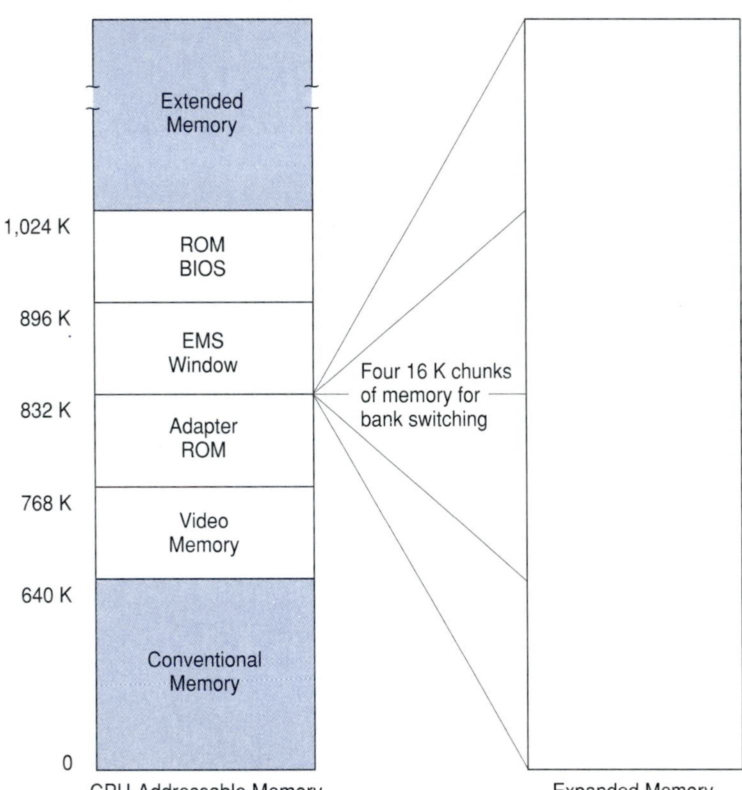

Figure 1–6
Conventional, extended, and expanded memories.

1–7   TYPES OF SECONDARY MEMORY

Since the main memory of a microcomputer is limited, expensive, and volatile, **secondary memory** storage devices are needed for mass data storage. Secondary storage is nonvolatile. Secondary storage devices are broadly classified into magnetic and optical. Let us briefly consider each group.

1–7–1   Magnetic Storage Devices

Magnetic storage devices include the diskette, mini floppy, hard disk, and Bernoulli box. The capacity of a diskette or a hard disk depends on its technical features.

There are three types of standard diskettes: 3½ inches, 5¼ inches, and 8 inches. The most recent floppy disk is a 2-inch floppy. Diskettes can be single density, double density, or high density. Density refers to the amount of information that can be stored on a disk. Diskettes can also be single sided or double sided. A 5¼-inch, single-sided, single-density floppy can hold roughly 125 K; a 5¼-inch, single-sided, double-density floppy can hold roughly 250 K; a 5¼-inch, double-sided, double-density floppy can hold roughly 360 K; a high-density (sometimes called quad-density) diskette can hold up to 1.2 MB. A 3½-inch, low-density floppy disk can store 720 K of data and a 3½-inch, high-density floppy can store 1.44 MB of data.

A hard disk (also called fixed disk or Winchester disk) can be 14, 8, 5¼ or less than 4 inches in diameter. The capacity of this device varies from 5 MB to 1 gigabyte.

A **Bernoulli box** is a removable medium. After finishing your computer work, you can pull this device out and store it in a safe location, which is not possible with a hard disk. A Bernoulli box uses high-capacity floppy disks to store 10 MB of data or more. Generally speaking, it is less prone to damage than a hard disk. This is true because the drive head of a Bernoulli box does not move as a hard disk head moves, often resulting in head crashes. In a Bernoulli box, the floppy disk moves toward the stationary read/write head through air currents. Figure 1–7 displays a Bernoulli box.

At the present time, the most commonly used secondary storage device is a 3½-inch floppy disk. However, at the beginning of the PC era, 5¼-inch floppy

Figure 1–7
A Bernoulli box.

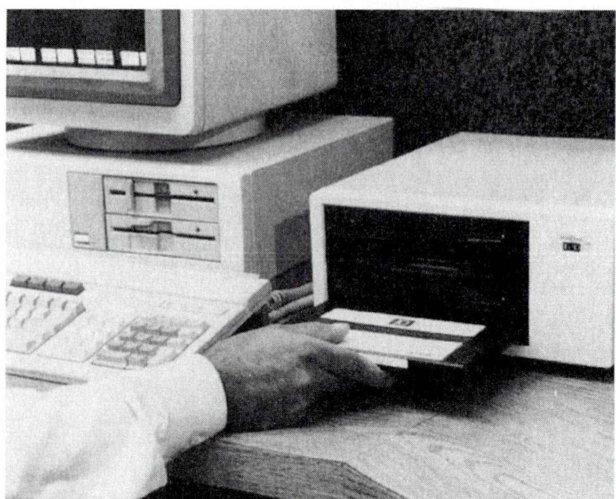

Figure 1–8
A 5¼-inch floppy disk.

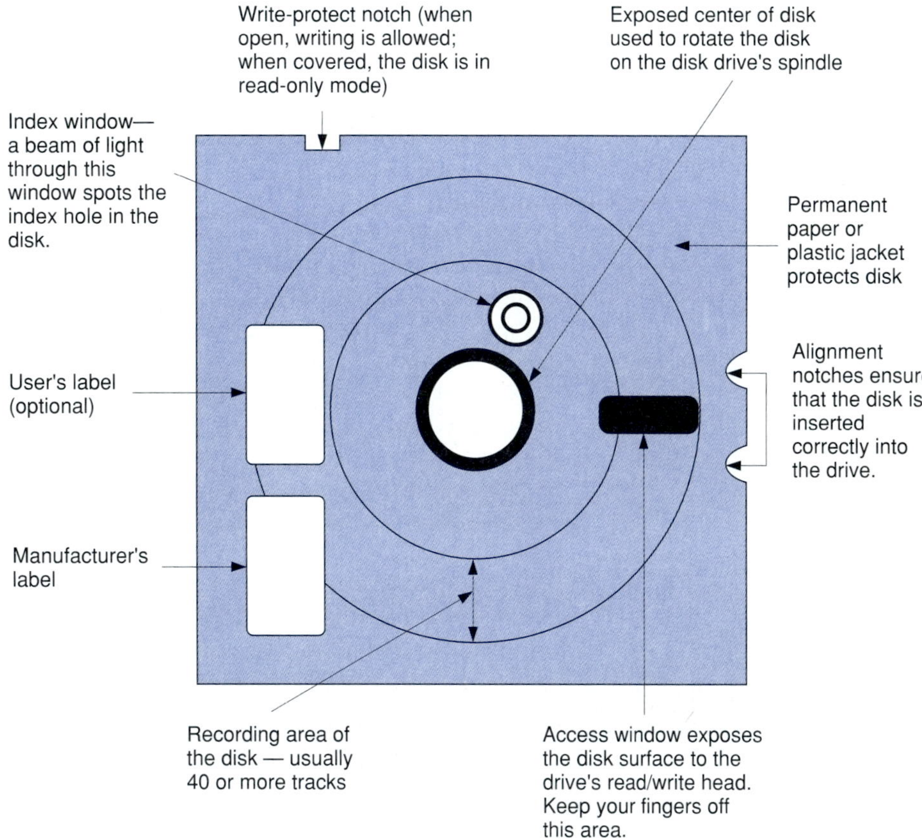

disks were the most commonly used secondary storage devices. A floppy disk is made of plastic material coated with magnetic material. A 5¼-inch disk is enclosed in a permanent vinyl jacket to protect the disk. After using a floppy disk, you should put it back in its paper cover to protect it from dirt and dust. Do not touch exposed portions of the disk or data loss may result. Figure 1–8 highlights important areas of a 5¼-inch diskette. Figure 1–9 displays a 3½-inch diskette. The 3½-inch diskettes are more durable and easier to handle than the 5¼-inch disks. They also store more information.

Figure 1–9
A 3½-inch floppy disk.

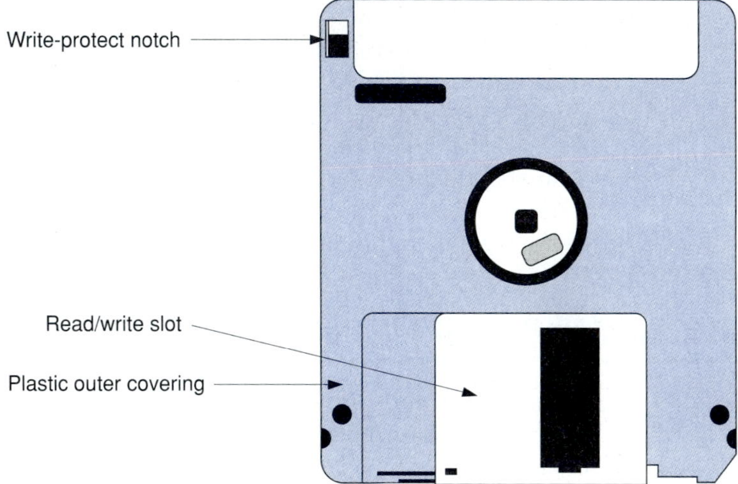

1–7–2   Optical Storage Technologies

Three types of optical storage have attracted much attention in recent years: CD-ROM, WORM, and erasable optical disk. The major advantages of optical technology devices are durability and massive storage capacity. The major drawback of optical technology is its slow speed; however, vendors are working rapidly to improve the technology. Let us briefly look at each type.

CD-ROM (compact disk, read-only memory), as the name indicates, is a permanent medium. In CD ROM, information is recorded by disk-mastering machines. A CD-ROM, which is similar to an audio compact disk, can be duplicated and distributed throughout an organization. Its major application is for large, permanent databases, for example, public domain databases such as libraries, real estate information, and corporate financial information.

A **WORM** (write once, read many) disk is also a permanent medium. Information can be recorded once and cannot be altered. A major drawback compared with CD-ROM is that you cannot duplicate a WORM disk. Its major application is for storing information that must be kept permanently, for example, information related to annual reports, nuclear power plants, airports, and railroads.

An **erasable optical disk** meets the needs of high-volume storage and updating. Information can be recorded and erased repeatedly.

Figure 1–10 illustrates each of the three types of optical storage.

1–8   MEMORY CAPACITY AND PROCESSOR SPEED

Microcomputer RAM capacity used to start at 512 or 640 K. Now PCs with capacities of 4 to 16 MB are becoming more common, and in the future, micros will approach minicomputer capacity.

For present and future planning, you should be able to calculate the memory requirements for your computing needs. For example, if you have a PC with 640 K of RAM, all of that memory may not be accessible to you. A large portion of that memory may be needed by software you use to carry out applications. As an example, Lotus Release 2.01 needs almost 200 K of RAM. So in your 640-K PC, you are left with only 440 K of memory to use (640 – 200 = 440).

Another consideration regarding memory is speed. The speed of the processor is measured in megahertz (MHz) and usually varies from 4 to 66. Vendors are rapidly extending this technology also. Soon, speeds of 100 MHz or more will be available. The higher the processor speed, the faster the computer.

Another factor that has direct impact on speed is the word size of the processor. Word size indicates the number of characters that can be processed simultaneously. Word size varies from 8 to 32 bits for microcomputers. The bigger the word size, the faster the computer.

The speed of your microcomputer may have a direct impact on your business operation. With a faster computer, you can process more information in a shorter period of time. However, always consider the additional cost incurred by buying a more powerful PC and the marginal benefit to be gained.

1–9   GENERAL CAPABILITIES OF MICROCOMPUTER SOFTWARE

A microcomputer can perform a variety of tasks by using either commercial software or software developed in-house. In-house developed software is usually more expensive than commercial software. However, software developed in-house

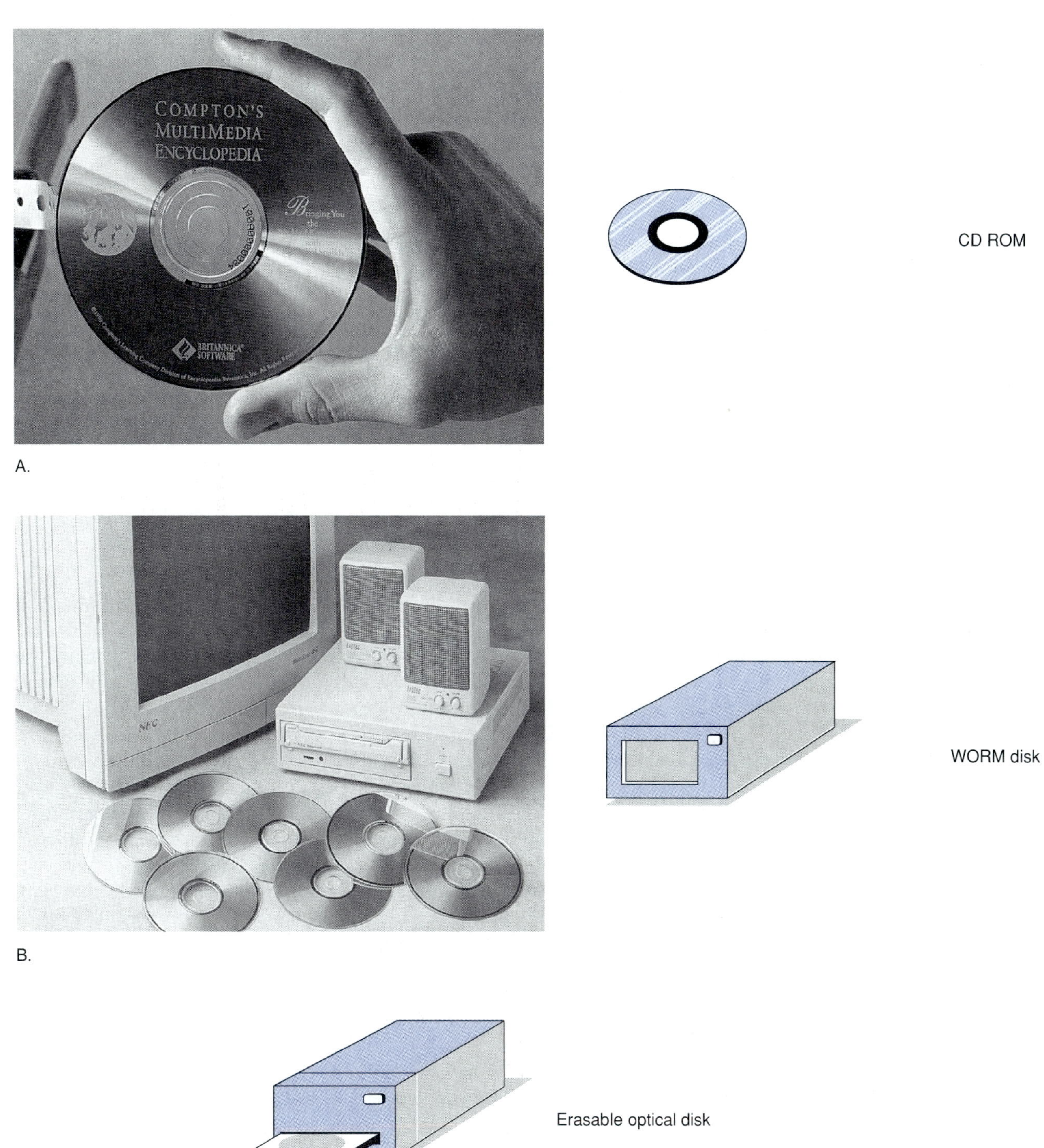

Figure 1–10

Optical storage devices for microcomputers. A. Close-up of CD-ROM (courtesy of Radio Shack, a division of Tandy Corp.). B. Disks and disk drive B (courtesy of NEC). C. Erasable optical disk.

is more customized and should better fit users' needs. Several thousands of software packages are available for PCs. For any task that can apply to several users, there is a software package on the market. The following are typical commercial packages and applications available for microcomputers.

1–9–1   Word Processing Software

A microcomputer that functions as a word processor is similar to a typewriter with a memory. With such a facility, you can generate documents, make deletions and insertions, and cut and paste. **Word processing software** is becoming more sophisticated. Some of the programs now provide limited graphics and data management features. Word processing programs allow users to save hundreds of hours by not typing the same document repeatedly. For example, organizations do not need to retype the letter that is sent to many of their customers. They need only change the names and addresses in the letters. Numerous word processing programs fill the marketplace. Some of the popular ones are WordPerfect (WordPerfect Corp.), Word (Microsoft Corporation), AmiPro (Lotus Development Corporation), and Wordstar (MicroPro International Corporation).

1–9–2   Grammar Checker Software

The ever-increasing speed and memory of microcomputers are promoting a new type of software. Most word processors now include spelling checkers, which are able to correct most of the typos in a document. The next challenge is the creation of documents that include correct verbs, subjects, adjectives, and a smooth style. Also, the creation of simple, easy-to-read, and simple sentences is of prime importance. **Grammar checker software** promotes good writing techniques.

Grammar checkers perform text analyses through linguistic analysis, parsing, and rule matching. Parsing means simply breaking long sentences into shorter ones. More sophisticated software includes more sophisticated parsers. Grammar checkers play an especially important role when multiple authors are involved in a project. In such cases, grammar checkers help create uniformity of tone, level, style, and usage. Grammar checkers are not 100 percent perfect yet, but they have come a long way. Among the more popular grammar checkers are Grammatik Windows and Grammatik IV (Reference Software International), PowerEdit (Artificial Linguistics, Inc.), and Correct Grammar for DOS (Writing Tools Group, Inc.).

1–9–3   Spreadsheet Software

A spreadsheet is a table of rows and columns. **Spreadsheet software** can be broadly classified into two types. One type is a dedicated spreadsheet; this means the program performs only spreadsheet functions. The other type of spreadsheet package can perform more than one type of function. Lotus 1-2-3, for example, is capable of performing spreadsheet functions as well as database and graphics functions. Other popular spreadsheet packages include Symphony (Lotus), Excel (Microsoft), SuperCalc (Computer Associates International, Inc.), and Quattro Pro (Borland International).

The number of jobs that can be performed by a spreadsheet program is unlimited. Generally speaking, any application suitable for analysis by row and column is a candidate for a typical spreadsheet. For example, say you decide to use a spreadsheet to prepare a budget. As soon as you have completed your budget, you can perform some impressive what-if analysis. This means you can manipulate variables on the spreadsheet. For example, reduce your income by 2 percent and direct the spreadsheet to calculate the effect of this change on other items in the spreadsheet.

1–9–4   Database Software

Database software is designed to perform database operations such as file creation, deletion, modification, search, sort, merge, and join (combining two files based on a common key). A file is a collection of a series of records. A record is a collection of a series of fields. A field is a collection of a series of characters. For example, the names, GPAs, and majors of all the students in our computer class constitute a student file. The name, GPA, and major of each student make up the record of each student. The name, GPA, or major is a field.

Popular database programs include dBASE III PLUS and IV (Borland), PC-File III (Buttonware, Inc.), Q&A (Symantec), Paradox (Borland), Omnis Quartz (Blyth Software), FoxBase and Fox Pro (Microsoft), and R-BASE (Microrim Corporation).

Think of a database as a table of rows and columns. The rows correspond to the occurrence of a record. The columns correspond to the fields within the record. Two common applications of database software are sorting and searching records. In sort operations, the user enters a series of records in any order, then asks the database program to sort the records in ascending or descending order based on the data in the fields. Search operations are even more interesting. You can search for data items that meet certain criteria, for example, all the MIS students who have GPAs greater than 3.60 and are younger than 20 years of age. Some databases (such as Q&A) allow you to search for key words within a text file.

1–9–5   Graphics Software

Graphics software has been designed to present data in graphic format. Data can be converted into a line graph to show a trend, to a pie chart to highlight the components of a data item, and to other types of graphs for various analyses. Masses of data can be converted to a graph and, in a glance, the reader can discover the general pattern of the data. Graphs can easily highlight patterns and the correlation of data items. They also make data presentation a more manageable job. Graphics can be done with integrated packages such as Lotus 1-2-3 or Quattro Pro or with dedicated graphics packages. Five popular graphics packages are Aldus Persuasion (Aldus Corporation), Hollywood Graphics (IBM Corporation), Harvard Graphics (Software Publishing Corporation), Freelance (Lotus), and Power Point (Microsoft Corporation).

1–9–6   Communications Software

Through a modem and **communications software**, your microcomputer can easily connect you to a wealth of information available in public and private databases. For example, several executives in different states or countries can work expeditiously on the same report by using communications software. The report is sent back and forth on computer to each location until it is completed. Communications software and a modem also make remote data entry an easy task. A modem converts computer signals (digital signals) to signals transferable on a telephone line (analog signals). Some software packages, such as Symphony by Lotus, include a communications program within the package itself. However, there are many communications software products on the market, among them Crosstalk

(Microstuf, Inc.), On-Line (Micro-Systems Software, Inc.), Pfs: Access (Software Publishing Corp.), and Smartcom II (Hayes Microcomputer Products, Inc.).

1–9–7   Desktop Publishing Software

Desktop publishing software allows you to produce professional-quality documents (with or without graphics) using relatively inexpensive hardware and software. All you need is a PC, a desktop publishing software package, and a laser or letter-quality printer. Desktop publishing has evolved as a result of three major factors: inexpensive PCs, inexpensive laser printers, and sophisticated and easy-to-use software.

With desktop publishing software, you can produce high-quality screen output and then transfer it to a printer—what you see is what you get (WYSIWYG). Today, newsletters, brochures, training manuals, transparencies, posters, and books are produced by means of desktop publishing.

Several desktop publishing software packages are available on the market. Pagemaker (Aldus) and Ventura Publisher (Xerox Corporation) are two popular ones. See Figure 1–11 for some of the output of desktop publishing software.

1–9–8   Financial Planning Software

Financial planning software works with large amounts of data and performs diverse financial analyses. These analyses include present value, future value, rate of return, cash flow analyses, depreciation analyses, and budgeting analyses. There are several packages for financial planning on the market. Among them are DTFPS (Desk Top Financial Solutions, Inc.), Excel (Microsoft), Finar (Finar Research Systems, Ltd.), Javelin (Javelin Software Corporation), Micro-DSS/Finance (Addison-Wesley Publishing Co.), Lotus 1-2-3 (Lotus), Quattro Pro (Borland), IFPS (Comshare), and Micro Plan (Chase Laboratories, Inc.).

Using these packages, you can plan and analyze your financial situation. For example, you can determine how much your $2,000 IRA will be worth at 5 percent interest in 30 years. Or, you can discount all future cash flows into today's dollars. You will know how much you have to deposit in the bank to have $90,000 in 10 years for your child's education.

1–9–9   Accounting Software

In addition to spreadsheet software which has widespread applications in the accounting field, there are dedicated **accounting software** packages that are able to perform many accounting tasks. The tasks performed by such software include general ledgers, account receivables, account payables, payrolls, balance sheets, and income statements. Depending on the price, these software packages vary in sophistication. Some of the popular accounting software packages are Business Works PC (Manzanita Software Systems), 4-in-1 Basic Accounting (Real World Corporation), Peachtree (Peachtree Software, Inc.), and DacEasy Accounting (Dac Software, Inc.).

1–9–10   Project Management Software

A project consists of a series of related activities. Building a house, designing an order entry system, or writing a thesis are examples of projects. The goal of **project management software** is to help decision makers keep time and budget under control by resolving scheduling problems. Project management software helps managers to plan and set achievable goals. Project management software highlights the bottlenecks and the relationships among different activities. This

A.

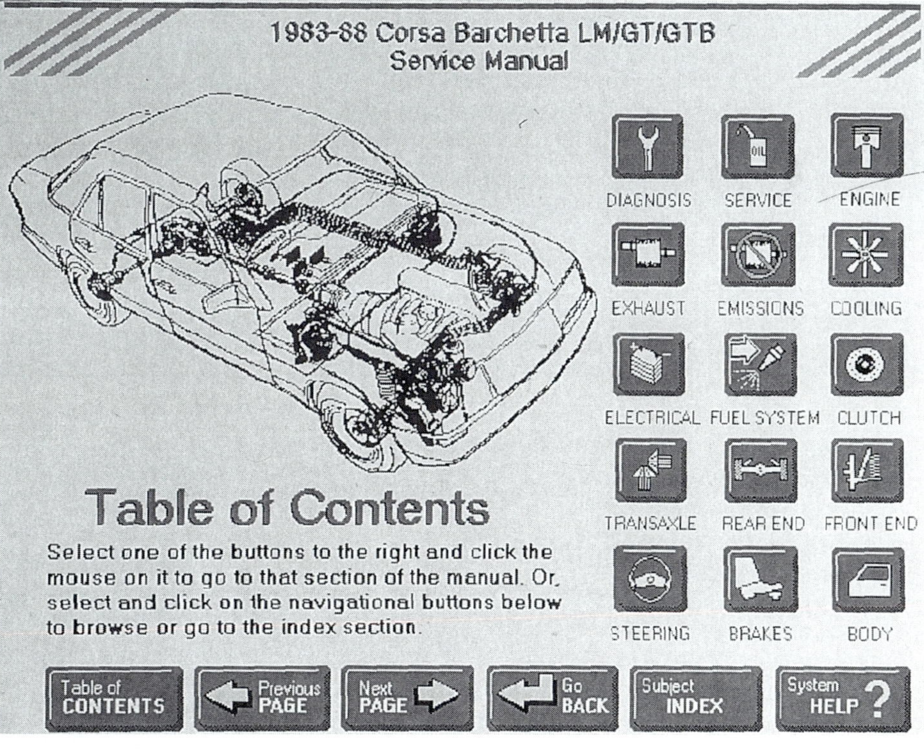

B.

Figure 1–11

Desktop publishing output. A. Desktop publishing combines text, graphics, and illustrations (courtesy of Aldus). B. With desktop publishing, business professionals can prepare high-quality documents on their own (courtesy of Ashton-Tate Corp.).

software allows the user to study the cost, time, and resource impacts of any change in the schedule. Several project management software packages are on the market: Harvard Total Project Manager (Software Publishing), Micro Planner 6 (Micro Planning International), Microsoft Project (Microsoft), Superproject Expert (Computer Associates) and Time Line (Symantec).

1–9–11   Computer-Aided Design (CAD) Software

Computer-aided design (CAD) software involves drafting and design. CAD software has replaced the traditional tools of drafting and design such as the T-square, triangle, and paper and pencil. It is used extensively in the architectural and engineering industries. CAD software no longer belongs only to large corporations. Because of the 386- and 486-based PCs and significant price reduction, small companies and individuals can afford this software. These new PCs have larger memory and are significantly faster than earlier PCs. With their enhanced power and sophistication, they are able to take advantage of most of the features offered by CAD programs. The home use of CAD software includes diverse architectural and engineering applications. There are several CAD programs on the market: AutoCAD (Autodesk), Cadkey (Cadkey), and VersaCAD (VersaCAD). See Figure 1–12 for some output from a CAD system.

A.

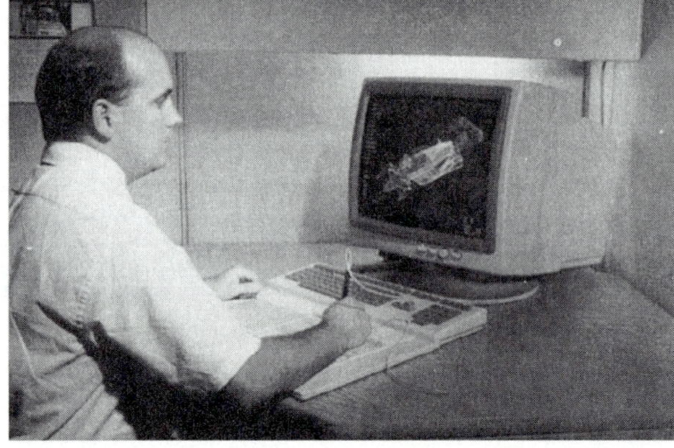

B.

Figure 1–12
A. CAD System for detailed architectural design (Larry Hamill/Macmillan). B. CAD system for design of a multicomponent product (courtesy of International Business Machines Corp.). C. CAD-supported design of aircraft landing gear (courtesy of International Business Machines Corp.).

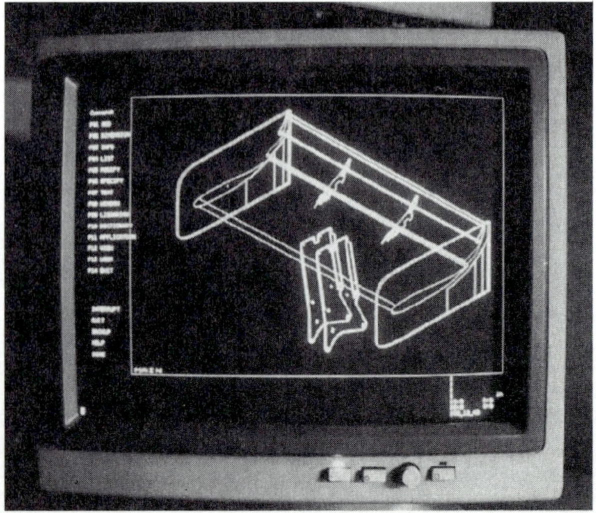

C.

1–9–12   Other Popular Software for Microcomputers

In addition to the 11 types of software just described, there are some others commonly used with microcomputers. Let us briefly consider them.

Utility software. These programs or utilities provide various DOS operations. Their goal is to simplify DOS operations for PC users. Depending on the sophistication of the program, various tasks are offered such as hard disk management, recovering a damaged disk or file, menu design, condensing a hard disk, and so forth.

Terminate & Stay Resident (TSR) Software. These programs are loaded when you start your PC and they stay in the background while other software applications are being used. TSR programs offer various features including screen printing, calendar, memo pad, and online calculator.

Investment Analysis Software. In addition to spreadsheet software, several other types of software are designed for investment analysis. By means of these programs, the user can track stocks, bonds, and other investment portfolios. Some of the programs are able to download financial data from public databases or stock exchanges. Others allow users to input their own financial data; then the programs perform financial analysis.

Tax Preparation software. This software assists a PC user in preparing taxes in a fairly straightforward manner. Some of the software packages enable the user to electronically download prepared tax forms to an IRS office.

Games software. Games probably form the oldest group of software for microcomputers, and they cover a broad range of activities. Although games are losing their popularity, they are still played by many PC users.

1–10   GUIDELINES FOR SUCCESSFUL SELECTION OF A MICROCOMPUTER

Because of the many microcomputers on the market, making a selection is a difficult task. The general guidelines provided here regarding the purchase and maintenance of a microcomputer may help you to choose a suitable computer and maintain it more easily.

Before you start the selection process, define your requirements. Sometimes this is called the "wish list" approach. You should have a clear idea of the type of microcomputer you *need* and the specific applications you want it to handle.

After you define your needs, think about software. Remember, if there is software on the market, there must be hardware to run it; but the reverse is not necessarily true. After defining the software and hardware you need and want, consider the technical support provided by vendors and reputation of vendors.

Important factors regarding selection and maintenance of a microcomputer are summarized next.

Software Selection

Good software should

- be easy to use
- be able to handle the business volume
- have good documentation
- have training available

- have updates available (free of charge or for a minimum charge)
- have local support
- come from a reputable vendor
- have a low cost

Hardware Selection (Processor and Keyboard)

Good hardware should

- have a comfortable keyboard
- have function keys
- have a general operating system (e.g., OS/2, MS-DOS, PC-DOS, Windows, or UNIX)
- have 16-bit or bigger processor (word) size
- have a high speed
- be expandable (memory and peripheral)
- have enough channel capacity or expansion slots (for attachment of peripherals)
- have a low cost

Hardware Selection (CRT)

A good monitor should

- have a separate CRT (not a built-in one)
- be easy to read (high resolution, super VGA or higher)
- have a standard number of characters per row and column

Hardware Selection (Disk Drive and Hard Disk)

A good disk drive should

- have a built-in, not separate, disk drive
- have adequate storage capacity (to load and run popular software)
- have a hard disk option

Hardware Selection (Printer)

A good printer should

- have a standard printer interface (without additional devices)
- produce high-quality output
- have high speed
- have a reasonable amount of noise suppression
- let you change tape, ribbons, or toner cartridge easily
- have a low cost

Vendor Selection

A good vendor should

- have a good reputation
- have a knowledgeable staff

- have training available for hardware and software
- have a hot line available
- support newsletters and user groups
- provide a "loaner" in case of breakdown
- provide updates (e.g., trade-in options)

Maintenance Contract Selection

A good contract should

- have a warranty period
- state a flexible time for repair
- limit downtime and inconvenience by providing flexible repair visits and timely repair of the computer
- have reasonable terms for contract renewal
- allow relocation and/or reassignment of the present contract
- observe confidentiality issues

1–11 TAKING CARE OF YOUR MICROCOMPUTER

To maintain the health of your microcomputer, consider the following factors:

- Protect your microcomputer against dirt, dust, and smoke.
- Make backup copies for security reasons and keep backups in different locations.
- Avoid any kind of liquid spills.
- Maintain steady power. Use surge protectors for power fluctuations and use lightning arresters in mountainous areas.
- Protect the system from static by using humidifiers or antistatic spray devices.
- Do not start your computer with a disk that you are not familiar with (avoid computer virus—the deadly program that erases and/or corrupts all your data).
- Do not download information to your computer from unknown bulletin boards. Downloading means importing information from other computers by using a modem and telephone line.
- Acquire insurance for your computer equipment.

1–12 ADVANTAGES OF MICROCOMPUTERS COMPARED WITH MAINFRAMES

Generally speaking, a microcomputer offers several advantages over a mainframe computer. Because of their extended memory and increased speed, microcomputers can perform many of the tasks performed by a mainframe but on a smaller scale. The advantages of microcomputers in comparison with mainframes follow:

- They are easier to use.
- They are less threatening to those who are not computer experts (e.g., they are smaller).
- They give the user more control.

- They are relatively inexpensive.
- They can be portable.

1–13   YOU AND YOUR PC: A HANDS-ON SESSION

If you place the DOS diskette or "boot disk" (disk that can be used to start the computer) in drive A, when you turn the computer on, your microcomputer will ask for the date. Remember, the majority of IBM or IBM-compatible systems come with a DOS disk. Either type the date in the desired format or press the Enter key to bypass the date. The computer then asks you for the time. Either type the time in the desired format or press the Enter key to bypass the time. Now you are at the A> prompt. This means your default drive is A.

If your computer has a hard disk, this start-up procedure is slightly different. You will get the system started from the hard disk and your prompt will be C> instead of A>. See Figure 1–13.

In any case, from this mode (the DOS mode), you can go to any application software.

For example, if the software (e.g., Lotus 1-2-3) is installed in the hard disk, use the DOS CD command to change to the directory that stores the software; then type *123* and press Enter. From the DOS mode, you can access any application software.

When you are at the C> prompt, you are in RAM. This area is called a working or temporary area. Any work you do in this area will disappear if you turn the computer off. To make your work permanent, you have to transfer it to a **permanent area**. The permanent area usually is either floppy disk or hard disk. Your work stays in the permanent area until you erase it.

While you are at the C> prompt, you can send any information to RAM by using the keyboard. This information can become permanent by saving it into a permanent medium. All application programs include a command for saving your work.

Beginning computer users are always worried about making mistakes! What happens if you make a mistake? Don't panic. Your mistake can be corrected easily. Some application programs have an UNDO command. If you realize you have made a mistake, you can recover from it by using the UNDO feature. All application programs include a feature for correcting mistakes. In the worst case, you can retype the correct statement over your previous material. Remember, any address (or cell) in the computer memory can hold only one value at a time. As soon as you type and enter a new value, the old one disappears.

1–14   WHAT IS A COMPUTER FILE?

A **computer file** is basically an electronic document. One way to create a document is to type and enter it using the keyboard. As soon as you save the document, you have generated a computer file.

To differentiate one file from another, you must save each file under a unique name—a file name. A file name is any combination of up to eight valid characters. Valid characters include letters of the alphabet (upper case or lower-

Figure 1–13
Getting the system started.

```
C>
```

case), digits 0 through 9, the underscore, and some special characters. If you provide a name longer than eight characters, some application programs give you an error message; others truncate the name and accept only the first eight characters.

In addition to a file name, a file is usually saved with a file extension. A file extension is similar to a file name but uses up to three characters. Some application programs automatically provide a file extension when you save the file. In other application programs, providing a file extension is the user's responsibility.

Several characters have special meanings in different application software. The asterisk (*) can represent any number of characters up to eight. The question mark (?) can represent any single character. These two characters are called wildcard characters. These **wildcards** can significantly improve your efficiency while you work with application programs. For example, all your Lotus 1-2-3 graphic files are identified by *.PIC. The * represents any file name and the PIC indicates that your file is a Lotus 1-2-3 graphic file. For example, if you want to copy all your Lotus 1-2-3 graphic files from the disk in drive A to the disk in drive B, type this DOS command at the A> prompt: *COPY *.PIC B:* (follow by pressing the Enter key). If you did not have this wildcard feature, you would have to repeat the COPY command as many times as the number of the graphic files. The file BRANCH?.* represents BRANCH1, BRANCH2, and so on. For example, in DOS if you type *DIR *.WK?* (and press Enter), your Lotus 1-2-3 files from version 1 and 1A (WKS) files, version 2 (WK1) files, version 3 (WK3) files, and student version (WKE) files will be displayed. The asterisk as the file extension indicates that the file can have any extension. Your entire disk can be identified by *.*. Using the COPY command, for example, at the A> prompt, to copy the entire disk in drive A to drive B, type *Copy *.* B:* (and press Enter).

1–15   TYPES OF DATA

Any application program or computer language accepts different types of data. The most commonly used data types are numeric and nonnumeric.

Numeric data include any combination of digits 0 through 9 and decimal points. Numeric data can be integer or real. Integer data include only whole numbers without any decimal points, for example, 656 or 986. Real data include digits and decimal points, for example, 696.25 or 729.793. Real data is sometimes called floating point data. Floating point means that the decimal point can move from right to left, for example, 222.2, 22.22, 2.222. Another type of real data is the fixed point, meaning that the decimal point is always fixed.

Nonnumeric data, or alphanumeric data, is sometimes called labels or strings. Any types of valid characters can be nonnumeric data, for example, Jackson or 123 Broadway Street. You cannot perform any arithmetic operations with nonnumeric data.

1–16   TYPES OF VALUES

Computers usually handle two types of values: variables and constants. **Variables** are valid computer addresses (locations) that hold different values at different times. For example, in A=65, A is the variable and 65 is the **constant**. B = "Brown": B is the variable and Brown is the constant. A variable holds a given value at any given time. As soon as you enter a new value into this variable, the old value disappears. The constant is always fixed. See Figure 1–14.

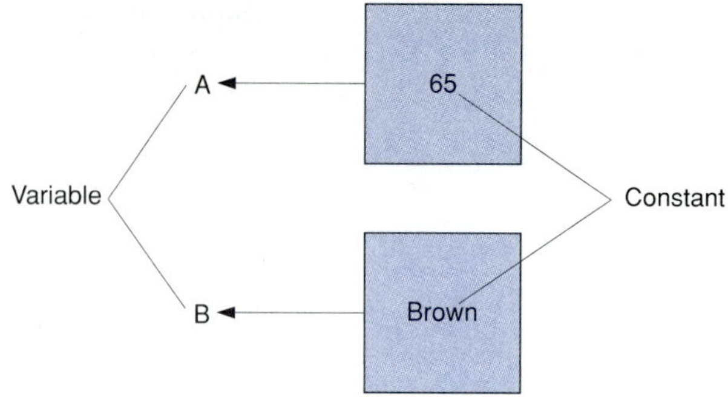

Figure 1–14
Example of a variable and a constant.

1–17   TYPES OF FORMULAS

Two types of formulas or functions are handled by computers: user-defined and built-in.

User-defined formulas or functions are a combination of computer addresses designed to perform a certain task. For example, the area of a triangle can be presented as A = B*H/2 (meaning base multiplied by height divided by 2). In this case, A is a formula or a function. When you enter different values for B and H, and a different value for A, the area of the triangle, will be calculated.

Built-in formulas or functions are already available within the application program or the computer language. As soon as the user provides values for a given variable or variables, the application program or the computer language dynamically calculates these formulas. For example, SQRT(X) is a function that calculates the square root of a variable, X. The X and any other information needed by these functions are called arguments. As soon as you provide a value for X, the square root is calculated; for example, SQRT(25) is equal to 5. The function FV(payment,interest rate,term) calculates the future value of a series of equal payments with a given interest rate over a period of time (term). This function can help you determine, for example, the future value of an IRA in which you plan to invest $2,000 for 30 years at a 10 percent interest rate.

1–18   PRIORITY OF ARITHMETIC OPERATIONS

When application programs perform arithmetic operations, they follow a series of rules. The rules for priority of arithmetic operations are as follows:

1. Expressions inside parentheses have the highest priority.
2. Exponentiation (raising to power) has the next highest priority.
3. Multiplication and division have the third highest priority.
4. Addition and subtraction have the fourth highest priority.
5. When there are two or more operations with the same priority, operations proceed from left to right.

The following examples should make the rules clear. First, an application program uses * (asterisk) for multiplication, ^ (caret) for exponentiation (raising the power), and / (slash) for division. If A=5, B=10, C=2, calculate the following:

$$A+B/C \quad = \quad 10$$
$$(A+B)/C \quad = \quad 7.5$$

$$A*B/C \quad = \quad 25$$
$$(A*B)/C \quad = \quad 25$$
$$A \wedge C/2 \quad = \quad 12.50$$

SUMMARY

This chapter focused on microcomputers in general. Input, output, and primary and secondary memory devices for microcomputers were described. The general capabilities of microcomputers were introduced. The chapter presented a series of guidelines for successful selection and maintenance of a microcomputer. It also listed the advantages of micros over mainframes. A hands-on session included the basics for getting started as a computer user. The chapter concluded with a definition of computer files, types of data, types of values, types of formulas, and priority of arithmetic operations.

REVIEW QUESTIONS

*These questions are answered in Appendix A.

1. What is a microcomputer? What are some of the capabilities of a micro?
*2. What are some typical input devices for a micro?
3. What are some typical output devices for a micro?
4. Explain the difference between a primary memory device and a secondary memory device.
5. What is RAM? ROM? PROM? EPROM?
*6. What are the most commonly used secondary storage devices for a micro?
7. What is extended memory? What is expanded memory?
8. Describe optical technologies. What are their advantages and disadvantages?
9. How do you measure the memory capacity of a micro?
10. Besides memory, what other attributes are important when you buy a micro?
11. What is the difference between a floppy disk and a hard disk?
12. Give the speed range for a typical microcomputer.
*13. What is the memory size of a typical micro?
14. What is a good software?
15. What is a good hardware?
16. What is a good maintenance contract? Who are the good vendors?
*17. How should you care for your micro?
18. List some application programs for a micro.
19. What are some of the advantages of a micro compared with a mainframe?
20. What is permanent memory in a PC? What is temporary memory?
21. How do you send information from RAM to a floppy or hard disk?
*22. How do you correct your mistakes?
23. Define a computer file.
24. What is a wildcard character?
25. Describe different types of data.
26. What is a variable? What is a constant?
*27. What is the priority of arithmetic operations?
28. List the symbols used for arithmetic operations.
29. Turn on a PC. What do you see? Turn it off. Insert the DOS disk in drive A and turn the computer back on. What do you see this time?

30. Enter the correct date and time in your computer. What happens if you make a mistake?

31. Type *DIR* and press the Enter key. What is displayed at this time?

32. What types of PCs do you have on your campus? Describe different input/output devices used by the PCs in your school's micro lab. Do you have a Bernoulli box in the lab? What are some of the advantages of Bernoulli box over a hard disk?

33. What are the most commonly used disks on your campus—3½ or 5¼? Compare and contrast these two types of storage devices.

34. Consult computer magazines to find out which computers use optical disks.

35. Which of the types of software packages introduced in this chapter are available on your campus? What are the applications of each?

36. If you want to buy a PC for personal use, how should you start shopping? What attributes makes a PC attractive?

KEY TERMS

Accounting software

Arithmetic logic unit (ALU)

Bernoulli box

Built-in formulas or functions

Central processing unit (CPU)

CD-ROM

Communications software

Computer-aided design (CAD) software

Computer file

Constants

Control unit

Conventional memory

Database software

Desktop publishing software

EPROM

Erasable optical disk

Expanded memory

Extended memory

Financial planning software

Floppy disk

Grammar checker software

Graphics software

Hard disk

Input device

Main memory

Micro

Microcomputer

Nonnumeric data

Numeric data

Output device

Permanent area

Personal computer (PC)

Primary memory

Priority of arithmetic operations

Project management software

PROM

Random-access memory (RAM)

RGB monitor

Read-only memory (ROM)

Secondary memory

Spreadsheet software

User-defined formulas or functions

Variables

Wildcard

Word processing software

WORM disk

ARE YOU READY TO MOVE ON?

Multiple Choice

1. Choose the correct ranking of monitor display resolutions from lowest to highest.
    a. VGA, CGA, XGA
    b. EGA, VGA, CGA
    c. EGA, CGA, VGA
    d. CGA, EGA, XGA
    e. XGA, CGA, EGA

2. Which of the following is *not* a typical adapter card?
    a. printer interface card
    b. clock card

    c. disk drive card
    d. display card
    e. punch card

3. Of the following types of main memory, which can the user control directly?
    a. ROM
    b. REM
    c. RAM
    d. PROM
    e. all of the above

4. What is now the most commonly used secondary storage device?
    a. 5¼ inch floppy disk and a hard disk
    b. 3½ inch floppy disk and a hard disk
    c. Bernoulli box and a hard disk
    d. hard disk with no floppy disk
    e. none of the above

5. What is the major advantage of optical storage technology?
    a. storage capacity
    b. cost
    c. durability
    d. both A and C
    e. all of the above

6. When we refer to memory and storage capacity sizes, we use kilobytes (as in 360 K). 1 K equals approximately
    a. 1 byte
    b. 1,000 bytes
    c. 1,000,000 bytes
    d. 1,048,576 bytes
    e. none of the above

7. Word size directly affects
    a. the speed of the computer
    b. the ability of the user to understand what is being said
    c. the maximum amount of data that can be displayed on the CRT
    d. the choice of which type of disk drive to use
    e. the meaning of the function keys on the keyboard

8. Which of the following are disadvantages of mainframes when compared with micro-computers?
    a. They are more difficult to use.
    b. They are more threatening to users who are not computer experts.
    c. The user has less control.
    d. They are relatively more expensive.
    e. All of the above are disadvantages.

9. After booting the computer with the DOS disk (loading DOS and entering the date and time), you are at
    a. the Lotus Access menu
    b. the DOS prompt (A> or C>)
    c. the parallel/serial interface
    d. the BASIC prompt
    e. none of the above

10. An example of alphanumeric data would be
    a. 123
    b. 123.25
    c. LOTUS-123
    d. A=(123-2)/4
    e. none of the above

True/False

1. The terms *personal computer*, PC, and *microcomputer* refer to different types of computers.

2. A typical microcomputer consists of input, output, and memory devices.

3. Monochrome CRTs cannot generate graphic output.

4. The purpose of function keys and special keys on a computer keyboard does not vary in different application programs.

5. The capacity of a hard disk is greater than the capacity of a floppy disk.

6. A WORM disk can be recorded and erased repeatedly when high-volume storage and updating are essential.

7. Typical microcomputer software packages and applications include spreadsheet, database, graphics, communications, and word processing.

8. The first step in selecting a microcomputer is to define your needs; then think about software.

9. The commands DIR *.* and DIR ????????.??? produce the same results.

10. Expressions inside parentheses have the lowest priority when it comes to performing arithmetic operations.

ANSWERS

Multiple Choice		True/False	
1.	d	1.	F
2.	e	2.	T
3.	c	3.	F
4.	b	4.	F
5.	d	5.	T
6.	b	6.	F
7.	a	7.	T
8.	e	8.	T
9.	b	9.	T
10.	c	10.	F

You and Your PC: The First Official Meeting

2

2–1   INTRODUCTION

In this chapter we consider the basics of the disk operating system (DOS) and define the differences between internal and external DOS commands. The system date and time are explained, and file specifications in the DOS environment are described. Important keys in the DOS environment, and the DIR and FORMAT commands, are highlighted. The chapter concludes with a review of different versions of MS-DOS and PC-DOS and the Help facility available in DOS 6.0.

2–2   TURNING ON YOUR PC

When you access a personal computer, the computer is either off or on. If the computer is off, put the **disk operating system** (DOS) disk in drive A and turn on the computer. This procedure is called a **cold boot** (boot means getting the computer started). If the computer is already turned on, insert the DOS disk in drive A and press the Ctrl, Alt, and Del keys simultaneously (Ctrl+Alt+Del). This procedure is called a **warm boot**. A warm boot is faster than a cold boot because the computer does not check its memory when you do a warm boot.

In some cases DOS is already installed in the C drive (the **hard disk drive**) when you use the computer, and this is the situation assumed in the examples in this book. If DOS is installed in the C drive, when you press Ctrl+Alt+Del you will see the C prompt (C>).

When the computer is booted from a floppy disk, it asks you to enter the current date. Enter the date in the format requested (mm-dd-yy) and press Enter. Your PC next asks for the current time. Enter the current time in the format requested (hh:mm:ss) and press Enter. (Note that DOS operates on a 24-hour clock, 2:30 p.m. is 14:30, 9:15 p.m. is 21:15, and so on.) Some computers have an internal clock and you do not need to enter the date and time—the computer keeps track automatically. This is the case in the examples in this book.

Now you should see the C> **DOS prompt,** which indicates that the necessary portions of DOS have been loaded into primary memory (RAM) and drive C is the default drive. The default drive is the disk drive that the PC will access if no other disk drive is specified. This is the drive the computer accesses for executing commands. For example, if you try to save a file, your file will be saved to this drive. If you ask for a directory listing, the directory of this drive will be highlighted. At this point, you should be able to access any internal or external DOS commands.

At boot-up time, if you do not want to enter date and time, you can bypass the prompts by pressing Enter twice. It is a good practice to enter both correct date and time when you start the PC. Your PC uses both the **system date** and **system time** when saving your files. The correct date and time will help you to determine the most or least recent versions of the files in the directory. A directory is a listing of all your files.

If you forget to enter the current date and time at boot-up, or if you decide to change date and time, you can enter this information any time by using the DATE and TIME commands. At the C> prompt type either DATE or TIME and press Enter to enter the information. The computer registers this information in its memory where it will be updated automatically until you turn off the PC.

Internal commands (sometimes called memory-resident commands) are those commands that are loaded into the computer memory at boot-up. Internal commands can be used without the DOS disk in any disk drive. CLS (clear screen) is an example of an internal DOS command. If you type CLS and press Enter, the screen will be cleared (erased).

    External commands (sometimes called nonmemory-resident commands) are those commands that can be executed only when the DOS disk is in one of the drives. These commands, which are sometimes called DOS utilities, are separate programs stored on the DOS disk. For example, DISKCOPY is an external DOS command. We will talk about these commands in detail in the next chapter.

2–3   DOS PROMPTS

Depending on how you get your PC started, you may see different prompts. If you have a hard disk in your system and you start the system from the hard disk, your prompt may be C>. The prompt indicates the current default drive. If a file is located on a disk that is not in the default drive, the default must be changed or the disk drive containing the file must be specified. Changing the default is an easy task. At the C> prompt type *A:* (remember the colon) and press Enter. Now the prompt is A>, which indicates that drive A is the default. You can change the default drive back to C> by typing *C:* and pressing Enter.

2–4   DOS FILE SPECIFICATIONS

DOS files follow the same conventions discussed in Chapter 1: File names can be up to eight characters long. File names can contain digits 0 through 9 and some special characters such as underscore (__) and the pound sign (#). File extensions can be up to three characters long and contain the same characters used in file names. Important extensions in **DOS file specifications** include the following:

- BAK (Backup). **Backup files** are generated by some word processing, spreadsheet, and database management programs. These files are backup copies of the original files.
- BAT (Batch). **Batch files** are text files generated by the user. This type of file contains DOS commands and statements that are executed when the name of the file is typed.
- COM (Command). This extension identifies **command files,** which can be executed by typing the name of the file.
- EXE (Executable). Like COM files, **executable files** can be executed by typing the file name.
- SYS (System). This extension identifies **system files,** which can be used only by DOS.

2–5   THE DIR COMMAND

With the DOS disk in drive C, you can generate a listing of your current directory by using the DIR command. If you type *DIR* and press Enter, information similar to that in Figure 2–1 is presented. At the top of Figure 2–1, the listing indicates that the volume in drive C is MS_DOS_6. This is the internal name for this disk.

    The DIR command displays the name and extension of each file, the size of the file in bytes, and the date and time that the file was created. At the end of the listing, the DIR command tells you the number of files and the amount of

Figure 2–1
Directory listing of DOS 6.0

```
Volume in drive C is MS_DOS_6
Volume Serial Number is 1C22-913B
Directory of C:\DOS

.                  <DIR>         06-06-92   12:24p
..                 <DIR>         06-06-92   12:24p
DBLSPACE BIN        51214 03-10-93    6:00a
FORMAT   COM        22717 03-10-93    6:00a
NLSFUNC  EXE         7036 03-10-93    6:00a
COUNTRY  SYS        17066 03-10-93    6:00a
KEYB     COM        14983 03-10-93    6:00a
KEYBOARD SYS        34694 03-10-93    6:00a
SETUP    EXE        71974 03-10-93    6:00a
DOSSETUP INI         3735 03-10-93    6:00a
ANSI     SYS         9065 03-10-93    6:00a
ATTRIB   EXE        11165 03-10-93    6:00a
CHKDSK   EXE        12907 03-10-93    6:00a
EDIT     COM          413 03-10-93    6:00a
EXPAND   EXE        16129 03-10-93    6:00a
EDLIN    EXE        12642 06-13-91    5:00a
MORE     COM         2546 03-10-93    6:00a
MSD      EXE       158470 03-10-93    6:00a
QBASIC   EXE       194309 03-10-93    6:00a
RESTORE  EXE        38294 03-10-93    6:00a
MIRROR   COM        18169 06-13-91    5:00a
SYS      COM         9379 03-10-93    6:00a
UNFORMAT COM        12738 03-10-93    6:00a
SMARTDRV SYS         8335 06-13-91    5:00a
OS2      TXT         6358 03-10-93    6:00a
NETWORKS TXT        20463 03-10-93    6:00a
README   TXT        44990 03-10-93    6:00a
DEBUG    EXE        15715 03-10-93    6:00a
FDISK    EXE        29333 03-10-93    6:00a
DOSSHELL VID         9462 03-10-93    6:00a
19C1DOSC BAT           16 01-23-93    3:05p
DEFAULT  SET         4207 01-02-94   10:49a
DOSSHELL GRB         4421 03-10-93    6:00a
CHOICE   COM         1754 03-10-93    6:00a
DEFRAG   EXE        75033 03-10-93    6:00a
PACKING  LST         2507 06-13-91    5:00a
DEFRAG   HLP         9227 03-10-93    6:00a
DOSSWAP  EXE        18756 03-10-93    6:00a
EGA      CPI        58870 03-10-93    6:00a
RECOVER  EXE         9146 06-13-91    5:00a
EGA      SYS         4885 03-10-93    6:00a
HIMEM    SYS        14208 03-10-93    6:00a
MEM      EXE        32150 03-10-93    6:00a
XCOPY    EXE        15820 03-10-93    6:00a
MONEY    BAS        46225 06-13-91    5:00a
MSHERC   COM         6934 06-13-91    5:00a
DELTREE  EXE        11113 03-10-93    6:00a
GORILLA  BAS        29434 06-13-91    5:00a
4201     CPI         6404 06-13-91    5:00a
4208     CPI          720 06-13-91    5:00a
5202     CPI          395 06-13-91    5:00a
MOVE     EXE        17823 03-10-93    6:00a
ASSIGN   COM         6399 06-13-91    5:00a
RAMDRIVE SYS         5873 03-10-93    6:00a
BACKUP   EXE        36092 06-13-91    5:00a
SMARTDRV EXE        42073 03-10-93    6:00a
```

```
COMP       EXE      14282  06-13-91     5:00a
DISPLAY    SYS      15789  03-10-93     6:00a
DOSHELP    HLP       5667  03-10-93     6:00a
DOSSHELL   COM       4620  03-10-93     6:00a
DOSSHELL   EXE     236378  03-10-93     6:00a
FASTHELP   EXE      11481  03-10-93     6:00a
GRAFTABL   COM      11205  06-13-91     5:00a
FASTOPEN   EXE      12034  03-10-93     6:00a
HELP       HLP     294741  03-10-93     6:00a
HELP       COM        413  03-10-93     6:00a
NIBBLES    BAS      24103  06-13-91     5:00a
REMLINE    BAS      12314  06-13-91     5:00a
MODE       COM      23521  03-10-93     6:00a
POWER      EXE       8052  03-10-93     6:00a
EXE2BIN    EXE       8424  06-13-91     5:00a
PRINT      EXE      15640  03-10-93     6:00a
JOIN       EXE      17870  06-13-91     5:00a
LCD        CPI      10753  06-13-91     5:00a
QBASIC     HLP     130881  03-10-93     6:00a
PRINTER    SYS      18804  06-13-91     5:00a
SHARE      EXE      10912  03-10-93     6:00a
DELOLDOS   EXE      17710  03-10-93     6:00a
SETVER     EXE      12015  03-10-93     6:00a
APPEND     EXE      10774  03-10-93     6:00a
APPNOTES   TXT       8660  06-13-91     5:00a
KEYBHP     COM      15997  06-13-91     5:00a
MODEHP     COM      23232  06-13-91     5:00a
SSTOR      SYS      37260  06-13-91     5:00a
DISKCOMP   COM      10620  03-10-93     6:00a
MOUSE      SYS      32730  06-13-91     5:00a
DISKCOPY   COM      11879  03-10-93     6:00a
B          BAT         46  06-06-92     1:53p
589DOSCM   BAT         16  01-23-93     3:01p
D5C0DOSC   BAT         16  01-23-93     6:49p
2688DOSC   BAT         16  01-23-93     3:08p
370CDOSC   BAT         16  01-23-93     4:12p
D923DOSC   BAT         16  01-23-93     5:50p
BA6EDOSC   BAT         16  01-23-93     6:43p
D329DOSC   BAT         16  01-23-93     6:49p
DRIVER     SYS       5406  03-10-93     6:00a
FC         EXE      18650  03-10-93     6:00a
FIND       EXE       6770  03-10-93     6:00a
GRAPHICS   COM      19694  03-10-93     6:00a
GRAPHICS   PRO      21232  03-10-93     6:00a
LABEL      EXE       9390  03-10-93     6:00a
SMARTMON   EXE      28672  03-10-93     6:00a
SMARTMON   HLP      10727  03-10-93     6:00a
SORT       EXE       6922  03-10-93     6:00a
LOADFIX    COM       1131  03-10-93     6:00a
MWBACKUP   EXE     309696  03-10-93     6:00a
MWBACKUP   HLP     400880  03-10-93     6:00a
REPLACE    EXE      20226  03-10-93     6:00a
SUBST      EXE      18478  03-10-93     6:00a
TREE       COM       6898  03-10-93     6:00a
DOSKEY     COM       5883  03-10-93     6:00a
VFINTD     386       5295  03-10-93     6:00a
MWBACKF    DLL      14560  03-10-93     6:00a
MWBACKR    DLL     111120  03-10-93     6:00a
MOUSE      COM      56408  03-10-93     6:00a
MSBACKUP   EXE       5506  03-10-93     6:00a
MSBACKUP   OVL     133952  03-10-93     6:00a
MSBACKFB   OVL      69066  03-10-93     6:00a
```

```
MSBACKFR OVL      72474 03-10-93      6:00a
CHKSTATE SYS      41600 03-10-93      6:00a
UNDELETE EXE      26420 03-10-93      6:00a
MWUNDEL  EXE     130496 03-10-93      6:00a
MWUNDEL  HLP      35741 03-10-93      6:00a
MWGRAFIC DLL      36944 03-10-93      6:00a
MSBACKUP HLP     314236 03-10-93      6:00a
WNTOOLS  GRP       2205 01-02-94      6:25p
MSBACKDB OVL      63098 03-10-93      6:00a
MSBACKDR OVL      66906 03-10-93      6:00a
MSBCONFG OVL      47210 03-10-93      6:00a
MSBCONFG HLP      45780 03-10-93      6:00a
DBLSPACE EXE     274388 03-10-93      6:00a
MEMMAKER INF       1652 03-10-93      6:00a
INTERLNK EXE      17197 03-10-93      6:00a
INTERSVR EXE      37314 03-10-93      6:00a
MSCDEX   EXE      25377 03-10-93      6:00a
DBLSPACE HLP      72169 03-10-93      6:00a
DBLSPACE INF       2178 03-10-93      6:00a
DBLSPACE SYS        339 03-10-93      6:00a
DBLWIN   HLP       8597 03-10-93      6:00a
DOSSHELL HLP     161323 03-10-93      6:00a
EMM386   EXE     115294 03-10-93      6:00a
MEMMAKER EXE     118660 03-10-93      6:00a
SIZER    EXE       7169 03-10-93      6:00a
MONOUMB  386       8783 03-10-93      6:00a
MSTOOLS  DLL      13424 03-10-93      6:00a
MSAV     EXE     172198 03-10-93      6:00a
MSAV     HLP      23891 03-10-93      6:00a
MSAVHELP OVL      29828 03-10-93      6:00a
MSAVIRUS LST      35520 03-10-93      6:00a
VSAFE    COM      62576 03-10-93      6:00a
MWAVDOSL DLL      44736 03-10-93      6:00a
MWAVDRVL DLL       7744 03-10-93      6:00a
AUTOEXEC UMB        703 01-01-94      5:34p
MOUSE    INI         28 01-01-94      5:34p
CONFIG   UMB        142 01-01-94      5:34p
MEMMAKER STS        851 01-01-94      5:40p
MWAVDLG  DLL      36368 03-10-93      6:00a
MSBACKUP INI         43 01-03-94      4:46p
MWAVSCAN DLL     151568 03-10-93      6:00a
MSBACKUP RST        608 04-13-92      7:07a
MSBACKUP TMP       5014 01-02-94     10:49a
MWAV     EXE     142640 03-10-93      6:00a
MWAVABSI DLL      54576 03-10-93      6:00a
MWAV     HLP      24619 03-10-93      6:00a
MWAVSOS  DLL       7888 03-10-93      6:00a
MWAVMGR  DLL      21712 03-10-93      6:00a
MWAVTSR  EXE      17328 03-10-93      6:00a
COMMAND  COM      52925 03-10-93      6:00a
MSAV     INI          0 01-01-94      3:01p
DEFAULT  BAK       4207 01-02-94      9:56a
MSBACKUP LOG     196811 01-02-94     10:54a
DEFAULT  SLT         64 01-02-94     10:49a
DEFAULT  SAV         64 01-02-94      9:56a
DOSSHELL INI      16424 01-02-94      1:02p
       176 file(s)      6563296 bytes
                      129966080 bytes free

C>
```

bytes available on this particular disk. To erase the screen, type *CLS* and press Enter.

The DIR command can be used with wildcard characters. Wildcard characters function as place holders for other characters in the file name or file extension. The two valid wildcards used by DOS are * and ?. The * takes the place of one or more characters in the file name or extension. For example, *.COM refers to any file name with the extension COM. The ? takes the place of only one character in the file name or extension.

You can use these wildcard characters in various combinations. For example, DIR *.COM displays all COM files. DIR *.PIC displays all Lotus 1-2-3 graphics files. DIR *.WK? displays 1-2-3 WK1, WKS, WK3, and WKE files. It also displays WKQ files.

2–6   USING DIR WITH SWITCHES

You can use the DIR command with different switches (parameters) to provide different types of listings. DIR/W provides a wide (horizontal) directory listing. In this case, only file names and extensions are listed. Figure 2–2 shows a wide listing. The DIR/P command displays one screen of the file listing at a time. You press a key to see another screen. Figure 2–3 shows a partial listing using the /P switch.

The DIR command can be used to provide a listing of files in any drive. You only have to specify the drive. For example, if the current drive is C, you can use the command DIR A:/W to display a wide directory of the files on drive A. Remember that there must be at least one space between the DIR command and the drive name when you issue the command.

2–7   IMPORTANT KEYS IN THE DOS ENVIRONMENT

Examine the picture of a typical keyboard presented in Figure 2–4. Several of the keys perform special tasks in the DOS environment. Table 2–1 briefly explains these keys.

2–8   THE FORMAT COMMAND

To use a newly purchased blank disk on your PC, you first must format the disk. To format a disk, put the blank disk in drive A, type *FORMAT A:* and press Enter. When the process is finished, DOS asks whether you would like to format another disk. If you answer Y, you are prompted to insert a new disk. If you answer N, the C> prompt returns.

When you format a disk, the operating system checks the entire disk for defective spots. It tells you whether your disk is usable. The FORMAT command divides a disk into tracks and sectors and creates the **file allocation table** (FAT). The FAT indicates where data is saved on a disk.

When you format a disk, remember that disk is completely erased. Make sure the disk you are formatting is either a brand new disk or an old disk with files you no longer need. Figure 2–5 shows the formatting procedure.

Formatting is discussed further in Chapter 3.

```
C>DIR/W

 Volume in drive C is MS_DOS_6
 Volume Serial Number is 1C22-913B
 Directory of C:\DOS

 [.]              [..]             DBLSPACE.BIN     FORMAT.COM       NLSFUNC.EXE
 COUNTRY.SYS      KEYB.COM         KEYBOARD.SYS     SETUP.EXE        DOSSETUP.INI
 ANSI.SYS         ATTRIB.EXE       CHKDSK.EXE       EDIT.COM         EXPAND.EXE
 EDLIN.EXE        MORE.COM         MSD.EXE          QBASIC.EXE       RESTORE.EXE
 MIRROR.COM       SYS.COM          UNFORMAT.COM     SMARTDRV.SYS     OS2.TXT
 NETWORKS.TXT     README.TXT       DEBUG.EXE        FDISK.EXE        DOSSHELL.VID
 19C1DOSC.BAT     DEFAULT.SET      DOSSHELL.GRB     CHOICE.COM       DEFRAG.EXE
 PACKING.LST      DEFRAG.HLP       DOSSWAP.EXE      EGA.CPI          RECOVER.EXE
 EGA.SYS          HIMEM.SYS        MEM.EXE          XCOPY.EXE        MONEY.BAS
 MSHERC.COM       DELTREE.EXE      GORILLA.BAS      4201.CPI         4208.CPI
 5202.CPI         MOVE.EXE         ASSIGN.COM       RAMDRIVE.SYS     BACKUP.EXE
 SMARTDRV.EXE     COMP.EXE         DISPLAY.SYS      DOSHELP.HLP      DOSSHELL.COM
 DOSSHELL.EXE     FASTHELP.EXE     GRAFTABL.COM     EDIT.HLP         FASTOPEN.EXE
 HELP.HLP         HELP.COM         NIBBLES.BAS      REMLINE.BAS      MODE.COM
 POWER.EXE        EXE2BIN.EXE      PRINT.EXE        JOIN.EXE         LCD.CPI
 QBASIC.HLP       PRINTER.SYS      SHARE.EXE        DELOLDOS.EXE     SETVER.EXE
 APPEND.EXE       APPNOTES.TXT     KEYBHP.COM       MODEHP.COM       SSTOR.SYS
 DISKCOMP.COM     MOUSE.SYS        DISKCOPY.COM     B.BAT            589DOSCM.BAT
 D5C0DOSC.BAT     2688DOSC.BAT     370CDOSC.BAT     D923DOSC.BAT     BA6EDOSC.BAT
 D329DOSC.BAT     DRIVER.SYS       FC.EXE           FIND.EXE         GRAPHICS.COM
 GRAPHICS.PRO     LABEL.EXE        SMARTMON.EXE     SMARTMON.HLP     SORT.EXE
 LOADFIX.COM      MWBACKUP.EXE     MWBACKUP.HLP     REPLACE.EXE      SUBST.EXE
 TREE.COM         DOSKEY.COM       VFINTD.386       MWBACKF.DLL      MWBACKR.DLL
 MOUSE.COM        MSBACKUP.EXE     MSBACKUP.OVL     MSBACKFB.OVL     MSBACKFR.OVL
 CHKSTATE.SYS     UNDELETE.EXE     MWUNDEL.EXE      MWUNDEL.HLP      MWGRAFIC.DLL
 MSBACKUP.HLP     WNTOOLS.GRP      MSBACKDB.OVL     MSBACKDR.OVL     MSBCONFG.OVL
 MSBCONFG.HLP     DBLSPACE.EXE     MEMMAKER.HLP     MEMMAKER.INF     INTERLNK.EXE
 INTERSVR.EXE     MSCDEX.EXE       DBLSPACE.HLP     DBLSPACE.INF     DBLSPACE.SYS
 DBLWIN.HLP       DOSSHELL.HLP     EMM386.EXE       MEMMAKER.EXE     SIZER.EXE
 MONOUMB.386      MSTOOLS.DLL      MSAV.EXE         MSAV.HLP         MSAVHELP.OVL
 MSAVIRUS.LST     VSAFE.COM        MWAVDOSL.DLL     MWAVDRVL.DLL     AUTOEXEC.UMB
 MOUSE.INI        CONFIG.UMB       MEMMAKER.STS     MWAVDLG.DLL      MSBACKUP.INI
 MWAVSCAN.DLL     MSBACKUP.RST     MSBACKUP.TMP     MWAV.EXE         MWAVABSI.DLL
 MWAV.HLP         MWAVSOS.DLL      MWAVMGR.DLL      MWAVTSR.EXE      COMMAND.COM
 MSAV.INI         DEFAULT.BAK      MSBACKUP.LOG     DEFAULT.SLT      DEFAULT.SAV
 DOSSHELL.INI
        176 file(s)      6563296 bytes
                       129966080 bytes free

 C>
```

Figure 2–2
Wide directory listing obtained with DIR/W command

2–9   DIFFERENT VERSIONS OF MS-DOS AND PC-DOS

PC-DOS is used in IBM microcomputers, and MS-DOS is used in IBM compatibles. Both of these operating systems have gone through several revisions from 1.0 to the latest version, 6.0. Each version has added new commands and corrected some of the bugs in the earlier versions. Versions 3.1 and later include commands for the LAN (local area network) environment. Major revisions are indicated by whole numbers (2.0, 3.0, and so on); minor revisions are indicated by fractions (2.01, 3.2, and so forth).

Versions of MS-DOS and PC-DOS are upwardly compatible. All the commands in earlier versions are available in the newer versions, but not vice versa.

```
C>DIR/P

 Volume in drive C is MS_DOS_6
 Volume Serial Number is 1C22-913B
 Directory of C:\DOS

 .               <DIR>         06-06-92   12:24p
 ..              <DIR>         06-06-92   12:24p
 DBLSPACE BIN       51214 03-10-93    6:00a
 FORMAT   COM       22717 03-10-93    6:00a
 NLSFUNC  EXE        7036 03-10-93    6:00a
 COUNTRY  SYS       17066 03-10-93    6:00a
 KEYB     COM       14983 03-10-93    6:00a
 KEYBOARD SYS       34694 03-10-93    6:00a
 SETUP    EXE       71974 03-10-93    6:00a
 DOSSETUP INI        3735 03-10-93    6:00a
 ANSI     SYS        9065 03-10-93    6:00a
 ATTRIB   EXE       11165 03-10-93    6:00a
 CHKDSK   EXE       12907 03-10-93    6:00a
 EDIT     COM         413 03-10-93    6:00a
 EXPAND   EXE       16129 03-10-93    6:00a
 EDLIN    EXE       12642 06-13-91    5:00a
 MORE     COM        2546 03-10-93    6:00a
 MSD      EXE      158470 03-10-93    6:00a
 QBASIC   EXE      194309 03-10-93    6:00a
 Press any key to continue . . .

 (continuing C:\DOS)
 RESTORE  EXE       38294 03-10-93    6:00a
 MIRROR   COM       18169 06-13-91    5:00a
 SYS      COM        9379 03-10-93    6:00a
 UNFORMAT COM       12738 03-10-93    6:00a
 SMARTDRV SYS        8335 06-13-91    5:00a
 OS2      TXT        6358 03-10-93    6:00a
 NETWORKS TXT       20463 03-10-93    6:00a
 README   TXT       44990 03-10-93    6:00a
 DEBUG    EXE       15715 03-10-93    6:00a
 FDISK    EXE       29333 03-10-93    6:00a
 DOSSHELL VID        9462 03-10-93    6:00a
 19C1DOSC BAT          16 01-23-93    3:05p
 DEFAULT  SET        4207 01-02-94   10:49a
 DOSSHELL GRB        4421 03-10-93    6:00a
 CHOICE   COM        1754 03-10-93    6:00a
 DEFRAG   EXE       75033 03-10-93    6:00a
 PACKING  LST        2507 06-13-91    5:00a
 DEFRAG   HLP        9227 03-10-93    6:00a
 DOSSWAP  EXE       18756 03-10-93    6:00a
 EGA      CPI       58870 03-10-93    6:00a
 RECOVER  EXE        9146 06-13-91    5:00a
 EGA      SYS        4885 03-10-93    6:00a
 Press any key to continue . . .

 (continuing C:\DOS)
 HIMEM    SYS       14208 03-10-93    6:00a
 MEM      EXE       32150 03-10-93    6:00a
 XCOPY    EXE       15820 03-10-93    6:00a
 MONEY    BAS       46225 06-13-91    5:00a
 MSHERC   COM        6934 06-13-91    5:00a
 DELTREE  EXE       11113 03-10-93    6:00a
 GORILLA  BAS       29434 06-13-91    5:00a
 4201     CPI        6404 06-13-91    5:00a
 4208     CPI         720 06-13-91    5:00a
 5202     CPI         395 06-13-91    5:00a
 MOVE     EXE       17823 03-10-93    6:00a
 ASSIGN   COM        6399 06-13-91    5:00a
 RAMDRIVE SYS        5873 03-10-93    6:00a
 BACKUP   EXE       36092 06-13-91    5:00a
```

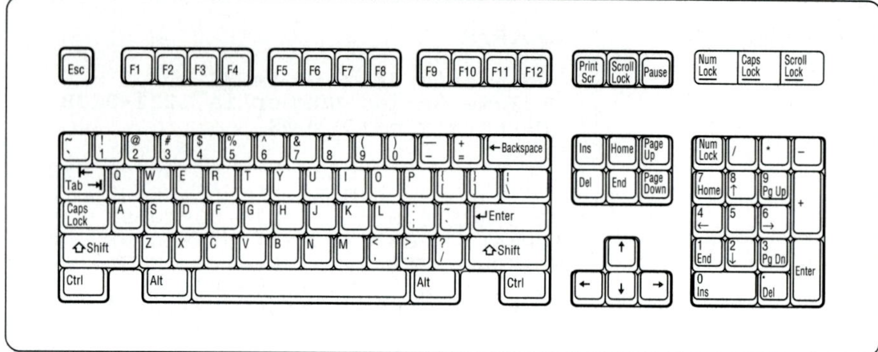

Table 2–1
Special keys on the keyboard

Keys	Description
Ctrl+Alt+Del	This key combination is used to warm boot the system. This is equivalent to turning your computer off, then turning it back on (without memory check).
Ctrl+C or Ctrl+Break	Cancels a command while it is being executed.
Ctrl+PrtSc or Ctrl+P	Sends a copy of each line on the screen to the printer, as it is being displayed (assuming that you are connected to a printer and the printer is on). This command toggles the printer on, meaning it will remain in effect until you press Ctrl and PrtSc or P again. When the printer is toggled on, everything displayed on screen also is printed on your printer.
Shift+PrtSc	Sends a copy of the screen to the printer. This command does not toggle the printer on. In enhanced keyboards, press the dedicated **Print Screen** key.
Ctrl+S or Ctrl+Num Lock	Pauses the directory listing for viewing.
F1 function key	Displays one character of the previous command with each press. Useful for editing a DOS command.
F3 function key	Displays the previous command. You can perform editing, or just press F3 and Enter to execute the command again.
F6 function key (equivalent to Ctrl+Z)	Marks the end of a batch file. It also stops an autoexec file (an autoexec file starts execution as soon as you start the co mputer).
Backspace	Backs up and erases the character typed.
Esc	Erases the current command or statement as it is being entered.

Figure 2–5
Formatting procedure

```
C>FORMAT A:
Insert new diskette for drive A:
and press ENTER when ready...

Checking existing disk format.
Saving UNFORMAT information.
Verifying 1.2M
Format complete.

Volume label (11 characters, ENTER for none)?

   1213952 bytes total disk space
   1213952 bytes available on disk

       512 bytes in each allocation unit.
      2371 allocation units available on disk.

Volume Serial Number is 293C-11CA

Format another (Y/N)?N


C>
```

To a typical microcomputer user, PC-DOS and MS-DOS are almost identical. To find out which version of DOS you are using, type *VER* at the C> prompt and press Enter. This command reveals the current version of DOS in the disk drive. Figure 2–6 illustrates this process. It shows that our version of DOS is 6.0. All the commands discussed in the text work with all versions of DOS unless otherwise specified.

2–10   ONLINE HELP FACILITY

While working with DOS 6.0, you can always request online help. There are several methods of requesting help. If you are working with the DOS shell or the Edit component of DOS 6.0 (discussed later in this book), press the F1 function key and the Help menu will appear.

At the DOS prompt you can ask for help by typing *HELP* and pressing Enter. You will then be presented with a screen similar to the one in Figure 2–7.

While the MS-DOS Help Command Reference (Figure 2–7) is displayed, you can move the cursor to any particular command and press Enter to receive online help on that command. For example, if you move the cursor to <Erase> and press Enter, you will be presented with a screen similar to the one in Figure 2–8.

If you are using a mouse, you can move the mouse pointer to a command and click the left button of the mouse. To exit the Help screen press Alt, F, X or, using the mouse, click on File, then on Exit.

Figure 2–6
Determining your version of DOS

```
C>VER

MS-DOS Version 6.00


C>
```

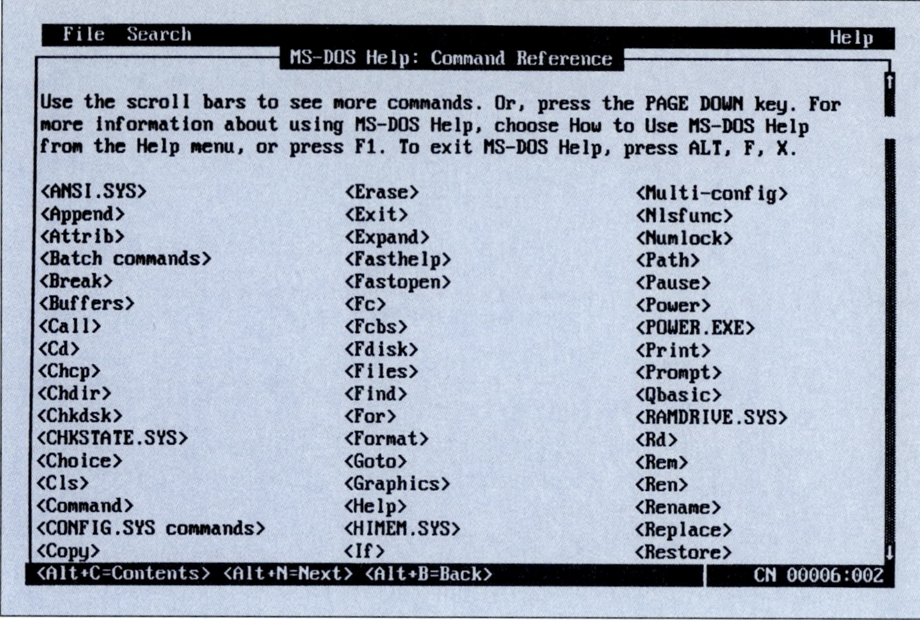

At the DOS prompt you can also type *HELP* followed by the command name to receive help. For example, type *HELP ERASE* (press Enter) to receive help on the Erase command.

You can use PgUp, PgDn, Tab, and arrow keys to navigate through the Help screen. You can also use the mouse to navigate through the Help screen. For example, you can click the scroll arrow (up or down) in the upper right or lower right of the Help screen to move to different sections of the screen. As you see at the bottom of the Help screen (Figure 2–7), you can press the following keys for various help options:

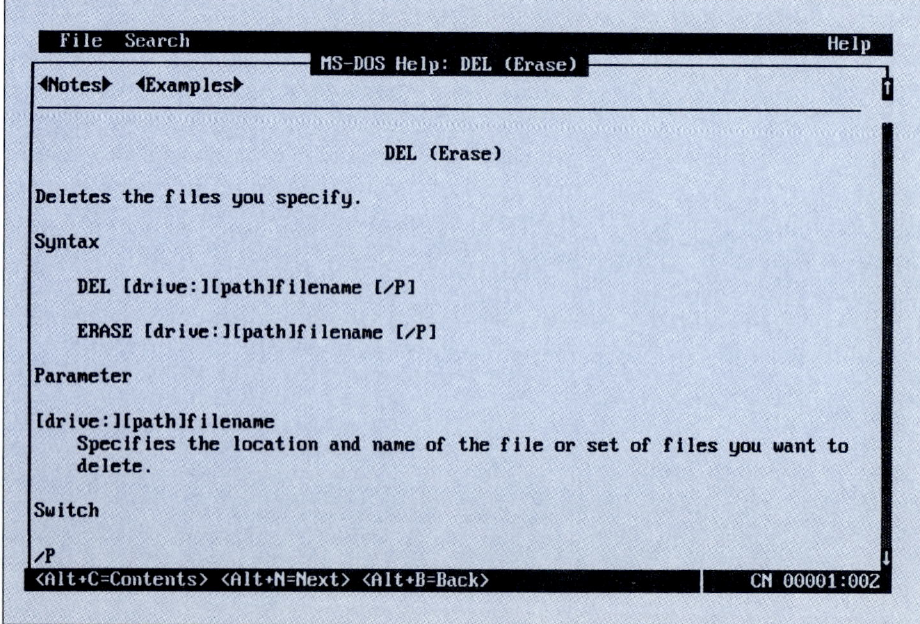

Figure 2–9
MS-DOS Help: How to use MS-DOS Help

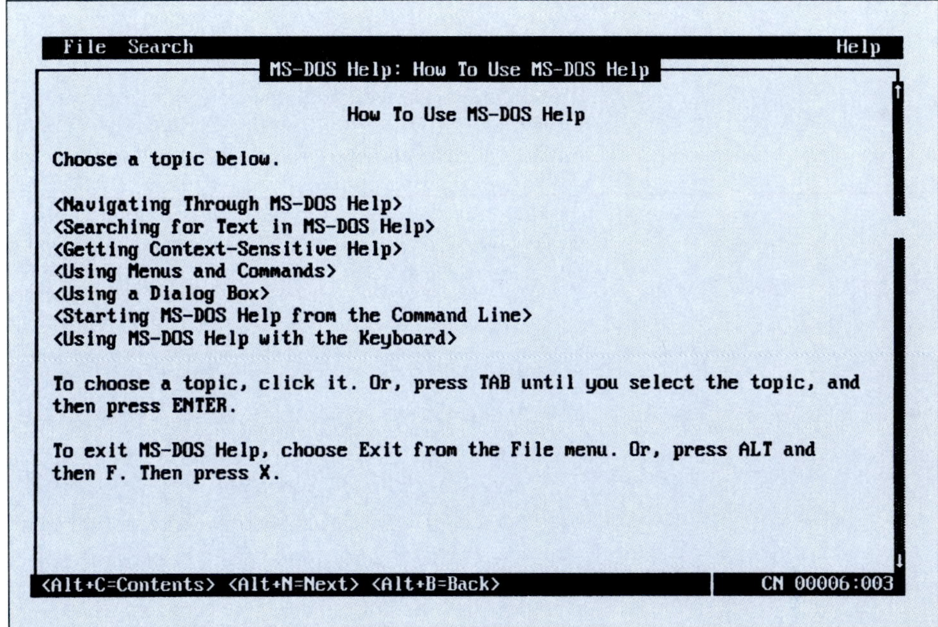

Alt + C	To display the help contents
Alt + N	To display the next screen
Alt + B	To display the previous screen

If you press the F1 function key while the MS-DOS Help Command Reference is displayed, you will see a screen similar to the one in Figure 2–9. You can select any of these options by moving the cursor to the option and pressing the Enter key.

You can also type *FASTHELP* at the DOS prompt to generate an alphabetical listing of all the DOS commands (see Figure 2–10).

Figure 2–10
Partial listing of FASTHELP

```
C:\>FASTHELP

For more information on a specific command, type FASTHELP command-name.
APPEND    Allows programs to open data files in specified directories as if
          they were in the current directory.
ATTRIB    Displays or changes file attributes.
BREAK     Sets or clears extended CTRL+C checking.
CD        Displays the name of or changes the current directory.
CHCP      Displays or sets the active code page number.
CHDIR     Displays the name of or changes the current directory.
CHKDSK    Checks a disk and displays a status report.
CLS       Clears the screen.
COMMAND   Starts a new instance of the MS-DOS command interpreter.
COMP      Compares the contents of two files or sets of files.
COPY      Copies one or more files to another location.
CTTY      Changes the terminal device used to control your system.
DATE      Displays or sets the date.
DBLSPACE  Sets up or configures DoubleSpace compressed drives.
DEBUG     Starts Debug, a program testing and editing tool.
DEFRAG    Reorganizes the files on a disk to optimize the disk.
DEL       Deletes one or more files.
DELOLDOS  Deletes the OLD_DOS.1 directory and the files it contains.
DELTREE   Deletes a directory and all the files and subdirectories in it.
DIR       Displays a list of files and subdirectories in a directory.
---More---
```

SUMMARY

This chapter reviewed elementary DOS operations and explained the difference between internal and external DOS commands. Types of DOS prompts and file name specifications in the DOS environment were highlighted. Use of the DIR command with different switches and important keys frequently used in the DOS environment were introduced. We also examined the FORMAT command. The chapter concluded with a brief discussion of different versions of DOS and DOS Help facility. In the next chapter, commonly used DOS commands are discussed.

REVIEW QUESTIONS

*These questions are answered in Appendix A.

1. What is a cold boot? Warm boot?
2. What are DOS internal commands? External commands?
3. What is the C> prompt? The A> prompt? How do you change the C> prompt to the A> prompt?
*4. Why should you always enter the correct date and time at boot-up? How do you bypass the date and time prompts?
5. What constitutes a valid DOS file name? An invalid DOS file name?
6. What are three examples of DOS file extensions?
7. What are the applications of the DIR command?
*8. What is the difference between DIR/W and DIR/P?
9. What are the applications of the F1 and F3 function keys in the DOS environment?
10. How do you generate a hard copy of the current screen?
*11. How do you stop the execution of a DOS command?
12. What are the applications of the Esc key?
13. How and where is the Ctrl key used?
14. Why does a new disk have to be formatted before it can be used?
15. What is actually done when you format a disk?
16. What is the first version of DOS? The latest version?
*17. How do you determine which version of DOS you are using?
18. How do you receive online help? How do you exit the Help screen?
19. What does FASTHELP do?

HANDS-ON EXPERIENCE

1. Turn on your PC. Enter the current date and time. Change the date to January 1, 1995. Change it to the current date. Change the time to 3:30 p.m. Change it to the current time.
2. List the directory of the DOS disk (use the DIR command). Erase the screen and display a wide directory of the disk (DIR/W). Erase the screen and list the directory with the pause switch (DIR/P).
3. Put a blank disk in drive A. Using the FORMAT A: command, format the disk. List the directory of the new disk. What are the contents of the disk?

4. Using a wildcard character, list all system files (system files have COM as their extension). Use the VER command to determine the version of DOS you are using.

5. Try to use all the keys presented in Table 2–1.

6. Display the directory of the default drive. Create a hard copy of this directory. What is the difference between Ctrl+PrtSc and Ctrl+P?

7. Can F1 and F3 perform the same task? If so, how?

8. Why are there many different versions of DOS? By consulting a DOS manual, name two specific improvements of DOS 6.0.

9. Using the instructions provided in this chapter, walk through various features of the Help menu. How do you receive online help on a specific command?

KEY TERMS

Backup file	DOS prompt	Internal command
Batch file	Executable file	System date
Cold boot	External command	System file
Command file	File allocation table	System time
Disk operating system	Hard disk	Warm boot
DOS file specification	Help facility	

KEY COMMANDS

A:, B:, C: (internal)	DATE (internal)	F6 function key (internal)
Backspace (internal)	DIR (internal)	FASTHELP (external)
CLS (internal)	DIR/P (internal)	FORMAT (external)
Ctrl+Alt+Del (internal)	DIR/W (internal)	HELP (external)
Ctrl+C (internal)	Esc (internal)	Shift+PrtSc (internal)
Ctrl+PrtSc or Ctrl+P (internal)	F1 function key (internal)	TIME (internal)
	F3 function key (internal)	VER (internal)
Ctrl+S or Ctrl+Num Lock (internal)		

MISCONCEPTIONS AND SOLUTIONS*

Misconception   You turn on your PC, and you see a message that is not familiar to you—non-system disk, for example.

> **Solution**   You either forgot to put the DOS disk into drive A, a data disk is in drive A, or you inserted your disk on the wrong side. Insert the DOS disk into drive A properly and reboot the system. If DOS is installed in drive C, remove any data disk from drive A and reboot the system.

---

* A complete listing of DOS error messages is provided in Appendix A.

Misconception   You are trying to format a disk and receive an ATTEMPTED WRITE-PROTECT VIOLATION error message.

> **Solution**   The disk in drive A has the write-protection notch covered. Either remove the protection or insert another disk.

Misconception   You are using the FORMAT command and receive a DRIVE NOT READY error message.

> **Solution**   Either the target drive door is not closed or there is no disk in that drive. Insert a disk in this drive, close the drive door, and press Enter.

Misconception   You are using a DOS command and receive a SYNTAX ERROR, BAD COMMAND, or FILENAME error.

> **Solution**   Check the spelling of the command. Most likely, you have misspelled a command.

ARE YOU READY TO MOVE ON?

Multiple Choice

1. The procedure known as warm boot means
   a. inserting the DOS disk in drive A and turning on the computer
   b. typing the name of the program to be run and pressing Enter
   c. simultaneously pressing the Ctrl, Alt, and Del keys
   d. formatting a disk
   e. none of the above

2. Which of the following prompts are you most likely to see after performing a cold boot with the DOS disk in drive C?
   a. A>
   b. B>
   c. C>
   d. OK
   e. B:/DOS>

3. If the correct date and time are not entered during the boot process or if you want to change them at any time, the commands are
   a. HOUR and DAY
   b. DAY and HOUR
   c. DATE and CLOCK
   d. DATE and TIME
   e. none of the above

4. To change the default drive from drive C to drive A, what should you type at the DOS prompt before pressing Enter?
   a. A
   b. DRIVE=A
   c. B=A
   d. GO TO A:
   e. A:

5. File names with these extensions can be executed by typing the name of the file:
   a. COM and SYS
   b. COM and EXE
   c. EXE and SYS

      d. BAK and SYS
      e. BAK and BAT

6. The command DIR/P will yield

      a. the same as DIR
      b. a wide directory listing
      c. one screen at a time of the directory listing
      d. a hard copy output to the printer
      e. nothing—it is not a valid command

7. The command to format a disk in drive B is

      a. ERASE B:
      b. DELETE *.*
      c. SYS B:
      d. FORMAT B:
      e. a or b

8. The file allocation table indicates

      a. where data is saved on a disk
      b. the maximum number of files that can be saved on disk
      c. how much disk space is available
      d. how much memory (RAM) is available
      e. none of the above

9. A typical computer response to the command VER is

      a. Disk Verified OK
      b. MS-DOS Version 6.0
      c. File Verified OK
      d. Insert new disk and strike Enter when ready
      e. a or b

10. When you format a disk,

      a. all data is erased
      b. a file allocation table is created
      c. the operating system checks for defective spots
      d. the disk is divided into sectors and tracks
      e. all of the above

True/False

1. If the computer is off and the system does not have a hard disk, the DOS disk must be placed in drive A to boot the computer.

2. A cold boot is faster than a warm boot because the computer does not check the memory.

3. Although DOS does not require the current date and time, it is good practice always to enter the correct information.

4. External DOS commands are those loaded into the computer memory at boot-up time.

5. The DOS prompt indicates the current default drive.

6. The DIR command generates a listing of the files in the default directory.

7. DOS wildcards act as placeholders for other characters and include *, ?, @, $, %, and .

8. DIR and DIR/W yield exactly the same information except that DIR/W places it in a wide format.

9. In general, a newly purchased disk cannot be used directly out of the box.

10. There is no help feature available in MS-DOS 6.0.

ANSWERS

Multiple Choice		True/False	
1.	c	1.	T
2.	c	2.	F
3.	d	3.	T
4.	e	4.	F
5.	b	5.	T
6.	c	6.	T
7.	d	7.	F
8.	a	8.	F
9.	b	9.	T
10.	e	10.	F

Commonly Used DOS Commands

3

3–1   INTRODUCTION

In this chapter we discuss some of the most common DOS commands. These commands are used in day-to-day operations and will help you improve your effectiveness while you are working with PCs. Various versions of the FORMAT command are discussed as are the DISKCOPY and COPY commands for copying an entire disk or selected files. The CHKDSK command, which is used for checking the space available on your disk and your PC is also covered. The RENAME (for changing a file name), DEL and ERASE (for erasing a file), and ATTRIB (for making a file read-only) commands are introduced.

3–2   FORMAT COMMAND

Any disk, floppy or hard, must be formatted before it can be used by your PC. **Formatting** a disk means checking the disk for defective spots and preparing storage areas. When the computer formats a disk, the disk is completely erased and a directory is generated that can be accessed by the DIR command. A file allocation table (FAT) is created, which provides the name, extension, size, date, and time a file is created. The FAT determines where data is saved. Remember that the FORMAT command is a destructive command. Be careful!

FORMAT is an external DOS command and has several variations (see Table 3–1). To use any of the commands shown in the table, the DOS disk must be in one of the drives. In our case, it is in the C drive. Although drive A is used in Table 3–1, these variations will work with any drive. Formatting a hard disk is explained in Chapter 4.

Table 3–1
Various FORMAT commands

Command	Function
FORMAT A:	Format a data disk with 9 or 15 sectors per track
FORMAT A:/S	Format a disk for self-booting. This command transfers system files IBMBIO.COM, IBM.COM, and COMMAND.COM to the newly formatted disk. This disk can then be used to boot the computer. This means the DOS disk is not needed to start up the system.
FORMAT A:/V	Format a disk with a volume label. A volume label is any valid name up to 11 characters. It follows the same conventions as the file name.
FORMAT A:/1	Format a one-sided disk
FORMAT A:/4	Format a double-sided disk in a high-capacity drive
FORMAT A:/8	Format an eight-sector-per-track disk
FORMAT A:/B	Format a disk for eight sectors and leave correct space for system files IBMBIO.COM and IBMDOS.COM. These files can be copied later.
FORMAT A:/F:size (DOS 3.3 and higher)	Specifies the size of the floppy disk to format, such as 360 K, 720 K, 1.2 MB or 1.44 MB, and so forth.

```
C>FORMAT A:
Insert new diskette for drive A:
and press ENTER when ready...

Checking existing disk format.
Saving UNFORMAT information.
Verifying 1.2M
Format complete.

Volume label (11 characters, ENTER for none)?

   1213952 bytes total disk space
   1213952 bytes available on disk

      512 bytes in each allocation unit.
     2371 allocation units available on disk.

Volume Serial Number is 293C-11CA

Format another (Y/N)?N


C>
```

Figure 3–1 illustrates an example of the FORMAT command. Insert an empty disk in the A drive. At the C> prompt, type *FORMAT A:* and press Enter. Follow the instructions at the prompt. When the disk is formatted, DOS asks whether you would like to format another disk. Answer N (for no). Remember, DOS commands are not case sensitive. This means there is no distinction between uppercase and lowercase.

Figure 3–2 illustrates formatting with a **volume label.** Insert a blank disk in drive A. At the C> prompt, type *FORMAT A:/V* and press Enter. Follow the instructions at the prompt. Enter a volume label up to 11 characters (Customers, for example) and press Enter. When you are finished, the computer displays

```
Format another (Y/N)?
```



```
C>FORMAT A:/V
Insert new diskette for drive A:
and press ENTER when ready...

Checking existing disk format.
Saving UNFORMAT information.
Verifying 1.2M
Format complete.

Volume label (11 characters, ENTER for none)? CUSTOMERS

   1213952 bytes total disk space
   1213952 bytes available on disk

      512 bytes in each allocation unit.
     2371 allocation units available on disk.

Volume Serial Number is 3F2F-19DB

Format another (Y/N)?N


C>
```

```
C>FORMAT A:/S/V
Insert new diskette for drive A:
and press ENTER when ready...

Checking existing disk format.
Saving UNFORMAT information.
Verifying 1.2M
Format complete.
System transferred

Volume label (11 characters, ENTER for none)? CUSTOMERS

   1213952 bytes total disk space
    119808 bytes used by system
   1094144 bytes available on disk

       512 bytes in each allocation unit.
      2137 allocation units available on disk.

Volume Serial Number is 371E-19DD

Format another (Y/N)?N


C>
```

Answer N to stop the format command. This disk now has a name—CUSTOMERS. When you list the directory of the disk, the volume name is displayed at the top of the directory listing. Labeling a disk internally is a good practice. This will help you to identify a disk if the external label (the sticker) is lost.

The switches, or parameters, for the FORMAT command can be combined. Figure 3–3 illustrates one example. Insert a blank disk in drive A. At the C> prompt, type *FORMAT A:/S/V*. Follow the instructions at the prompt, and enter a volume label. This command creates a system disk with a volume label that can be used to boot the system.

3–3   LABEL COMMAND

If you forget to give a volume label to a disk when formatting, you can always add the volume label later with the LABEL command. This command also can be used to change an existing volume label.

Figure 3–4 illustrates this procedure. Insert the data disk with the CUSTOMERS volume label in drive A. At the C> prompt, type *LABEL A:* and press Enter. Enter *SUPPLIERS* as the volume label and press Enter. Now you have changed the volume label from CUSTOMERS to SUPPLIERS.


```
C>LABEL A:
Volume in drive A is CUSTOMERS
Volume Serial Number is 371E-19DD
Volume label (11 characters, ENTER for none)? SUPPLIERS

C>
```

By using the VOL (volume) command, you can find out if a disk has a label or not. Just type *VOL* at the DOS prompt and press Enter.

3–4　　DISKCOPY COMMAND

The DISKCOPY command generates an exact duplicate of a disk. When you use the DISKCOPY command, the target disk does not need to be formatted because the DISKCOPY command formats while it is copying. Remember that only non-protected disks can be copied. Protected disks are designed by the vendors to guard against illegal copying of their programs. Figure 3–5 illustrates the DISKCOPY command. If your computer has two external drives of the same size, insert the disk to be copied in drive A and a blank disk in drive B, type *DISKCOPY A: B:* and press Enter. Follow the prompts. When copying is complete, answer N to stop the DISKCOPY command. Now you have created an exact copy of the disk in drive A in drive B. If you have a computer with only one external drive, type *DISKCOPY A: A:* and press Enter. The computer reads the first disk; next you pull this disk out and insert the second disk in the same drive. So the one disk is functioning as both A and B. Be aware, however, that you may have to swap the disks several times before you are finished copying.

Whenever you are working with a DOS command that deals with two drives or two separate locations in one drive, the command always works on a from-to basis. The first drive or location is the source (from) and the second is the target (to).

Figure 3–5
DISKCOPY command

```
C>DISKCOPY A: A:

Insert SOURCE diskette in drive A:

Press any key to continue . . .

Copying 80 tracks
15 sectors per track, 2 side(s)

Insert TARGET diskette in drive A:

Press any key to continue . . .

Insert SOURCE diskette in drive A:

Press any key to continue . . .

Insert TARGET diskette in drive A:

Press any key to continue . . .

Insert SOURCE diskette in drive A:

Press any key to continue . . .

Insert TARGET diskette in drive A:

Press any key to continue . . .

Volume Serial Number is 1CC9-2C39

Copy another diskette (Y/N)? N

C>
```

```
C>DISKCOMP A: A:

Insert FIRST diskette in drive A:

Press any key to continue . . .

Comparing 80 tracks
15 sectors per track, 2 side(s)

Insert SECOND diskette in drive A:

Press any key to continue . . .

Insert FIRST diskette in drive A:

Press any key to continue . . .

Insert SECOND diskette in drive A:

Press any key to continue . . .

Compare OK

Compare another diskette (Y/N) ?
```

3–5   DISKCOMP COMMAND

The DISKCOMP command is used to verify whether the copy generated by the DISKCOPY command is 100 percent correct. Figure 3–6 illustrates this process. If your computer has a hard disk (drive C) and two external drives (A and B) of the same size, follow these steps. At the C> prompt, insert the desired disk in drive A and the disk for comparison (the duplicate) in drive B, type *DISKCOMP A: B:,* and press Enter. Follow the instructions at the prompt. You will see the message

```
Compare OK
```

if your disks are identical. If your computer has only one drive, or its drives are not of the same size, you can use drive A for both drives. Type *DISKCOMP A: A:* and follow the prompts.

3–6   CHKDSK COMMAND

You use the CHKDSK command to determine the memory status of your disk or your computer. It tells you the total amount of disk space in bytes (free or unused), bytes on the disk, memory available on your PC, and the memory being used. Figure 3–7 illustrates this command. At the C> prompt insert the desired disk in drive A, and then type *CHKDSK A:.* Press Enter and you will see the information provided in Figure 3–7. We used a sample disk that includes SYS files from DOS 6.0.

The CHKDSK command can be used with the V and F parameters. The V parameter enables you to view the files and their paths on a given disk. Figure 3–8 illustrates this command. At the C> prompt, we inserted the sample disk in drive A. We typed *CHKDSK A:/V* and pressed Enter.

```
C>CHKDSK A:

Volume SUPPLIERS    created 01-03-1994 10:26a
Volume Serial Number is 11E5-2152

   1213952 bytes total disk space
    131072 bytes in 3 hidden files
    248832 bytes in 14 user files
    834048 bytes available on disk

       512 bytes in each allocation unit
      2371 total allocation units on disk
      1629 available allocation units on disk

    655360 total bytes memory
    574960 bytes free

C>
```

Using CHKDSK with the F parameter enables you to correct errors in the directory or file allocation table on a given disk. If there is no error, the normal output is generated, which is similar to that of the CHKDSK command alone. Figure 3–9 illustrates this command. At the C> prompt, insert the desired disk in drive A, type *CHKDSK A:/F*, and press Enter. In drive A, we inserted the sample disk that included SYS files from DOS 6.0.


```
CHKDSK A:/V

Volume SUPPLIERS    created 01-03-1994 10:26a
Volume Serial Number is 11E5-2152
Directory A:\
A:\IO.SYS
A:\MSDOS.SYS
A:\COUNTRY.SYS
A:\DBLSPACE.BIN
A:\KEYBOARD.SYS
A:\ANSI.SYS
A:\SMARTDRV.SYS
A:\EGA.SYS
A:\HIMEM.SYS
A:\RAMDRIVE.SYS
A:\DISPLAY.SYS
A:\PRINTER.SYS
A:\SSTOR.SYS
A:\DRIVER.SYS
A:\MOUSE.SYS
A:\CHKSTATE.SYS
A:\DBLSPACE.SYS

   1213952 bytes total disk space
    131072 bytes in 3 hidden files
    248832 bytes in 14 user files
    834048 bytes available on disk

       512 bytes in each allocation unit
      2371 total allocation units on disk
      1629 available allocation units on disk

    655360 total bytes memory
    574960 bytes free

C>
```

Figure 3–9
CHKDSK/F command

```
C>CHKDSK A:/F

Volume SUPPLIERS    created 01-03-1994 10:26a
Volume Serial Number is 11E5-2152

   1213952 bytes total disk space
    131072 bytes in 3 hidden files
    248832 bytes in 14 user files
    834048 bytes available on disk

       512 bytes in each allocation unit
      2371 total allocation units on disk
      1629 available allocation units on disk

    655360 total bytes memory
    574960 bytes free

C>
```

3–7   SYS COMMAND

The SYS command is used to copy the DOS hidden files from the DOS disk to another disk. To use this command, you must have formatted the desired disk using the FORMAT/B command. This disk will not be a self-booting disk until you transfer COMMAND.COM from the DOS disk. With a self-booting disk, you do not need the DOS disk to get your computer started. The self-booting disk does the job by itself. Figure 3–10 illustrates the procedure. Insert the disk that has been formatted with the FORMAT/B command in drive A. At the C> prompt, type *SYS A:* and press Enter.

If you list the directory of the disk in drive A with the DIR command, you will see nothing new, because only the hidden files are transferred. To verify the process, you can measure the space available on this disk by using the CHKDSK command before and after execution of the SYS command. You can tell that something, indeed, has been transferred; you can see it by using the CHKDSK/V command.

3–8   COPY COMMAND

The COPY command is used for copying one or several files from one disk to itself or to another disk. If you are making a duplicate copy of a file on the same disk, you must use a different file name for the target (duplicate) file, otherwise you will receive an error message. The COPY command, combined with wildcard characters, can be very powerful. Table 3–2 shows several versions of the COPY command. In these examples, the default drive is C. FILE1 is any valid file name and EXT is any valid file extension.

Figure 3–11 illustrates one example of the COPY command. Insert a formatted disk in drive A. At the C> prompt, type *COPY *.SYS A:* and press Enter.

Figure 3–10
SYS command

```
C>SYS A:
System transferred

C>
```

Table 3–2
Various COPY commands

Command	Description
COPY FILE1.EXT B:	Copy FILE1.EXT from C to B
COPY B:FILE1.EXT	Copy FILE1.EXT from B to C
COPY *.COM B:	Copy all files with COM extension from C to B
COPY B:*.COM	Copy all files with COM extension from B to C
COPY *.* B:	Copy all files from C to B
COPY B:*.*	Copy all files from B to C
COPY FILE1.EXT File2.EXT	Copy a file from C to C with a different name
COPY B:FILE1.EXT B:File2.EXT	Copy a file from B to B with a different name
COPY FILE1.EXT+File2.EXT File3.EXT	Combine File1 and File2 and generate a third file (File3) in C (There must be one space between FILE2.EXT and FILE3.EXT)
COPY FILE1.EXT B:/V	Copy FILE1.EXT from C to B and verify the process

This command copies all SYS files from drive C to A. You can verify this by checking the directory of drive A with *DIR A:* command.

3–9   COPY VERSUS DISKCOPY

There are four major differences between the COPY *.* and DISKCOPY commands. First, the COPY *.* command can be used to duplicate a disk; however, the target disk must be formatted first. DISKCOPY formats while it is copying. Second, COPY *.* does not transfer the hidden files from the source disk to the target disk. If you want to maintain the information on the target disk, do not use the DISKCOPY command—this command erases the target disk. You must always use the COPY command instead. Third, COPY *.* copies files contiguously (files are stored in adjacent sectors), reorganizing the files and speeding up access of files. Fourth, when you use the COPY command, it is not necessary to have the DOS disk in one of your drives (COPY is an internal command). When using the

Figure 3–11
Example of COPY command

```
C>COPY *.SYS A:
COUNTRY.SYS
KEYBOARD.SYS
ANSI.SYS
SMARTDRV.SYS
EGA.SYS
HIMEM.SYS
RAMDRIVE.SYS
DISPLAY.SYS
PRINTER.SYS
SSTOR.SYS
DRIVER.SYS
MOUSE.SYS
CHKSTATE.SYS
DBLSPACE.SYS
        14 file(s) copied

C>
```

```
C>COMP DRIVER.SYS
Name of second file to compare: A:DRIVER.SYS
Option :
Comparing DRIVER.SYS and A:DRIVER.SYS...
Files compare OK

Compare more files (Y/N) ? N

C>
```

DISKCOPY command, the DOS disk must be in one of your drives (DISKCOPY is an external command).

3–10   COMP COMMAND

The COMP command is used to verify whether a particular file has been copied correctly. The two files can be on one disk or on different disks. Figure 3–12 illustrates one example of this command. At the C> prompt, insert the sample disk in drive A. Suppose that we want to compare DRIVER.SYS on these two disks. At the C> prompt, type *COMP DRIVER.SYS* and press Enter. The computer asks you to enter the second file name. Type *A:DRIVER.SYS* and press Enter. (In DOS 5.0, press Enter twice to bypass the Option choice.) DOS responds

```
Files compare OK
```

Remember, you always must use the driver identification if the two files are not on the same disk.

3–11   RENAME COMMAND

You use the RENAME command to change the name of a file or several files. Figure 3–13 shows an example of this command. At the C> prompt, insert the sample disk in drive A. Suppose that you want to change DRIVER.SYS to JACKSON.SYS in drive A. At the C> prompt, type *RENAME A: DRIVER.SYS JACKSON.SYS* and press Enter. You can check your work by looking at the directory for the A drive. The RENAME command can be used with wildcard characters, which means you can rename several files at once. For example, RENAME *.COM *.XYZ renames all COM files to XYZ files in your default drive.

3–12   DELETE AND ERASE COMMANDS

You can use either the DELETE (DEL) or the ERASE command to erase one file or the entire disk. For example, to erase EDLIN.COM from drive A, type *DEL*


```
A>RENAME DRIVER.SYS JACKSON.SYS

A>
```

```
C>ATTRIB +R COMMAND.COM

C>
```

A:EDLIN.COM at the C> prompt. To erase the entire disk in drive A, type *DEL A:*.** at the C> prompt. An alternative method of erasing is to use the ERASE A:EDLIN.COM or ERASE A:*.* commands. Be careful, however; these commands can be dangerous, especially when they are combined with wildcard characters.

3–13   ATTRIB COMMAND

The ATTRIB command protects a file from being deleted accidentally. This command can be very helpful to protect essential commands such as COMMAND.COM, without which you cannot boot the system. Figure 3–14 illustrates an example of this command. At the C> prompt, type *ATTRIB +R COMMAND.COM* and press Enter. This file is now a **read-only file.** If you try to delete it with either the ERASE or the DEL command, you will receive an Access Denied message.

If you would like to remove the read-only status from this file, type *ATTRIB –R* and the file name. Remember the ATTRIB command is available only in DOS versions 3 and above.

To make your entire disk a read-only disk, issue the command *ATTRIB +R *.** and press Enter.

SUMMARY

This chapter reviewed commonly used DOS commands—FORMAT, DISKCOPY, CHKDSK, DISKCOMP, COMP, COPY, RENAME, DEL, ERASE, and ATTRIB. Understanding these commands makes it easier to work with DOS. In the next chapter, we talk about directories and subdirectories.

REVIEW QUESTIONS

*These questions are answered in Appendix A.

1. What version of the FORMAT command is the most commonly used?

*2. What version of the FORMAT command is used to make a disk self-booting?

3. What version of the FORMAT command is used to leave the correct space for system files?

4. What is a volume label? Why should you always use a volume label? How do you change an existing volume label?

*5. When do you use the DISKCOPY command? Do you need to format the target disk to use the DISKCOPY command?

6. When do you use the DISKCOMP command?

7. What are the applications of the CHKDSK command?

8. To find out how much space is available on your disk, what command should you use?

9. What are the two possible parameters that can be used with the CHKDSK command? What are the applications of each?

*10. What are the applications of the SYS command?

11. How do you verify whether a SYS command issued earlier has been successful?

12. What command do you use to transfer all the EXE files from drive C to a formatted disk in drive A?

*13. What command do you use to combine FILEA.ABC and FILEB.ABC into a third file called FILEC.ABC?

14. What version of the COPY command should you use to verify the COPY procedure?

15. What version of the COPY command should you use to copy the entire disk A to disk B without losing the existing contents of disk B?

*16. What are the differences between COPY *.* and DISKCOPY?

17. What are the applications of the COMP command? The RENAME command?

18. What version of the DEL command should you use to erase the entire disk in drive A?

19. What are the applications of the ATTRIB command?

HANDS-ON EXPERIENCE

1. This exercise assumes DOS is installed in your C drive. Insert a blank disk in drive A and do the following:
   a. Format the disk in drive A.
   b. Format the disk in drive A as a self-booting disk.
   c. Format the disk in drive A with 9 or 15 sectors per track.
   d. Format the disk in drive A with a volume label called TRY.
   e. Change the volume label from TRY to EXERCISE.

2. Using the DISKCOPY command, generate a duplicate of a sample disk in drive A. Using the DISKCOMP command, verify whether this is a correct copy. Using the CHKDSK command, find out how much unused space exists on your disk. Use the DEL *.* command to erase the entire disk in drive A.

3. Use the appropriate command to transfer DOS hidden files from drive C to A. Copy all COM files from C to A, and then erase the entire disk in drive A.

4. Copy the COMMAND.COM file from C to A. Now, by using the ATTRIB command, make this file a read-only file. How do you know a file is read-only? Remove the read-only status from the file.

5. Copy the COMMAND.COM file from drive C to A. Use the RENAME command to rename this file to TRY.ABC.

6. Select any two files from the DOS disk. By using the COPY command, combine these two files into a file called COMBINE.XYZ in drive A. Now copy this file to drive B or C by using the COPY/V command. Using the ERASE command, erase the file.

KEY TERMS

Formatting

Read-only file

Volume label

KEY COMMANDS

ATTRIB (external) DISKCOMP (external) LABEL (external)
CHKDSK (external) DISKCOPY (external) RENAME (internal)
COMP (internal) ERASE (internal) SYS (external)
COPY (internal) FORMAT (external) VOL (internal)
DELETE (DEL) (internal)

MISCONCEPTIONS AND SOLUTIONS

Misconception   You are using command FORMAT A:/ and receive an Invalid Parameter message.

Solution   You must include either the V or S parameter when you use / with the FORMAT command.

Misconception   You are working with the COPY command and receive the error message

```
FILE CANNOT BE COPIED TO ITSELF O FILE(S) COPIED.
```

Solution   You are either using the same name on the same disk or left out the drive identifier for the second file. Either use a different name for the second file or copy the same file with the same name to a different disk.

ARE YOU READY TO MOVE ON?

Multiple Choice

1. The command to format a self-booting disk with a volume label using drive A is
   a. FORMAT A:
   b. FORMAT B:
   c. FORMAT A:/V
   d. FORMAT B:/V
   e. FORMAT A:/S/V

2. To change the name (volume label) of a disk, the command to use is
   a. VOLUME
   b. LABEL
   c. NAME
   d. TYPE
   e. none of the above

3. The CHKDSK command tells you all of the following except
   a. the amount of memory available
   b. the amount of memory being used
   c. the version of DOS being used
   d. the amount of disk space available
   e. the amount of disk space used

4. The SYS command transfers the following file(s) to the disk:
   a. IBMBIO.COM
   b. IBMDOS.COM
   c. COMMAND.COM
   d. both a and b
   e. All of the above

5. The COPY command can do all of the following except
    a. format the disk
    b. copy from/to floppy disk and hard disk
    c. copy selected files
    d. verify that the files have been copied correctly
    e. copy more than one file at a time

6. An advantage of COPY over DISKCOPY is that the COPY command
    a. formats the disk
    b. copies protected files
    c. copies the hidden files
    d. maintains the files already on the target disk
    e. none of the above

7. To remove only the file TEST.MIS from the disk in the default drive, the command is
    a. DELETE TEST.MIS
    b. DELETE *.MIS
    c. DELETE TEST.*
    d. DELETE *.*
    e. REMOVE TEST.MIS

8. To generate a new file FILE3 by combining FILE1 and FILE2, the command is
    a. COPY FILE1, FILE2, FILE3
    b. COPY FILE1+FILE2 FILE3
    c. COPY FILE1 AND FILE2 TO FILE3
    d. FILE1+FILE2=FILE3
    e. none of the above

9. Which of the following is/are *not* true about the DISKCOPY command?
    a. It formats the target disk.
    b. It is destructive.
    c. It cannot be used with a single disk drive.
    d. It cannot be used to copy to/from a hard disk.
    e. all of the above

10. Which command verifies that the file FILE1.EXT was copied correctly to drive B?
    a. DISKCOPY FILE1.EXT B:
    b. COPY FILE1.EXT B:
    c. VER FILE1.EXT B:
    d. CHECK FILE1.EXT B:
    e. COMP FILE1.EXT B:/V

True/False

1. Only floppy disks need to be formatted.

2. The target disk does not need to be formatted when using the DISKCOPY command.

3. DISKCOPY only works with a hard disk.

4. DISKCOPY automatically checks and verifies that it has copied correctly.

5. CHKDSK/V enables you to see the files and their paths on a disk, including the DOS hidden files.

6. Assuming that all disks are formatted and that there are no system files, DISKCOPY A: B: and COPY A:*.* B: copy the same files from A to B.

7. There is no command to verify that the command COPY FILE1.ABC B: has copied FILE1.ABC correctly.

8. You must change the file name if you want to make a copy of a file on the same disk.

9. DELETE is used to remove one or more files; ERASE is used only to clear the entire disk.

10. The ATTRIB command can be used to protect a file from being accidentally deleted.

ANSWERS

	Multiple Choice		True/False
1.	e	1.	F
2.	b	2.	T
3.	c	3.	F
4.	d	4.	F
5.	a	5.	T
6.	d	6.	T
7.	a	7.	F
8.	b	8.	T
9.	c	9.	F
10.	e	10.	T

Directories and Subdirectories

4

4–1   INTRODUCTION

In this chapter we consider the process of establishing directories and subdirectories on a floppy or hard disk. Commands for creating a directory, changing a directory, and removing or erasing a directory are explained. The chapter concludes with information on hard disk management. This includes preparing a hard disk, backing it up, and restoring it in case of a crash. Directory operations enable you to manage your hard disk very effectively.

4–2   DEFINING A DIRECTORY

When you format a disk, DOS automatically creates a **directory** for you. This directory usually is called the **root directory.** Because of the advances in disk technology, more and more files can be stored on a disk. These files are stored based on the date that they were created. When the number of these files increases, it becomes extremely difficult to manage them properly. It becomes a time-consuming process to locate one file among several hundred. By using a directory, you can store all your graphics files in one location, and all your word processing files in another location, and so on.

There is a limit to the number of files that can be stored on a floppy or a hard disk. The root directory on a single-sided disk can hold up to 64 files; on a double-sided disk there can be up to 112 files. A high-density disk can hold up to 224 files, and a hard disk up to 512 files. To create a better mechanism for storing and maintaining files and to bypass these limitations, you can create subdirectories.

A **subdirectory** is basically an electronic folder that contains a listing of files that you have grouped together based on a given scheme. (Subdirectory names follow the same conventions as file names.)

Consider a file cabinet in your office. Suppose that you store all important sales documents in this file cabinet. One method of storage is to throw all the sales documents in the cabinet as they arrive. In this case, retrieving information is a very difficult task. Another method is to divide the file cabinet into three separate parts (three subdirectories) by using some kind of folders. You can then divide the folders into more logical parts (lower level subdirectories). After this segmentation, you can put each document into its proper folder. This method improves the retrieval time. Figure 4–1 illustrates this example.

The directory below the root directory is considered a subdirectory to the root directory. A directory immediately below a subdirectory is considered a subdirectory to that subdirectory. In Figure 4–1, the WEST, SOUTH, and EAST regions are subdirectories to the root directory. OREGON and CALIFORNIA are subdirectories to the WEST region. We can break this down further into SOUTHERN and NORTHERN California, and so on.

As another example, suppose that on your hard disk you create four subdirectories for WordPerfect, Lotus 1-2-3, dBASE, and Quattro. All your word processing documents will be saved under the WORDPERFECT directory, all your spreadsheets will be saved under the 1-2-3 directory, and so forth. Under 1-2-3, you may want to create two subdirectories, one for your graphics files and one for your database files. This can continue for several levels, based on your specific needs.

The root directory is always identified by a back slash (\). The current subdirectory is identified by a period (.) and the parent subdirectory (the directory immediately above the current directory) is identified by two periods (..).

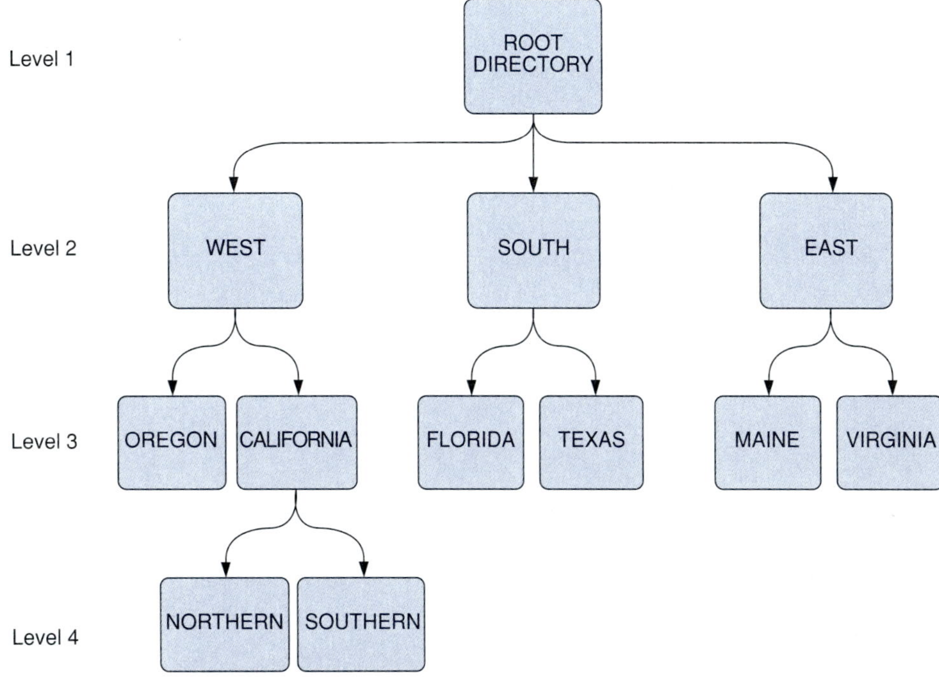

Figure 4–1
Example of directory structure

4–3   IMPORTANT COMMANDS FOR DIRECTORIES

To create a subdirectory, use the DOS command MKDIR (make directory), or MD. You must be in the directory immediately above the subdirectory you are creating.

To change to a subdirectory or make a subdirectory the current directory, use the CHDIR (change directory), or CD, command. The CD command uses several different parameters as shown in Table 4–1.

To remove a subdirectory, you first must erase all the files and subsequent subdirectories by using either the DEL or ERASE command. Then use the RMDIR (remove directory), or RD, command.

If you do not know in which directory you are working, use the PROMPT PG command to solve the problem. At the DOS prompt, type *PROMPT PG*. The default prompt changes to a prompt that identifies the current directory. For example, if you are working in the OREGON directory in drive A, your new prompt will read

```
A\OREGON>
```

Table 4–1
CD command parameters

Parameter	Function
CD.	Displays the current directory
CD..	Moves up one directory level
CD\	Moves up to the root directory from any directory level
CD..\..	Moves up two directory levels
CD\WEST\OREGON	OREGON becomes the current directory

To display the structure of your directory, use the TREE command. The command TREE/F displays each directory on your disk and the files stored within each directory.

Another powerful command that you can use with directories is the PATH command. This command establishes a search path. Suppose that you are working with a data disk in drive A. If you issue an external DOS command from drive A, you will receive an error message (because the DOS disk is in drive C). If you type *PATH C:* at the C> prompt, DOS searches the root directory on drive C for any commands that it cannot find in the current drive or directory (in our case drive A). You also can establish multiple search paths by using the PATH command and a semicolon (;). Suppose that you want to tell your computer to search for DOS commands in drive A and in a subdirectory on drive C called EXTERNAL. The following search path will do the job:

PATH A:\; C:\EXTERNAL

When you establish a search path, it remains in effect until you turn off your PC. To cancel a search path, type *PATH* and press Enter.

One very powerful command for working with directories is XCOPY. The XCOPY command enables you to copy all the directories and the files included within them from source drive/directory to the destination drive/directory. As an example, consider the disk in drive A which includes 205 files in Lotus, dBASE, and WordPerfect directories. To copy all these files and these directories from the A drive to the B drive the command is (default is C drive)

XCOPY A:*.* B:/S

The S parameter indicates that all subdirectories will be copied as well as the files. The S parameter copies all the subdirectories except the empty ones. The E parameter copies all the subdirectories including the empty ones. For the above example, the XCOPY command with the E parameter would be

XCOPY A:*.* B:/E

4–4   MOVE AND DELTREE COMMANDS

DOS 6.0 offers two very useful commands when working with directories, MOVE and DELTREE. The **MOVE** command moves (cuts and pastes) files and directories from one directory or drive to another directory or drive. You can rename a file or directory at the same time that you are moving it. Example:

C> MOVE A:TEST.BAT B:SAMPLE.BAT

This command removes TEST.BAT from drive A and copies and renames it to SAMPLE.BAT on drive B.

The **MOVE /Y** command moves all files and directories and bypasses user confirmation. As mentioned earlier, the MOVE command can also move directories. For example, MOVE A:WEST B:WEST moves the WEST directory to drive B. You can also rename while moving.

The **DELTREE** command deletes a directory, including all files and subdirectories in that particular directory. You can use the DELTREE command alone or with the **/Y** parameter. The /Y parameter instructs DELTREE not to prompt you for confirmation before executing the command.

4–5   EXAMPLE 1: DIRECTORY CREATION

Start DOS and format a blank disk. Insert the formatted disk in drive A. At the C> prompt, type *PROMPT PG* and press Enter. From now on you will know which directory you are working with. Type *DIR A:* followed by Enter to see the contents of your disk before directory creation. In our case the disk is empty. Remember that DOS commands are not case sensitive.

Type *A:* followed by Enter. This changes the default from C> to A>. To create three directories named WEST, SOUTH, and EAST, type the following commands and press Enter after each:

    MD WEST
    MD SOUTH
    MD EAST

Type *DIR* and press Enter. You will see the information presented in Figure 4–2. It shows there are three directories.

Type *CD\WEST* to make WEST the current directory. To create the subdirectories OREGON and CALIFORNIA, type the following commands and press Enter after each:

    MD OREGON
    MD CALIFORNIA

Next, type *CD* to return to the root directory and type *CD\SOUTH* to make SOUTH the current directory (remember to press Enter after each command). Create the subdirectories FLORIDA and TEXAS with the following commands (remember to press Enter after each one):

    MD FLORIDA
    MD TEXAS

Type *CD* to return to the root directory. Type *CD\EAST* to make EAST the current directory and enter the following:

    MD MAINE
    MD VIRGINIA

Type *CD* to go back to the root directory. Enter the command *CD\WEST\CALIFORNIA* to make CALIFORNIA the current directory. Next,

Figure 4–2
Three subdirectories within the
root directory

```
A>DIR

   Volume in drive A is SUPPLIERS
   Volume Serial Number is 371E-19DD
   Directory of A:\

WEST            <DIR>       01-01-93     9:12p
SOUTH           <DIR>       01-01-93     9:12p
EAST            <DIR>       01-01-93     9:12p
         3 file(s)              0 bytes
                        1140736 bytes free

A>
```

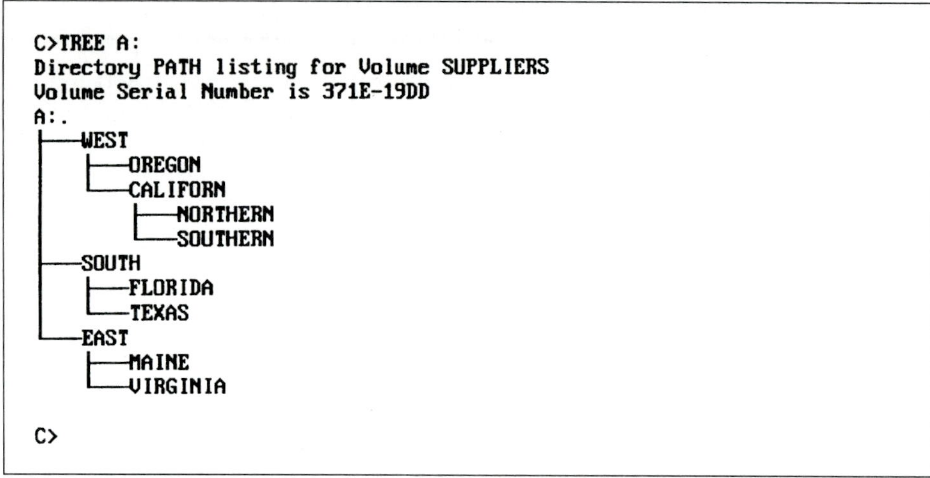

```
C>TREE A:
Directory PATH listing for Volume SUPPLIERS
Volume Serial Number is 371E-19DD
A:.
    ├──WEST
    │   ├──OREGON
    │   └──CALIFORN
    │       ├──NORTHERN
    │       └──SOUTHERN
    ├──SOUTH
    │   ├──FLORIDA
    │   └──TEXAS
    └──EAST
        ├──MAINE
        └──VIRGINIA

C>
```

type the following commands to create the NORTHERN and SOUTHERN sub-directories:

> MD NORTHERN
> MD SOUTHERN

You have now constructed the diagram presented in Figure 4–1. Type *CD* to return to the root directory. At the C> prompt, type *TREE A:,* and press Enter. You will see information similar to that shown in Figure 4–3.

4–6   EXAMPLE 2: COPYING TO DIRECTORIES

Copying to directories is similar to copying files. However, in a directory environment, you must provide a specific path for a given file.

Start DOS and insert the disk you just created in drive A. Suppose that you want to copy all files with the COM extension from drive C (the DOS disk) to the WEST subdirectory. From the C> prompt, type

> COPY *.COM A:\WEST

Now you can check the contents of WEST (by using the DIR command) to verify your work.

Suppose that you want to copy COMMAND.COM from drive C to subdirectory SOUTHERN. The command is

> COPY COMMAND.COM A:\WEST\CALIFORNIA\SOUTHERN

If you check the contents of the SOUTHERN directory, you will see COMMAND.COM residing there.

4–7   EXAMPLE 3: COPYING FROM ONE SUBDIRECTORY TO ANOTHER

Suppose that you want to copy COMMAND.COM from the SOUTHERN subdirectory to the NORTHERN subdirectory. The command for this from the C> prompt is

COPY A:\WEST\CALIFORNIA\SOUTHERN\COMMAND.COM
A:\WEST\CALIFORNIA\NORTHERN

Generate a directory listing of both the SOUTHERN and NORTHERN subdirectories. They should be identical.

4–8   EXAMPLE 4: REMOVING A DIRECTORY

You decide to remove both the SOUTHERN and NORTHERN subdirectories. Start DOS and insert the disk you have been working with in drive A. To remove a directory, first you must erase all the files and subsequent directories. At the C> prompt type the following:

DEL A:\WEST\CALIFORNIA\NORTHERN\COMMAND.COM
DEL A:\WEST\CALIFORNIA\SOUTHERN\COMMAND.COM

Now both the NORTHERN and SOUTHERN subdirectories are empty. Type *CD* and press Enter to return to the root directory. (You must be in either the root directory or in a directory one level above the subdirectory to be removed.) Enter the following commands, remembering to press Enter after each line:

RD A:\WEST\CALIFORNIA\NORTHERN
RD A:\WEST\CALIFORNIA\SOUTHERN

4–9   HARD DISK MANAGEMENT

As a result of decreasing costs and advancements in hard disk technology, hard disks are becoming more popular among PC users. The major difference between a hard disk and a floppy disk is the massive storage space available on a hard disk. You can store all your application programs on a hard disk and relieve yourself of the pain of dealing with hundreds of floppy disks. It is also safer to store application programs on the hard disk. Damaging a floppy disk is more likely than damaging the hard disk.

Generally speaking, hard disks are more durable than floppy disks; however, hard disks are prone to crashing. A hard disk **crash** happens when the drive head comes in contact with the surface of the disk. Experts recommend that you use the programs SHIPDISK.COM or PARK.COM to park the drive head before turning off the system. These two utilities are not on the DOS disk, but you can get them from the vendors of your computer. To use these programs, insert the disk containing these commands in drive A. From the A> prompt, type the command *PARK.COM* or *SHIPDISK.COM* and follow the prompts.

To be able to work with a hard disk, you should be able to perform the following tasks:

- Partition the hard disk (using the FDISK command)
- Back it up (using the BACKUP command)
- Restore the files if the hard disk crashes (using the RESTORE command)

We discuss these commands in the next few pages. Remember that all the DOS commands you have learned so far except DISKCOPY and DISKCOMP work in a hard disk environment. These two commands do not work because there is a significant size difference between a floppy and a hard disk. Hard disk commands can be used with DOS 2.0 and above.

```
                         MS-DOS Version 6
                      Fixed Disk Setup Program
                 (C)Copyright Microsoft Corp. 1983 - 1993

                            FDISK Options

Current fixed disk drive: 1

Choose one of the following:

1. Create DOS partition or Logical DOS Drive
2. Set active partition
3. Delete partition or Logical DOS Drive
4. Display partition information


Enter choice: [1]



Press Esc to exit FDISK
```

Figure 4–4
FDISK menu

4–10   PARTITIONING A HARD DISK

A hard disk provides huge amounts of storage space compared with a floppy disk. To better manage this storage, you should **partition** the hard disk. Partitioning simply means dividing your hard disk into smaller chunks. You can partition a hard disk into separate drives, such as C, D, E, and so forth. You can install different operating systems besides DOS on your system. These may include UNIX, OS/2, or Windows. You may need to do this if you are using software packages that require operating systems other than DOS.

In any event, partitioning helps you to better manage your hard disk. To use the FDISK program, at the C> prompt type *FDISK* and press Enter. You will see the screen shown in Figure 4–4. This is a menu-driven system—you can walk through it and select the options you need.

4–11   PREPARING A HARD DISK

Just like floppy disks, hard disks also need to be formatted. Remember, you format the hard disk only once. If you mistakenly format a hard disk that you are using, all the valuable information is lost permanently (you better have a backup!). To format your hard disk, put the disk that includes the FORMAT command in drive A. At the A> prompt, type *FORMAT C:/S/V*. The S parameter is used to transfer system files to the hard disk and to make it a self-booting system. The V parameter is used to provide a volume label for the hard disk.

<table>
<tr><td>Table 4–2
BACKUP command parameters</td><td>

Parameter	Function
/S	Backs up the entire disk (files and directories)
/M	Backs up files that have been modified since the last time that the BACKUP command was used
/A	Adds new backup files to an existing backup disk without erasing any of the current files
/D	Backs up files that have been modified on or after a given date. The format for the date is [month-day-year] ([01-25-94], for example).

</td></tr>
</table>

4–12 BACKING UP A HARD DISK

Because your hard disk includes thousands of important files and data items, you should **back up** your hard disk periodically. You can back up a hard disk on floppies or you can use a tape backup system. The command for backing up a hard disk is BACKUP, and it can take several parameters, as shown in Table 4–2.

The following are some specific examples of the BACKUP command:

- C> BACKUP C :*.* A:/S

  Backs up the entire drive C to drive A.
- C> BACKUP C :*.* A:/S/M

  Backs up all the new files that have been modified since the last backup.
- C> BACKUP C :*.* A:/S/A/D 10/10/94

  Backs up all the files created since 10/10/94 and adds them to the disk in drive A without erasing any of the files in this drive.

Figure 4–5 illustrates an example of the BACKUP command. Also see BACKUP and RESTORE facilities of MS-DOS 6.0 in Chapter 7, Section 7–5.

4–13 RESTORING A CRASHED HARD DISK

If your hard disk fails, it is not a difficult task to put it back to normal if you have a backup. To restore your disk, you must use the DOS RESTORE command. From the C> prompt, type

RESTORE A : C :*.* /S

Figure 4–5
BACKUP command

```
C>BACKUP C:\*.* A:/S

Insert backup diskette 01 in drive A:

WARNING! Files in the target drive
A:\ root directory will be erased
Press any key to continue . . .

*** Backing up files to drive A: ***
Diskette Number: 01
```

```
C:\>RESTORE A: C:\*.*/S

Insert backup diskette 01 in drive A:
Press any key to continue . . .

*** Files were backed up 01-06-1994 ***

*** Restoring files from drive A: ***
Diskette: 01
```



```
C>DIR A:

 Volume in drive A is BACKUP   001
 Directory of A:\

BACKUP    001    1210880 01-03-94   10:29a
CONTROL   001       2661 01-03-94   10:29a
        2 file(s)     1213541 bytes
                            0 bytes free

C>
```

Figure 4–6 illustrates a sample screen of the RESTORE command. This example assumes that your hard disk is technically sound and that the only problem is the data on it has been lost. If your hard disk has been damaged, you must repair or replace it first, then use the RESTORE command to put all the data back on it.

If you have several disks and you want to discover whether a disk is a backup or an original, you can use the DIR command. If the disk is a backup, at the top of your directory you will see the backup disk by its number. See Figure 4–7.

SUMMARY

This chapter reviewed directory and subdirectory operations. We discussed commands for directory creation, changing a directory, and removing a directory. We also discussed the TREE command for displaying the structure of a directory and the PROMPT command for customizing the DOS prompt in a tree-structured environment. The chapter concluded with valuable information on hard disk management.

REVIEW QUESTIONS

*These questions are answered in Appendix A.

1. What is a directory? A subdirectory?
2. Is there a limit on the number of directories on a disk (hard or floppy)?
*3. Why are subdirectories important, particularly in a hard disk environment?
4. What constitutes valid directory names?
5. How is the root directory identified?
6. What does a back slash (\) mean? A single period? Double periods?

4. To make another subdirectory the current directory, the command to use is
   a. CD
   b. RD
   c. MD
   d. GOTO
   e. none of the above

5. The command to allow DOS to display the current directory is
   a. DISPLAY PG
   b. SHOW PG
   c. SEE PG
   d. DIR PG
   e. PROMPT PG

6. Formatting the hard disk will
   a. divide the disk into sectors and tracks
   b. partition the disk into C:, D:, E:, and so forth
   c. erase all data
   d. both a and b
   e. both a and c

7. One of the best methods of protecting your data is to
   a. create subdirectories
   b. back up the disk
   c. run CHKDSK periodically
   d. run TREE/F periodically
   e. format the disk

8. If the disk you have is a backup, a directory listing will show
   a. THIS IS A BACKUP DISK
   b. BACKUP ***
   c. DOS BACKUP
   d. BACKUP @ @ @ or its number
   e. none of the above

9. If you want to place the files from a backup disk onto the hard disk, use the command
   a. RESTORE
   b. DUMP
   c. REPLACE
   d. BACKUP/R
   e. none of the above

10. Subdirectories are useful because they
    a. prevent loss of data from a head crash
    b. eliminate the need to back up the disk
    c. provide better file management and organization
    d. prevent unauthorized access
    e. all of the above

True/False

1. When you format a disk, DOS automatically creates the root directory for you.
2. There is no limit to the number of files that can be stored in the root directory.
3. Subdirectories are directories created below the root directory or existing subdirectories.
4. The root directory is always identified by two periods (..).
5. Removing a subdirectory with the RMDIR or RD command will erase all files in the subdirectory.

6. The PATH command enables DOS automatically to search various subdirectories for commands that it cannot find in the current directory.

7. Experts recommend that you use a utility to park the heads of a hard disk before turning off the computer.

8. All partitions of the hard disk must have the same operating system on them.

9. One cannot overemphasize the importance of maintaining a current backup of the hard disk.

10. BACKUP/M is used to back up the entire disk.

ANSWERS

Multiple Choice		**True/False**	
1.	b	1.	T
2.	c	2.	F
3.	d	3.	T
4.	a	4.	F
5.	e	5.	F
6.	e	6.	T
7.	b	7.	T
8.	d	8.	F
9.	a	9.	T
10.	c	10.	F

Creating and Editing Batch Files with EDLIN

5

5–1 INTRODUCTION

In this chapter, we discuss batch files. Batch files can simplify PC use in a variety of settings. All the DOS commands that you have learned can be included in a batch file and can be executed simply by typing the name of the file. We look at AUTOEXEC.BAT as a special type of a batch file, and we discuss EDLIN, the DOS line editor. All the important EDLIN commands are explained, and specific commands for batch files are highlighted.

5–2 DEFINING A BATCH FILE

A **batch file** is a permanent file stored on a disk that includes a series of DOS commands and statements. All the DOS commands that you have learned so far can be used in a batch file.

5–3 WHEN TO USE BATCH FILES

Batch files can improve the efficiency and effectiveness of a PC user. Specifically, these files are used to

- Customize a system prompt
- Direct a user to a subdirectory
- Start an application program
- Save time by including several commands in one file
- Direct the contents of a file to a printer
- Simplify PC use for novice users

Suppose that you want to change the DOS prompt from C> to A>, generate a directory of drive A, clear the screen, and change the drive back to C. This is a simple operation; however, you must type four separate commands every time you want to do this. To save time, you can include all these steps in a batch file. You only have to type the name of the file to execute all these commands.

5–4 GENERATING A BATCH FILE

A batch file can be generated by any word processing program (such as WordPerfect), by any editor (such as EDLIN), or simply by using a special version of the COPY command—COPY CON.

A batch file name must follow the same conventions as any other file name. However, the extension must always be BAT (batch). Each command must be typed on one line, and each line must be ended by pressing Enter. To terminate a batch file, press Ctrl+Z or the function key F6, followed by Enter.

To generate a batch file to execute the four commands mentioned earlier, get the system started and put a formatted disk in drive A. At the C> prompt, type the following commands (press Enter at the end of each line):

```
COPY CON A:SIMPLE.BAT
A:
DIR
CLS
C:
```

Press Ctrl+Z or F6 and Enter to end this batch file.

Line one uses the COPY CON command to generate a file called SIM-PLE in drive A. You can create this file in any drive. Line two changes the drive from C to A. Line three generates a directory of the current drive (which is drive A). Line four clears the screen. The fifth line changes the drive from A back to C. And pressing Ctrl+Z terminates this process. To invoke this batch file at the C> prompt, type *A:SIMPLE* followed by Enter, and watch the screen. To stop the execution of a batch file, press Ctrl+Break.

A batch file can become a self-booting file by naming it AUTOEXEC.BAT. An **autoexec file** is executed as soon as you start the system. In fact, DOS always searches for this file first. If you include this file in your default drive, all the commands in it are executed automatically as soon as you start the system.

AUTOEXEC.BAT files can be very helpful for customizing a complex task for first-time users. Batch files are also very helpful if you have to do a series of repetitive operations over and over.

5–5   CREATING BATCH FILES USING EDLIN

The major disadvantage of the COPY CON command is that you cannot edit a file after it has been created. In other words, COPY CON does not offer any editing features. To edit this file, you must call it in EDLIN or any other text editor that accepts this format. For this reason, you should use either a word processing program or a **line editor** to create your batch files. **EDLIN**[1] is an editor available in DOS 3.0 and above, and is available on your DOS disk. You can perform a variety of tasks using EDLIN:

- Create a batch file
- Display it on screen
- Insert additional lines
- Delete unwanted lines
- Copy a line or series of lines to another location in the file
- Move a line or series of lines to another location in the file
- Replace characters with other characters
- Perform searches
- Transfer lines to another file

5–6   GETTING IN AND OUT OF EDLIN

Boot your PC and insert a formatted disk in drive A. At the C> prompt type

        EDLIN A:CH5-1.BAT

and press Enter. You will see the screen presented in Figure 5–1. EDLIN responds with

        New file

---

[1]A much more powerful editing program will be introduced in Chapter 8: the EDIT program available in DOS 5.0 and DOS 6.0.

```
C>EDLIN A:CH5-1.BAT
New file
*
```



```
C>EDLIN A:CH5-1.BAT
New file
*I
        1:*
```

which indicates that you are creating a new file.

To start the creation of text, press I (for insert) and press Enter. EDLIN responds with

```
1:*
```

meaning that you are in the first line of your desired file. The * indicates that you are in EDLIN mode. Figure 5–2 illustrates this process.

To end the input process, press Ctrl+C. You will be back in the * mode. To return to the C> prompt, type *E* at the * mode. This command saves your file and exits to the C> prompt.

5–7　　YOUR FIRST EDLIN FILE

Using EDLIN, we would like to create a batch file that displays two messages and executes four commands as follows:

```
IT IS A NICE DAY
TIME
DATE
DIR/P
CLS
IT WAS FUN
```

We will call this file CH5-3.BAT. Insert your formatted disk in drive A. At the C> prompt, type

```
EDLIN A:CH5-3.BAT
```

and press Enter. Press I and Enter. At this point, type the following batch file, remembering to press Enter after each line:

```
ECHO    IT IS A NICE DAY
TIME
DATE
DIR/P A:
CLS
ECHO    IT WAS FUN
```

Figure 5–3
Batch file generated with EDLIN

```
C>EDLIN A:CH5-1.BAT
New file
*I
        1:*ECHO IT IS A NICE DAY
        2:*TIME
        3:*DATE
        4:*DIR/P A:
        5:*CLS
        6:*ECHO IT WAS FUN
        7:*^C

*E

C>
```

Press Ctrl+C to end the input process. You can also press Ctrl+Z or F6.

You are returned to the * mode. Type *E* (and press Enter) to save the file and return to the C> prompt. Figure 5–3 displays this file.

Now you can execute this batch file at the C> prompt by typing *A:CH5-3.BAT* and pressing Enter. If you do this, the "IT IS A NICE DAY" message is displayed (the ECHO command displays the message written after it). The computer asks for the time, so enter the correct time and press Enter. Next, the computer asks for the date. Enter the correct date and press Enter. The directory of the A drive will be displayed one page at a time. Finally, the screen is cleared and the "IT WAS FUN" message is displayed.

You could also use a batch file with the PATH command to access several subdirectories from any drive. The subdirectories can be in your hard disk or any other drive. As an example, we have created three subdirectories in the C drive. They are 1-2-3, dBASE, and WP. In drive A, we created the following batch file (remember to press Enter after each line):

```
C> EDLIN A:GO.BAT
PROMPT $P$G
PATH C:\1-2-3; C:\dBASE; C:\WP
Ctrl+Z
E
```

Now at the A> prompt, type *GO* to activate the batch file. At the A> prompt you can access 1-2-3, dBASE, or WP (WordPerfect) by just typing *123* (for 1-2-3), *dbase* (for dBASE), and *wp* (for WordPerfect). This may slow down the processing time, but you will save much time by not switching from one subdirectory to another to load an application program.

5–8   EDITING AN EXISTING FILE

Many times you may be interested in editing an old file. You may want to add to it, delete from it, or simply modify some of the information in the file. EDLIN enables you to perform all these tasks easily.

Suppose that in your CH5-3.BAT file you want to add another line after IT IS A NICE DAY that says EDLIN IS EASY TO LEARN, you want to delete DIR/P A:, and you want to add a last line to the file that says WE SHALL RETURN.

Insert the data disk containing CH5-3.BAT file in drive A, then, at the C> prompt, type

        EDLIN A:CH5-3.BAT

and press Enter. An *End of input file* message will be displayed. To see your file, type *L* and press Enter.

Because the first task is to insert a line right after the first line (before line 2), type *2I.* Press Enter and type

        EDLIN IS EASY TO LEARN (press Enter)

Press Ctrl+C to get out of the insert mode. At this point, if you generate a listing of your file (by pressing L and Enter), you will see that the new line has been inserted.

To delete DIR/P A:, type *5D* and press Enter. Because DIR/P A: is now the fifth line of your file, you use 5D. To delete any line, just type the line number followed by the letter D and press Enter. You can verify your work by typing *L* and reviewing the current status of your file.

The final task is adding the new line

        WE SHALL RETURN

One method of doing this is to type *7I.* Because your file presently has only six lines, 7I will insert text right before line 7, which does not exist. Your file now includes seven lines. To save this file to your disk, press Ctrl+C to get out of the insert mode. Then type *E* and press Enter.

Table 5–1 provides a summary and a brief explanation of all EDLIN commands.

5–9   SPECIAL COMMANDS IN BATCH FILES

Besides all the DOS commands, which can be used in any batch file, there are some other commands that can be used in a batch file. The most commonly used include ECHO, GOTO, PAUSE, and REM. Brief descriptions of these commands can be found in Table 5–2.

5–10   SETTING UP MENUS USING EDLIN

To demonstrate one useful application of batch files and EDLIN, consider the following example. Suppose that you have a computer with a hard disk (drive C). In drive C, you have installed five programs—1-2-3, dBASE, Quattro, WordPerfect, and Wordstar—under five directories with these names.

You want to create a menu that will be displayed as soon as you turn your computer on. Or you can display the menu by typing a particular name. With EDLIN in your default drive (drive C), type the following lines as shown:

Table 5–1
EDLIN commands summary

Command	Function
EDLIN FIRST.BAT	Creates a new file called FIRST.BAT in the default drive. EDLIN responds with New File.
EDLIN FIRST.BAT	Brings an old file called FIRST.BAT into memory for editing purposes. EDLIN responds with an End of Input File message.
C	Copies from one location to another
1,5,30C	Copies lines 1 through 5 to before line 30
1,1,15C	Copies line 1 to before line 15
D	Deletes the current line. The current line is always marked with * (asterisk).
1,15D	Deletes line 1 through 15 inclusive
20D	Deletes line 20
I	Inserts after the current line. It is also used to create a new file.
10I	Inserts text before line 10.
L	Displays the entire file
1,15L	Displays lines 1 through 15 inclusive
20L	Displays from line 20 to the end
1,20,60M	Moves lines 1 through 20 to before line 60
1,3 ?R OLD STRING F6 (Ctrl+Z) NEW STRING	Replaces the OLD STRING with the NEW STRING, and then displays the line with the change. The user can accept the change by pressing Y or reject it by typing N. If you say N, the change will not take place.
1,5 SNICE	Searches lines 1 through 5 for the string NICE. It displays the line containing the first occurrence of the string. Press Enter to see the subsequent occurrences of the string.
5TA:SECOND.BAT	Transfers SECOND.BAT from drive A to the top of line 5 of the current file
10W	Writes the first 10 lines to disk. This file has the same name as the current file but the extension is BAK.
P	Displays 23 lines of the current file beginning with the current line
5,10P	Displays lines 5 through 10 inclusive
E	Ends the EDLIN session and saves the file on the disk
Q	Enables you to abort the editing session without saving the changes. If you abort the session you will return to the DOS prompt.
. or line number	Displays the current line or a specific line for editing purposes. For example if you type *10* and press Enter, line 10 will be displayed, and you can edit it. By moving the right arrow you can display the line one character at a time, add to it, or delete from it.

Table 5–2
Common batch file commands

Command	Function
ECHO message	Displays a given message
ECHO ON	Displays all the commands in a batch file to the screen while they are being executed
ECHO OFF	Prevents the display of commands on the screen during the execution of a batch file
REM	Enables you to document your batch file. For example, you may type REM This program was written on January 1, 1994. This kind of message is only for the user of the program. The computer ignores any line that starts with the REM statement.
PAUSE	Halts the execution of a batch file until you press any key
GOTO label	Transfers control to the line following the one containing the label. In batch files, a label is inserted right afte r the colon. Following is an example: :Good morning Then you can type *GOTO Good morning.*

Command	Function
C> EDLIN AUTOEXEC.BAT	Creates an AUTOEXEC.BAT file on your default drive. This file will be executed as soon as the computer is started. You can call it MENU.BAT or any other name. When your computer is started, you must type this name to display the menu.
I	Starts the creation of the menu
ECHO OFF	Prevents on-screen display of commands in your batch file
ECHO+++++++++++++++	Displays 15 plus signs for cosmetic reasons
ECHO TO SELECT AN OPTION	
ECHO PRESS THE LETTER NUMBER	A message to the user
ECHO A - LOTUS 1-2-3	Shows that Option A is 1-2-3
ECHO B - dBASE III PLUS	Shows that Option B is dBASE III Plus
ECHO C - QUATTRO	Shows that Option C is Quattro
ECHO D - WORDPERFECT	Shows that Option D is Wordperfect
ECHO E - WORDSTAR	Shows that Option E is Wordstar
ECHO+++++++++++++++	Displays 15 plus signs for cosmetic reasons
F6	Terminates the input process
E	Saves the file on the default drive

At this point the menu is complete. Now you must create five batch files with the names A, B, C, D, and E. Type batch file A as follows (remember to press Enter after each line):

```
C> EDLIN A.BAT
I
CD 1-2-3
123
F6
E
```

Batch file B is as follows:

```
C> EDLIN B.BAT
I
CD dBASE
dBASE
F6
E
```

Batch file C is as follows:

```
C> EDLIN C.BAT
I
CD Quattro
Q
F6
E
```

Batch file D is as follows:

```
C> EDLIN D.BAT
I
CD Wordperfect
WP
F6
E
```

Finally, batch file E is as follows:

```
C> EDLIN E.BAT
I
CD Wordstar
WS
F6
E
```

At this point, you have constructed the entire menu and its related batch files. When you turn your computer on, the menu will be displayed. If you press letters A through E, the designated software will be started. Batch files are very helpful for users who do not have much computer training. The entire process of setting your computer can become an automatic process.[2]

Remember, if you edit an existing file and finalize your editing session with the E command, the original file is saved with a BAK extension. (The original file does not include any of the editing performed on the file.) The BAK stands for backup. You cannot edit a BAK file using EDLIN. Rename the file with another extension to edit it using EDLIN.

---

[2]For additional examples of batch files, see Appendix A.

SUMMARY

This chapter reviewed the principles of batch files and explained their specific applications. AUTOEXEC.BAT as a special type of batch file for self-booting your system was introduced. EDLIN, the line editor available on your DOS disk, was described. We also discussed different commands for batch file creation, modification, search, and display using EDLIN. The chapter introduced several commands commonly used in batch files. It concluded with a comprehensive example that highlighted the usefulness and power of EDLIN and batch files.

REVIEW QUESTIONS

*These questions are answered in Appendix A.

1. What is a batch file?
2. What are some of the applications of batch files?
3. How is a batch file created?
*4. What are some of the limitations of the COPY CON command for batch file creation?
5. Can you edit a batch file created by the COPY CON command?
6. How is a batch file executed?
7. What is the file extension of a batch file?
*8. What are some of the specific commands used in a batch file?
9. What are the applications of the ECHO command? REM? PAUSE? GOTO?
10. Why should you use a word processor or a line editor for creating a batch file?
*11. What is EDLIN?
12. What are some of the capabilities of EDLIN?
*13. How do you get EDLIN started?
14. In what version(s) of DOS is EDLIN available?
15. How do you exit EDLIN and, at the same time, save your work?
16. How do you abort EDLIN without saving your work?
17. Using EDLIN, what command do you use to display a file? To delete 10 lines? To move 5 lines?
18. How do you edit an existing file?
*19. What is the EDLIN prompt for a new file? For an old file?
20. How do you search for all occurrences of a string while using EDLIN?

HANDS-ON EXPERIENCE

1. Using the COPY CON command, create a batch file to perform the following tasks:
   a. To change from drive C to drive A
   b. To display the contents of the disk in drive A
   c. To erase the screen
   d. To display the version of DOS in use
   e. To ask for the current time
   f. To ask for the current date

2. Do the preceding exercise using the EDLIN program. What are the advantages of EDLIN compared with COPY CON? Why is EDLIN preferred?

3. Generate an AUTOEXEC.BAT file that performs the following tasks:

     a. Display the message WELCOME TO THE LAB
     b. Ask for the current date
     c. Ask for the current time
     d. Clear the screen

4. Create a batch file that uses ECHO, PAUSE, REM, and GOTO.

5. Using EDLIN, create a file that includes the following two messages:

> EDLIN IS A POWERFUL PROGRAM.
> THERE ARE TWO TYPES OF COMMANDS IN DOS: INTERNAL AND
> EXTERNAL.

Perform the following tasks on this file:
     a. Using an appropriate command, replace "A POWERFUL" with "AN EASY."
     b. Add a third line to this file that says

> AUTOEXEC.BAT IS A SPECIFIC TYPE OF BATCH FILE

     c. Using the W command, write this file to the disk.
     d. Under which name is this file saved?
     e. Copy the third line to just before line 1.
     f. Delete the first line.

6. Using EDLIN, design an AUTOEXEC file that, when it is loaded, displays the following message:

> AT A> PROMPT INSERT THE SYSTEM DISK IN DRIVE A AND TYPE
> LOTUS.

KEY TERMS

Autoexec file	EDLIN
Batch file	Line editor

KEY COMMANDS

C (copy) (EDLIN)	GOTO (batch file)	Q (abort) (EDLIN)
COPY CON (internal)	I (insert) (EDLIN)	R (replace) (EDLIN)
Ctrl+Z or F6 (internal)	L (list) (EDLIN)	REM (remark) (batch file)
D (delete) (EDLIN)	M (move) (EDLIN)	S (search)
E (save) (EDLIN)	P (display) (EDLIN)	T (transfer) (EDLIN)
ECHO (batch file)	PAUSE (batch file)	W (write) (EDLIN)

ARE YOU READY TO MOVE ON?

Multiple Choice

1. Customizing a system prompt and combining several DOS commands in one file are characteristics of
     a. the operating system
     b. batch files
     c. the FORMAT command

    d. network topologies
    e. none of the above

2. Batch files can be created by

    a. a word processing program
    b. a text editor
    c. the COPY command
    d. both a and b
    e. all of the above

3. The extension of a batch file must be

    a. BAT
    b. COM
    c. EXE
    d. SYS
    e. WK1

4. To generate a batch file, one possible command is

    a. BATCH file name
    b. WRITE CON file name
    c. COPY CON file name
    d. PRINT file name
    e. none of the above

5. A DOS text editor used to create batch files is

    a. BATCH
    b. EDITOR
    c. WRITER
    d. EDLIN
    e. none of the above

6. Which character prompt indicates that you are in EDLIN mode?

    a. *
    b. >
    c. !
    d. \
    e. @

7. The EDLIN command to have the batch file display a particular message is

    a. DISPLAY
    b. PRINT
    c. SAY
    d. ECHO
    e. Ctrl+C

8. The EDLIN command to delete lines 3 through 8 inclusive is

    a. D3,8
    b. 3,8D
    c. M3,8
    d. 3,8M
    e. 3,8L

9. By typing the line number of a specific line while in EDLIN, you can then

    a. erase the line automatically
    b. rename the file
    c. edit the line
    d. execute the batch file from that line
    e. none of the above

10. To stop the execution of the batch file momentarily, use the command

    a. HALT
    b. STOP

c. WAIT
d. ECHO
e. PAUSE

True/False

1. A batch file is a permanent file stored on a disk that includes a series of DOS commands or statements.
2. Batch files do not improve the efficiency or the effectiveness of a PC user.
3. The COPY CON command enables you to generate a batch file and edit it after it has been created.
4. A batch file can be made self-booting by naming it AUTOEXEC.BAT.
5. To start creation of text in EDLIN, enter the command I (for insert).
6. To stop the text input process in EDLIN and return to the * mode, enter E for exit.
7. EDLIN cannot be used to edit a batch file once it has been created and saved.
8. The EDLIN command to see the file is L (for List).
9. Only DOS commands can be used in batch files.
10. The command REM in a batch file is used to document the file with comments; these lines are not executed.

ANSWERS

Multiple Choice		True/False	
1.	b	1.	T
2.	e	2.	F
3.	a	3.	F
4.	c	4.	T
5.	d	5.	T
6.	a	6.	F
7.	d	7.	F
8.	b	8.	T
9.	c	9.	F
10.	e	10.	T

Additional DOS Commands and Features

6–1   INTRODUCTION

In this chapter we discuss additional features of DOS. Redirection of standard input and output is explained, and piping as a means for connecting two or more DOS commands is introduced. We examine three important filters—SORT, FIND, and MORE. We also review the PRINT, MODE, VERIFY, RECOVER, and FILES commands. The chapter concludes with a quick review of DOS utilities and the trend in MS-DOS and PC-DOS development.

6–2   REDIRECTING INPUT AND OUTPUT

In the previous chapters, you have directed the output of a command, such as DIR, to a standard output device, your monitor. It is possible to direct output to other devices besides the CRT. To do so, you use the > (greater-than) sign after the command followed by the name of the device. For example, the command

C>DIR>PRN

displays the listing of your directory to your default printer. You can also **redirect** the listing to a disk file, such as FIRST, by typing

C>DIR>A:FIRST

A listing of all your files in the default directory (C) is stored in a file called FIRST on drive A:. You can see the contents of this file by typing *TYPE A:FIRST*. DOS does not assign any extension to this file. Figure 6–1 illustrates this command.

If you direct the listing of your directory to an existing file such as FIRST, the contents of this file will be erased. If you are interested in keeping the contents of this file, you must use two greater-than signs (>>). In this example, you must type

C>DIR>>A:FIRST

You can also redirect the input device with the < (less-than) sign. For example, at the C> prompt, type

DIR<A:FIRST

Then the command DIR will receive its input from A:FIRST.

6–3   DEFINING FILTERS

So far, you have not had any control over the DIR command. By control, we mean the way in which a directory is displayed, how much of it is displayed, and what file should be displayed. DOS provides you with three **filters** that give you control over the DIR command and your files. These filters are SORT, FIND, and MORE.

6–3–1   SORT Command

The SORT command organizes a directory of a disk or a file either in **ascending order** or **descending order**. It also enables you to choose a specific column in which you can sort your file or directory. Table 6–1 gives variations of the SORT command.

```
C>TYPE A:FIRST

 Volume in drive C is MS_DOS_6
 Volume Serial Number is 1C22-913B
 Directory of C:\DOS

 .              <DIR>         06-06-92   12:24p
 ..             <DIR>         06-06-92   12:24p
 DBLSPACE BIN      51214 03-10-93    6:00a
 FORMAT   COM      22717 03-10-93    6:00a
 NLSFUNC  EXE       7036 03-10-93    6:00a
 COUNTRY  SYS      17066 03-10-93    6:00a
 KEYB     COM      14983 03-10-93    6:00a
 KEYBOARD SYS      34694 03-10-93    6:00a
 SETUP    EXE      71974 03-10-93    6:00a
 DOSSETUP INI       3735 03-10-93    6:00a
 ANSI     SYS       9065 03-10-93    6:00a
 ATTRIB   EXE      11165 03-10-93    6:00a
 CHKDSK   EXE      12907 03-10-93    6:00a
 EDIT     COM        413 03-10-93    6:00a
 EXPAND   EXE      16129 03-10-93    6:00a
 EDLIN    EXE      12642 06-13-91    5:00a
 MORE     COM       2546 03-10-93    6:00a
 MSD      EXE     158470 03-10-93    6:00a
 QBASIC   EXE     194309 03-10-93    6:00a
 RESTORE  EXE      38294 03-10-93    6:00a
 MIRROR   COM      18169 06-13-91    5:00a
 SYS      COM       9379 03-10-93    6:00a
 UNFORMAT COM      12738 03-10-93    6:00a
 SMARTDRV SYS       8335 06-13-91    5:00a
 OS2      TXT       6358 03-10-93    6:00a
 NETWORKS TXT      20463 03-10-93    6:00a
 README   TXT      44990 03-10-93    6:00a
 DEBUG    EXE      15715 03-10-93    6:00a
 FDISK    EXE      29333 03-10-93    6:00a
 DOSSHELL VID       9462 03-10-93    6:00a
 19C1DOSC BAT         16 01-23-93    3:05p
 DEFAULT  SET       4207 01-02-94   10:49a
 DOSSHELL GRB       4421 03-10-93    6:00a
 CHOICE   COM       1754 03-10-93    6:00a
 DEFRAG   EXE      75033 03-10-93    6:00a
 PACKING  LST       2507 06-13-91    5:00a
 DEFRAG   HLP       9227 03-10-93    6:00a
 DOSSWAP  EXE      18756 03-10-93    6:00a
 EGA      CPI      58870 03-10-93    6:00a
 RECOVER  EXE       9146 06-13-91    5:00a
 EGA      SYS       4885 03-10-93    6:00a
 HIMEM    SYS      14208 03-10-93    6:00a
 MEM      EXE      32150 03-10-93    6:00a
 XCOPY    EXE      15820 03-10-93    6:00a
 MONEY    BAS      46225 06-13-91    5:00a
 MSHERC   COM       6934 06-13-91    5:00a
 DELTREE  EXE      11113 03-10-93    6:00a
 GORILLA  BAS      29434 06-13-91    5:00a
 4201     CPI       6404 06-13-91    5:00a
 4208     CPI        720 06-13-91    5:00a
 5202     CPI        395 06-13-91    5:00a
 MOVE     EXE      17823 03-10-93    6:00a
 ASSIGN   COM       6399 06-13-91    5:00a
 RAMDRIVE SYS       5873 03-10-93    6:00a
 BACKUP   EXE      36092 06-13-91    5:00a
 SMARTDRV EXE      42073 03-10-93    6:00a
```

```
COMP      EXE     14282 06-13-91   5:00a
DISPLAY   SYS     15789 03-10-93   6:00a
DOSHELP   HLP      5667 03-10-93   6:00a
DOSSHELL  COM      4620 03-10-93   6:00a
DOSSHELL  EXE    236378 03-10-93   6:00a
GRAFTABL  COM     11205 06-13-91   5:00a
EDIT      HLP     17898 03-10-93   6:00a
FASTOPEN  EXE     12034 03-10-93   6:00a
HELP      HLP    294741 03-10-93   6:00a
HELP      COM       413 03-10-93   6:00a
NIBBLES   BAS     24103 06-13-91   5:00a
REMLINE   BAS     12314 06-13-91   5:00a
MODE      COM     23521 03-10-93   6:00a
POWER     EXE      8052 03-10-93   6:00a
EXE2BIN   EXE      8424 06-13-91   5:00a
PRINT     EXE     15640 03-10-93   6:00a
JOIN      EXE     17870 06-13-91   5:00a
LCD       CPI     10753 06-13-91   5:00a
QBASIC    HLP    130881 03-10-93   6:00a
PRINTER   SYS     18804 06-13-91   5:00a
SHARE     EXE     10912 03-10-93   6:00a
DELOLDOS  EXE     17710 03-10-93   6:00a
SETVER    EXE     12015 03-10-93   6:00a
APPEND    EXE     10774 03-10-93   6:00a
APPNOTES  TXT      8660 06-13-91   5:00a
KEYBHP    COM     15997 06-13-91   5:00a
MODEHP    COM     23232 06-13-91   5:00a
SSTOR     SYS     37260 06-13-91   5:00a
DISKCOMP  COM     10620 03-10-93   6:00a
MOUSE     SYS     32730 06-13-91   5:00a
DISKCOPY  COM     11879 03-10-93   6:00a
B         BAT        46 06-06-92   1:53p
589DOSCM  BAT        16 01-23-93   3:01p
D5C0DOSC  BAT        16 01-23-93   6:49p
2688DOSC  BAT        16 01-23-93   3:08p
370CDOSC  BAT        16 01-23-93   4:12p
D923DOSC  BAT        16 01-23-93   5:50p
BA6EDOSC  BAT        16 01-23-93   6:43p
D329DOSC  BAT        16 01-23-93   6:49p
DRIVER    SYS      5406 03-10-93   6:00a
FC        EXE     18650 03-10-93   6:00a
FIND      EXE      6770 03-10-93   6:00a
GRAPHICS  COM     19694 03-10-93   6:00a
GRAPHICS  PRO     21232 03-10-93   6:00a
LABEL     EXE      9390 03-10-93   6:00a
SMARTMON  EXE     28672 03-10-93   6:00a
SMARTMON  HLP     10727 03-10-93   6:00a
SORT      EXE      6922 03-10-93   6:00a
LOADFIX   COM      1131 03-10-93   6:00a
MWBACKUP  EXE    309696 03-10-93   6:00a
MWBACKUP  HLP    400880 03-10-93   6:00a
REPLACE   EXE     20226 03-10-93   6:00a
SUBST     EXE     18478 03-10-93   6:00a
TREE      COM      6898 03-10-93   6:00a
DOSKEY    COM      5883 03-10-93   6:00a
VFINTD    386      5295 03-10-93   6:00a
MWBACKF   DLL     14560 03-10-93   6:00a
MWBACKR   DLL    111120 03-10-93   6:00a
MOUSE     COM     56408 03-10-93   6:00a
MSBACKUP  EXE      5506 03-10-93   6:00a
MSBACKUP  OVL    133952 03-10-93   6:00a
MSBACKFB  OVL     69066 03-10-93   6:00a
```

```
MSBACKFR OVL      72474 03-10-93     6:00a
CHKSTATE SYS      41600 03-10-93     6:00a
UNDELETE EXE      26420 03-10-93     6:00a
MWUNDEL  EXE     130496 03-10-93     6:00a
MWUNDEL  HLP      35741 03-10-93     6:00a
MWGRAFIC DLL      36944 03-10-93     6:00a
MSBACKUP HLP     314236 03-10-93     6:00a
WNTOOLS  GRP       2205 01-02-94     6:25p
MSBACKDB OVL      63098 03-10-93     6:00a
MSBACKDR OVL      66906 03-10-93     6:00a
MSBCONFG OVL      47210 03-10-93     6:00a
DBLSPACE EXE     274388 03-10-93     6:00a
MEMMAKER HLP      17081 03-10-93     6:00a
MEMMAKER INF       1652 03-10-93     6:00a
INTERLNK EXE      17197 03-10-93     6:00a
INTERSVR EXE      37314 03-10-93     6:00a
MSCDEX   EXE      25377 03-10-93     6:00a
DBLSPACE HLP      72169 03-10-93     6:00a
DBLSPACE INF       2178 03-10-93     6:00a
DBLSPACE SYS        339 03-10-93     6:00a
DBLWIN   HLP       8597 03-10-93     6:00a
DOSSHELL HLP     161323 03-10-93     6:00a
EMM386   EXE     115294 03-10-93     6:00a
MEMMAKER EXE     118660 03-10-93     6:00a
SIZER    EXE       7169 03-10-93     6:00a
MONOUMB  386       8783 03-10-93     6:00a
MSTOOLS  DLL      13424 03-10-93     6:00a
MSAV     EXE     172198 03-10-93     6:00a
MSAV     HLP      23891 03-10-93     6:00a
MSAVHELP OVL      29828 03-10-93     6:00a
MSAVIRUS LST      35520 03-10-93     6:00a
VSAFE    COM      62576 03-10-93     6:00a
MWAVDOSL DLL      44736 03-10-93     6:00a
MWAVDRVL DLL       7744 03-10-93     6:00a
AUTOEXEC UMB        703 01-01-94     5:34p
MOUSE    INI         28 01-01-94     5:34p
CONFIG   UMB        142 01-01-94     5:34p
MEMMAKER STS        851 01-01-94     5:40p
MWAVDLG  DLL      36368 03-10-93     6:00a
MSBACKUP INI         43 01-03-94     4:46p
MWAVSCAN DLL     151568 03-10-93     6:00a
MSBACKUP RST        608 04-13-92     7:07a
MSBACKUP TMP       5014 01-02-94    10:49a
MWAV     EXE     142640 03-10-93     6:00a
MWAVABSI DLL      54576 03-10-93     6:00a
MWAV     HLP      24619 03-10-93     6:00a
MWAVSOS  DLL       7888 03-10-93     6:00a
MWAVMGR  DLL      21712 03-10-93     6:00a
MWAVTSR  EXE      17328 03-10-93     6:00a
COMMAND  COM      52925 03-10-93     6:00a
MSAV     INI          0 01-01-94     3:01p
DEFAULT  BAK       4207 01-02-94     9:56a
MSBACKUP LOG     196811 01-02-94    10:54a
DEFAULT  SLT         64 01-02-94    10:49a
DEFAULT  SAV         64 01-02-94     9:56a
DOSSHELL INI      16424 01-02-94     1:02p
       176 file(s)      6563296 bytes
                      129966080 bytes free

C>
```

These specific columns (designated by n) are the default settings for your directory. The file names start in column 1, the file extensions start in column 10, and so forth. If you design a specific file, you can sort on any given column.

Using EDLIN, we generated the following file called A:SAMPLE.TEX:

```
55   THOMAS
33   JONES
11   BROWN
22   ADAM
44   SMITH
```

There are five students and their assigned numbers. The numbers begin in column 1 and the names begin in column 6. We have included three spaces between numbers and names.

We want to perform some sort operations with this file. At the C> prompt put the disk that includes SAMPLE.TEX in drive A. Type

```
SORT<A:SAMPLE.TEX
```

and press Enter. The output will be

```
11   BROWN
22   ADAM
33   JONES
44   SMITH
55   THOMAS
```

As you see, the file is sorted by the student numbers from 11 to 55. In this example, the SORT filter receives its input from A:SAMPLE.TEX.

To sort the names alphabetically, at the C> prompt, type

```
SORT/+6<A:SAMPLE.TEX
```

and press Enter. The output will be

```
22   ADAM
11   BROWN
33   JONES
44   SMITH
55   THOMAS
```

Table 6–1

Variations of the SORT command

Command	Description
SORT	Sorts in ascending order
SORT/R	Sorts in descending order
SORT/+n	Sorts by one of five parameters:
	n = 1 by file name (default value)
	n = 10 by file extension
	n = 14 by file size
	n = 24 by date the file was created
	n = 34 by time the file was created

This file has been sorted alphabetically by the names (remember, names are in column 6).

Next, at the C> prompt, type

SORT/R/+6<A:SAMPLE.TEX

and press Enter. The output will be

```
55    THOMAS
44    SMITH
33    JONES
11    BROWN
22    ADAM
```

This file is sorted in descending order based on the names.

You can combine both input and output redirection using SORT as a filter. For example, type

SORT<A:SAMPLE.TEX>PRN

at the C> prompt to sort the contents of SAMPLE.TEX based on the character in the first column, and then direct the result to the printer. You also can direct the result to a disk file.

6–3–2 FIND Command

The FIND command searches and finds a specific string or character in a directory or a file. The FIND command uses the parameters shown in Table 6–2.

To make these options clearer, we use the SAMPLE.TEX file from our previous example. Insert the disk that includes SAMPLE.TEX in drive A. At the C> prompt, type

FIND "SMITH" <A:SAMPLE.TEX

The output is

```
44    SMITH
```

Because FIND is an external DOS command, you must have the DOS disk in one of your drives. The < sign causes the FIND command to receive its input from A:SAMPLE.TEX in drive A.

With the disk that includes SAMPLE.TEX in drive A, type

C>FIND/C "SMITH" <A:SAMPLE.TEX

Table 6–2
FIND command parameters

Parameter	Description
/C	Displays only the number of lines (the total) that include a particular string
/N	Displays each line where a particular string is encountered and its line number
/V	Displays each line that does not contain a particular string

The output will be 1, because there is only one SMITH in this file. Remember, the C parameter counts the number of occurrences of a particular string. If you type

    C>FIND/N "SMITH" <A:SAMPLE.TEX

the output will be

```
[5]44    SMITH
```

This output indicates that there is one SMITH and it is in line 5. If you type

    C>FIND/V "SMITH" <A:SAMPLE.TEX

the output will be

```
55    THOMAS
33    JONES
11    BROWN
22    ADAM
```

The output does not include the given string, which is SMITH.

6–3–3   MORE Command

The MORE command generates one screen of a directory or a file at a time. Then it waits for you to respond if you want to see more. This command is similar to the DIR/P command with one difference. The MORE command can also be used with the TYPE command. Therefore, you can see one screen of the contents of a file at a time as well. Figure 6–2 illustrates an example of the MORE command. This is a partial listing of the MS-DOS 6.0 directory.

6–4   DEFINING PIPING

Piping takes place when you combine two or more commands by using the ¦ sign (found on the back slash key). For example, A>DIR ¦ SORT sorts the contents of drive A alphabetically. A>DIR ¦ SORT>THIRD sorts the contents of drive A and directs the output to a file called THIRD. A>DIR ¦ SORT>PRN sorts the contents of drive A and directs the output to the default printer. The command

    C>DIR ¦ FIND "COM" ¦ SORT/R

sorts all the files in drive C that contain "COM" either in their names or extensions in descending order.
The command

    C>DIR ¦ FIND "WK1" ¦ SORT

sorts all the 1-2-3 worksheet files in drive C in ascending order. The results of these commands can be directed to a file or a printer.

Figure 6–2
Example of the MORE command

```
C>DIR|MORE


 Volume in drive C is MS_DOS_6
 Volume Serial Number is 1C22-913B
 Directory of C:\DOS

 .              <DIR>        06-06-92    12:24p
 ..             <DIR>        06-06-92    12:24p
 DBLSPACE BIN      51214     03-10-93     6:00a
 FORMAT   COM      22717     03-10-93     6:00a
 NLSFUNC  EXE       7036     03-10-93     6:00a
 COUNTRY  SYS      17066     03-10-93     6:00a
 KEYB     COM      14983     03-10-93     6:00a
 KEYBOARD SYS      34694     03-10-93     6:00a
 SETUP    EXE      71974     03-10-93     6:00a
 DOSSETUP INI       3735     03-10-93     6:00a
 ANSI     SYS       9065     03-10-93     6:00a
 ATTRIB   EXE      11165     03-10-93     6:00a
 CHKDSK   EXE      12907     03-10-93     6:00a
 EDIT     COM        413     03-10-93     6:00a
 EXPAND   EXE      16129     03-10-93     6:00a
 EDLIN    EXE      12642     06-13-91     5:00a
 MORE     COM       2546     03-10-93     6:00a
 MSD      EXE     158470     03-10-93     6:00a
 -- More --

 QBASIC   EXE     194309     03-10-93     6:00a
 RESTORE  EXE      38294     03-10-93     6:00a
 MIRROR   COM      18169     06-13-91     5:00a
 SYS      COM       9379     03-10-93     6:00a
 UNFORMAT COM      12738     03-10-93     6:00a
 SMARTDRV SYS       8335     06-13-91     5:00a
 OS2      TXT       6358     03-10-93     6:00a
 NETWORKS TXT      20463     03-10-93     6:00a
 README   TXT      44990     03-10-93     6:00a
 DEBUG    EXE      15715     03-10-93     6:00a
 FDISK    EXE      29333     03-10-93     6:00a
 DOSSHELL VID       9462     03-10-93     6:00a
 19C1DOSC BAT         16     01-23-93     3:05p
 DEFAULT  SET       4207     01-02-94    10:49a
 DOSSHELL GRB       4421     03-10-93     6:00a
 CHOICE   COM       1754     03-10-93     6:00a
 DEFRAG   EXE      75033     03-10-93     6:00a
 PACKING  LST       2507     06-13-91     5:00a
 DEFRAG   HLP       9227     03-10-93     6:00a
 DOSSWAP  EXE      18756     03-10-93     6:00a
 EGA      CPI      58870     03-10-93     6:00a
 RECOVER  EXE       9146     06-13-91     5:00a
 EGA      SYS       4885     03-10-93     6:00a
 -- More --

 HIMEM    SYS      14208     03-10-93     6:00a
 MEM      EXE      32150     03-10-93     6:00a
 XCOPY    EXE      15820     03-10-93     6:00a
 MONEY    BAS      46225     06-13-91     5:00a
 MSHERC   COM       6934     06-13-91     5:00a
 DELTREE  EXE      11113     03-10-93     6:00a
 GORILLA  BAS      29434     06-13-91     5:00a
 4201     CPI       6404     06-13-91     5:00a
 4208     CPI        720     06-13-91     5:00a
 5202     CPI        395     06-13-91     5:00a
 MOVE     EXE      17823     03-10-93     6:00a
 ASSIGN   COM       6399     06-13-91     5:00a
 RAMDRIVE SYS       5873     03-10-93     6:00a
 BACKUP   EXE      36092     06-13-91     5:00a
 SMARTDRV EXE      42073     03-10-93     6:00a
```

6–5 MISCELLANEOUS DOS COMMANDS

In the remaining part of this chapter we look at several new DOS commands that will be helpful while you are using advanced features of DOS.

6–5–1 PRINT Command

By using the PRINT command, you can instruct the computer to print a file while you are using the computer for other purposes. You should use the PRINT command only for printing **ASCII files.** All files created by EDLIN, EDIT, and COPY CON are examples of ASCII files.

It is easy to find out if a file is in ASCII. Insert the disk that includes the ASCII file in drive A and, at the C> prompt, type *TYPE A:FILENAME.EXT*. If a file is listed in standard keyboard characters, it is an ASCII file, otherwise it is not. To use PRINT command at the C> prompt, type *PRINT A:FILENAME.EXT*. If the file is not in drive A, you must use the drive identifier or a path to the file.

If you are connected to more than one printer, the computer may ask you to which printer you would like to send the output. To cancel the printing process before it is completed, type *PRINT/T* and press Enter.

6–5–2 MODE Command

The MODE command can perform a variety of tasks. One of these tasks is setting up the width of your output from the printer. To see the effect of this command, get your computer started and turn on the printer. At the C> prompt, type

  MODE LPT1 : 132,8

LPT1 is your default printer; you can also use LPT2, LPT3, and so on. Number 132 indicates the number of characters per line and number 8 indicates number of vertical lines per inch. The default value for the MODE command is MODE LPT1:80,6. The vertical lines per inch can be either 6 or 8. The number of characters per line can be either 80 or 132.

You can perform other tasks with the MODE command such as switching monitor display mode, setting protocol for a serial port, and redirecting parallel port output to a serial port. For more information, consult your DOS manual.

6–5–3 VERIFY Command

The VERIFY command verifies that the data written onto a disk has been properly recorded. VERIFY can be either ON or OFF. To set it on, at the C> prompt type *VERIFY ON* and press Enter. It stays in effect until you type *VERIFY OFF*. When verify is on, your system will run slower because the computer is performing more than the normal number of tasks.

6–5–4 RECOVER Command

The RECOVER command is used to rescue a file or a series of files from a damaged disk. To execute this command, insert the damaged disk in drive A and at the C> prompt, type

  C>RECOVER A:FIRST

This command recovers the file FIRST from the disk in drive A. C>RECOVER A: recovers the entire drive A.

6–5–5   FILES Command

The FILES command allows you to specify the maximum number of files that can be opened concurrently. The default is 8 files and the maximum is 255. The format is

$$FILES\ =\ Y$$

where Y is greater than or equal to 8 and less than or equal to 255.

6–6   DOS UTILITIES

DOS utilities, or shells, are programs that simplify DOS operations. These programs are usually menu driven and easy to use. Depending on their sophistication, they perform one or a series of the following functions:

- Menu creation
- File backup
- Disk backup
- Management of files in subdirectories
- File protection by password creation
- Macro creation (combining a series of keystrokes into one keystroke)
- Undo command (allows you to change your mind if making a mistake)
- General hard disk management

There are many DOS utilities on the market. Among the popular ones are Norton Utilities (Peter Norton Computing, Inc.), PC Tools Deluxe (Central Point Software), Superkey (Borland International), and Xtree Pro (Executive Systems).

6–7   THE TREND IN MS-DOS AND PC-DOS DEVELOPMENT

The newer versions of DOS have added new capabilities and have also fixed some of the previous bugs. Most recently, DOS 6.0 has attracted much attention in the microcomputer community.

DOS 6.0 has gained popularity by the support of Intel 80386, 80486, and Pentium microprocessors. The new DOS has several specific goals:

- Expanded memory, beyond the traditional 640 K
- Multitasking
- Multiprocessing
- Upward compatibility
- Ease of use, or user-friendliness

Memory expansion is essential to access more sophisticated software. Also, to improve user-friendliness, the system may have to use DOS shells, spelling checkers, electronic mail, notepads, pull-down windows, and so on. All these require enhanced and expanded memory.

Multitasking and multiprocessing add a new dimension to the microcomputer environment. These features allow a user to run more than one task or more than one program at the same time. They assist a PC user in performing more sophisticated operations. The multiprocessing (networking) feature enables more than one user to access the same application program. This feature makes a PC more cost-effective. A multiprocessing system may, however, run slower than single-tasking systems and may cause compatibility problems.

Upward compatibility allows PC users to upgrade to better and more powerful operating systems without losing what they already have.

User-friendliness is of significant importance to PC users. A typical user often does not have much experience with computers. The easier the system is to use, the more attractive it is to the user. User-friendliness can be improved by DOS shells or through a graphical interface, such as the graphical interface available on Apple's Macintosh. IBM developed Top View, and Microsoft developed the popular graphical interface called Windows. To include such features in DOS, the PC must have expanded memory.

IBM's Personal System 2 (PS/2) and compatibles perform multitasking, use the 16-megabyte and more address space of the 80386, 80486, and Pentium microprocessors, and work with a DOS-compatible environment. At the same time, OS/2 (another operating system for PS/2) addresses one gigabyte of virtual memory. Virtual memory enables a user to extend his or her computer memory beyond the available memory. OS/2 also includes many features for programmers and application developers.

The new microprocessors—386, 486, and Pentium—can benefit immensely from the new DOS. DOS users should remember that AT&T's UNIX operating system may be a major competitor to MS-DOS and PC-DOS. One version of UNIX was introduced in 1971. This operating system has gone through major changes and is being marketed under different names. Initially, it was created for minicomputers. It has been designed to perform multitasking and multiprogramming. Newer versions of UNIX are available for all types of computers, from mainframe to some high-powered microcomputers. The major advantages of UNIX over MS/PC-DOS are its adaptability to a wide variety of computers and its extensive library of tools created for application developers. However, at the present time, it is too complex for novice computer users.

We will discuss more advanced features of DOS 6.0 in detail in Chapters 7 and 8.

SUMMARY

This chapter reviewed additional features of DOS. Redirection and piping were discussed. Three important filters, SORT, FIND, and MORE, were explained. These filters enable you to exercise more control over your files and directories. The chapter briefly introduced the PRINT, MODE, VERIFY, RECOVER and FILES commands. We concluded with a brief discussion on DOS utilities and the trend in MS-DOS and PC-DOS development.

REVIEW QUESTIONS

*These questions are answered in Appendix A.

1. What is redirection?

2. Why is redirection needed?

*3. How do you redirect your directory listing to the printer?

4. Can you redirect a directory listing to a file? If yes, how?

5. Can you use input redirection as opposed to output redirection? If yes, how?

*6. What are filters? How many filters does DOS have?

7. How do you sort your directory based on the date of creation? Based on file extension?

8. How many parameters are available in the FIND command?

9. What does the /V parameter do in the FIND command? /C parameter? /N parameter?

10. What are the applications of the MORE filter?

*11. What is the difference between the DIR/P and MORE commands?

12. What symbol is used for piping?

*13. Why is piping used?

14. What are the applications of the PRINT command?

15. Can the PRINT command be used with any types of files? Discuss.

16. What are the applications of the MODE command?

17. Where and when may you use the VERIFY command?

18. What are the applications of the RECOVER command?

*19. What are the applications of the FILES command?

20. What are some examples of DOS utilities? What do they do?

21. What are some of the features of DOS 6.0? How do these features help novice users?

22. By consulting computer magazines, compare and contrast the OS/2 and UNIX operating systems. Why may UNIX become the operating system of the future?

HANDS-ON EXPERIENCE

1. Insert a formatted disk into drive A. At the C> prompt, do the following:
   a. Redirect the directory listing of DOS to your printer.
   b. Redirect the directory listing of DOS to a file in drive A called TRY.
   c. Print the contents of TRY.
   d. Does TRY have any extension?

2. Insert a formatted disk into drive A. At the C> prompt, perform the following tasks:
   a. Sort the DOS files based on file names and direct the result into a file called S1 in drive A.
   b. Sort the DOS files based on the dates the files were created, in descending order, and direct the results into a file called S2 in drive A.
   c. Sort the DOS files based on the file sizes in descending order and direct the result into a file called S3 in drive A.

3. Insert a formatted disk into drive A. At the C> prompt, perform the following tasks:
   a. Using the FIND command, display the number of files with the COM extension.
   b. Using the FIND command, display all the files with the COM extension.
   c. Using the FIND command, display all the files that do not have the COM extension.
   d. Using the MORE command, display the drive A directory one page at a time.
   e. Using the piping technique, generate a directory of drive A and sort it and direct the result to a file called S4 in drive C.

4. Send one of the DOS files to the printer by using the PRINT command. What is the difference between the PRINT command and Shift+PrtSc (or Print Screen in enhanced keyboards)?

5. If you have access to a printer by using the MODE command, change the default mode to 132 and 8. This means 132 characters per line and 8 lines per inch. Now print a listing of your directory to see the difference in the output.

6. Design a batch file that sets the number of files to 15 (use the FILES command).

7. Conduct some research on Norton Utilities. What are offered by these utilities? How may these utilities make your job easier? Who will benefit the most from these utilities?

KEY TERMS

Ascending order   DOS utilities   Piping
ASCII file   Filter   Redirect
Descending order

KEY COMMANDS

FILES (internal)   MORE (external)   SORT (external)
FIND (external)   PRINT (external)   TYPE (internal)
MODE (internal)   RECOVER (external)   VERIFY (internal)

ARE YOU READY TO MOVE ON?

Multiple Choice

1. Output redirection is accomplished by using

   a. >
   b. <
   c. =
   d. +
   e. #

2. DOS filters include

   a. SORT
   b. MORE
   c. DIR
   d. both a and b
   e. all of the above

3. In the command SORT/+n, the "n" refers to the

   a. name of the file to sort
   b. column number on which to sort
   c. number of files to sort
   d. types of characters allowed
   e. none of the above

4. The command SORT/R<LIST will

   a. sort the contents of LIST in ascending order
   b. place the output of the sort into a file called LIST
   c. sort the contents of LIST in descending order
   d. both a and b
   e. both b and c

   Questions 5 and 6 refer to the following file, called MAJORS.BPA:

9086	ROBERT	MIS
1011	MARY	ACC
3032	JOHN	MIS
2098	AMY	FIN
3856	JIM	MKT

5. The output of FIND/N "MKT"<MAJORS.BPA is

    a. 9086 ROBERT MIS
    b. [3] 3032 JOHN MIS
    c. both a and b
    d. [4] 2098 AMY FIN
    e. [5] 3856 JIM MKT

6. The output of FIND/C "MIS"<MAJORS.BPA is

    a. 1
    b. 2
    c. 3
    d. 4
    e. one of the above

7. The character used to combine DOS commands is

    a. <
    b. >
    c. /
    d. \
    e. |

8. The MODE command can be used to

    a. set the width of printer output
    b. switch monitor display mode
    c. redirect parallel port output to a serial port
    d. all of the above
    e. none of the above

9. To have DOS determine whether data written onto a disk has been properly recorded, use the command

    a. CHKDSK
    b. VERIFY
    c. RECOVER
    d. VER
    e. none of the above

10. To allow 10 files to be open at the same time, enter

    a. FILES=10
    b. FILES<10
    c. SET FILES TO 10
    d. LET FILES=10
    e. none of the above

True/False

1. It is not possible to direct the output of any DOS commands to other devices besides the CRT.

2. DIR>LIST will place a directory listing into a file called LIST.

3. DIR>LIST and DIR<LIST mean the same thing.

4. DOS filters allow more control over commands such as DIR.

5. The FIND command searches and finds files with the specified file name and is similar to the DIR command.

6. The MORE command generates one screen of a directory or a file at a time and can be used with both DIR and TYPE.

7. Only two DOS commands can be piped together.

8. PRINT file name and TYPE file name>PRN will produce the same output.

9. The VERIFY command has no effect on system speed.

10. DOS utilities are available to help simplify DOS operations.

ANSWERS

Multiple Choice		True/False	
1.	a	1.	F
2.	d	2.	T
3.	b	3.	F
4.	c	4.	T
5.	e	5.	F
6.	b	6.	T
7.	e	7.	F
8.	d	8.	T
9.	b	9.	F
10.	a	10.	T

DOS 6.0 Advanced Features: Part I

7

7–1   INTRODUCTION

In this chapter we first review DOS 6.0 in general. We consider the unique features of DOS 6.0. Next we discuss memory management, the online help facility, and the DOS shell in detail. As you will see, DOS 6.0 makes DOS work a little more easily. In the next chapter we cover macros and full-screen editing features.

7–2   DOS 6.0: AN OVERVIEW

PC-DOS 6.0 and MS-DOS 6.0 represent a major step forward in the operating systems for IBM and IBM compatibles. DOS 6.0 is fully compatible with earlier versions of MS-DOS and PC-DOS. It is considered a major advancement because of the increased power it offers by the addition of many sophisticated features and the enhancement of many of its previously offered features.

DOS 6.0 includes several new commands, additional options for some of the existing commands, a shell program (also available in DOS 5.0), and a full-screen editing feature. Two of the new commands are the UNDELETE and UNFORMAT commands, which assist the user in the rescue of data that has been lost through the use of DELETE and FORMAT commands. (These two commands were also available in DOS 5.0. However, they include new switches, now.) Previously, these important features were available only through programs such as Norton Utilities or PC Tools.

Upgrading to DOS 6.0 does entail certain hardware requirements. Nevertheless, the process of upgrading is not too painful. The following hardware requirements must be met:

- Minimum of 256 K of memory
- DOS version 2.11 or later
- Minimum of 4.0 MB of free hard disk space, if upgrading to a hard disk
- Note: When installing DOS 6.0, the installation program conveniently saves all of your old DOS files. If problems occur during the installation process or subsequent use of DOS, DOS 6.0 can be "uninstalled," thereby resetting the system back to the original version of DOS that was on the computer before installation of DOS 6.0.

Although DOS 6.0 can be used on older hardware, some of its new features will only benefit those who have more advanced PCs, for example, PCs with 386, 486, or higher processors. Several new features characterize DOS 6.0:

- Disk compression by using the DBLSPACE program that can approximately double the capacity of your hard disk
- Back up and restore utilities by using the MSBACKUP program for easy backing up and restoring your hard disk
- Anti-virus feature by using the MSAV program, which scans and removes over 1,000 known viruses
- Memory management by using the MEMMAKER program, which can increase your conventional memory by up to 100 K
- Advanced communications capabilities for accessing files and peripherals on other PCs with compatible software
- Ease of use by improving the online help

■ New commands such as MOVE for moving files and directories and DELTREE for deleting a directory and its contents

We have already talked about some of these features. The rest will be discussed in this chapter and Chapter 8.

7–3 USING THE COMPRESSION FEATURE

DOS 6.0 performs an efficient disk compression task using the **DBLSPACE** program. DBLSPACE is capable of increasing hard disk capacity by a factor of almost 2. The rate of compression depends on the type of files on your hard disk. EXE files, for example, will give less compression. On the other hand, uncompressed text and graphics files will give more.

After installing DOS 6.0, you are invited to use DBLSPACE. Double-space creates a CVR (Compressed Volume File), negating the need to reformat your hard disk.

If you do not use DBLSPACE during the installation, you can always use it later by typing DBLSPACE (followed by Enter) at the DOS prompt.

The compression operation leaves a lot of empty spaces in the hard disk when the double-space operation is complete. Following compression, use the **DEFRAG** command to rearrange the files on your hard disk. The DEFRAG command reorganizes the files on a disk to optimize disk performance. A particular file may be fragmented and stored in several noncontiguous sections of the hard disk. The DEFRAG command will take care of all these problems. Do not use the DEFRAG command when you are running Windows.

7–4 ANTI-VIRUS TOOLS

A computer virus is a series of self-propagating program codes that are triggered by a specified time or event within the computer system. When the program or the operating system containing the virus is used again, the virus copies onto another program and the cycle continues. The seriousness of computer viruses varies, ranging from springing a joke on a user to completely destroying computer programs and data. Computer viruses are relatively new in the United States, but they have been around much longer in European countries.

Virus infections can also be transmitted through a network. Bulletin boards are databases that are accessed by a number of computer users by using a modem. This type of virus can infect anyone who accesses the bulletin board, and bulletin boards had become notorious as carriers of viruses in recent years. However, due to stringent efforts by bulletin board operators to keep the board clean, this particular source of viruses has become almost virus-free.

DOS 6.0, similar to many popular utility programs, includes a virus protection program. The virus protection is performed by the **MSAV** command. MSAV scans for and removes virus-infected files. According to Microsoft, this program is capable of removing over 1,000 known viruses. The MSAV command comes with several switches. Table 7–1 summarizes commonly used switches.

In addition to checking for known viruses, the anti-virus program will add a checksum to existing executable files and warns the user if these files have been changed.

Let us say you want to check for any known viruses in drive A. At the DOS prompt, type *MSAV/C A:* and press Enter. You will be presented with a

Table 7–1
MSAV commonly used switches

Switch	Function
/A	Scans all drives except floppy disk drives A: and B:
/C	Scans for and removes any viruses found. You have to identify the drive.
/R	Creates a report listing of all scanned files and all viruses found and removed and saves the report to the default file MSAV.RPT. By default this option is off. You have to identify the drive.
/S	Scans selected drives for viruses, but does not remove viruses that MSAV finds. You have to identify the drive.

Figure 7–1
Microsoft anti-virus screen

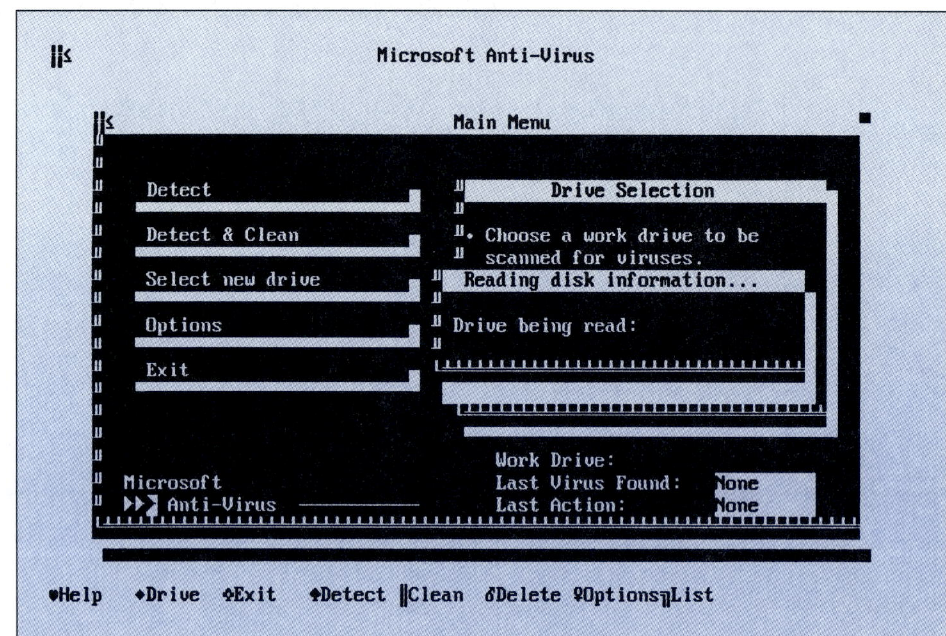

screen similar to the one in Figure 7–1. In a few seconds MSAV checks all the files in drive A and removes any known viruses from this drive.

7–5   BACKUP AND RESTORE FACILITIES

In addition to BACKUP and RESTORE commands (discussed in Chapter 4), MS-DOS 6.0 includes the MSBACKUP program for backing up your computer hard disk and restoring it in case of a hard disk failure. This is how you back up a hard disk.

1. At the DOS prompt, type *MSBACKUP* and press Enter. The program scans drive C by default and saves the information in the default setup file named DEFAULT.SET. It reads its directories and then presents the starting screen. See Figure 7–2.

2. Select the **BACKUP** button. You can do this by clicking on the Backup option if using a mouse or by using the Tab key to move the cursor to the

Figure 7–2
The starting screen of Microsoft
Backup

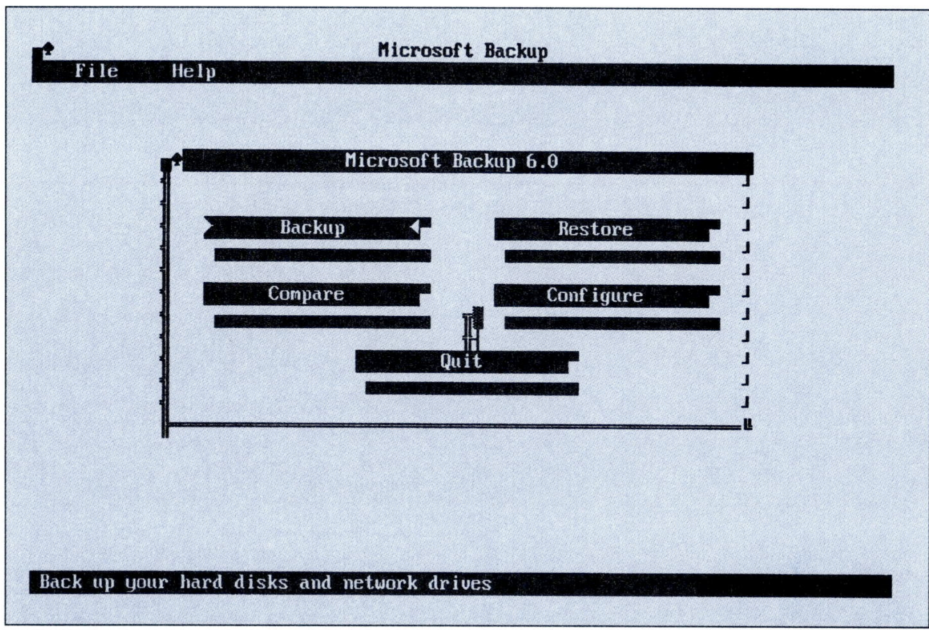

Figure 7–3
The Backup program screen

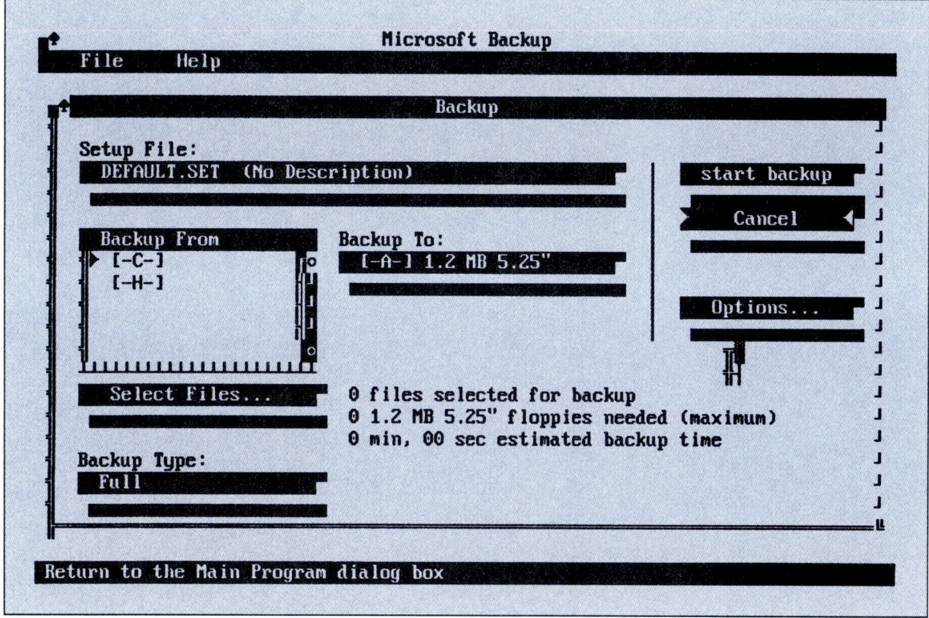

Backup option then pressing Enter. As soon as you select the Backup option you
will be presented with a screen similar to the one in Figure 7–3. As shown in Figure 7–3, the default setup file is loaded and by default the selected backup type is
Full. You can change this if you so desire. If you select this option, you will be presented with a screen similar to the one in Figure 7–4.

   The Incremental option backs up all selected files that have changed
since the last full or incremented backup, as well as the new files in selected directories. This backup type is useful if you want to keep copies of all your data files
as they change. The Incremental option lowers the archive flags; then the program knows what has been backed up to this point. The Differential option per-

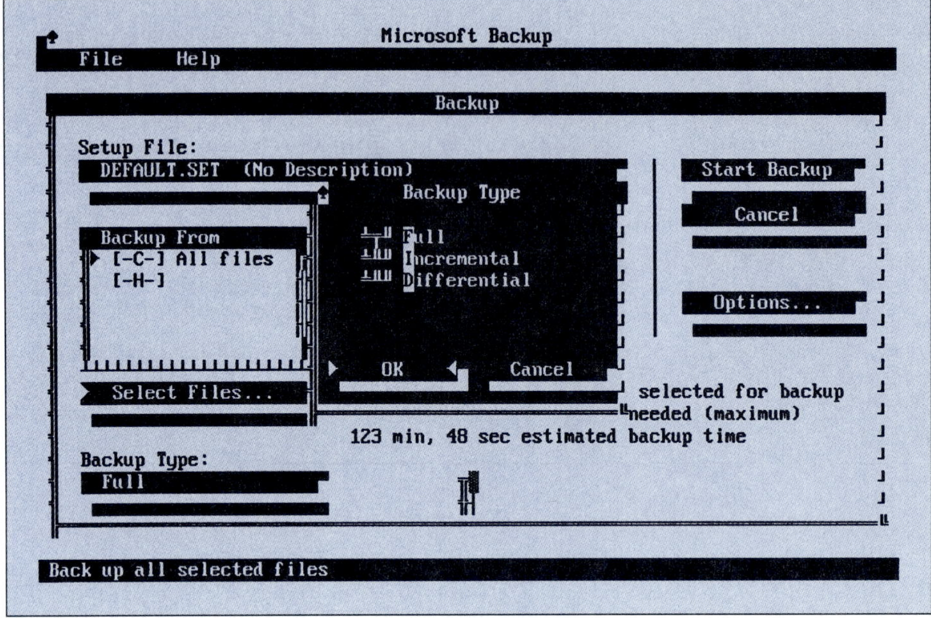

forms the same exact task as the Incremental, but does not lower the archive flags. This type of backup would be useful if you want to back up all files that have changed since your last full backup. This would be very practical if you want a single backup set that contains all of your changed files.

To start a full backup, choose the drive you want to back up from the **Backup From** list (Figure 7–3) by double-clicking the appropriate drive, or by using the arrow-movement keys to move to the desired drive and pressing the Enter key. As you start the backup process, the backup screen shows you what is required. You may receive a message similar to the following:

```
2,292 files (with catalog) selected for backup
41 1.44 MB 3.5" floppies needed (maximum)
26 min, 30 sec estimated backup time
```

The Backup program formats any target disks that are not formatted and compresses the data on the backup disk to reduce the number of disks required.

3. Select **Start Backup** (Figure 7–3). The MSBACKUP program starts by creating the backup catalog and listing the files to be backed up. You will receive the following message:

```
Insert diskette #1 into drive A:
```

Insert a disk in the diskette drive and press the **Continue** button. As soon as the backup process starts, you may see a screen like the one in Figure 7–5.

4. As soon as the disk is full, the MSBACKUP prompts you to insert the next disk. This process will continue until the backup is complete. For documentation purposes, label each disk as Backup #1, Backup #2, . . . as you remove them. This will help you to easily identify and use these disks when they are needed.

In case of hard disk failure, you can restore your hard disk from the backup disks. To do so, select **Restore** button in Figure 7–2. The Restore option in the MSBACKUP program enables you to restore an individual file, selected

Figure 7–5
Backup progress screen

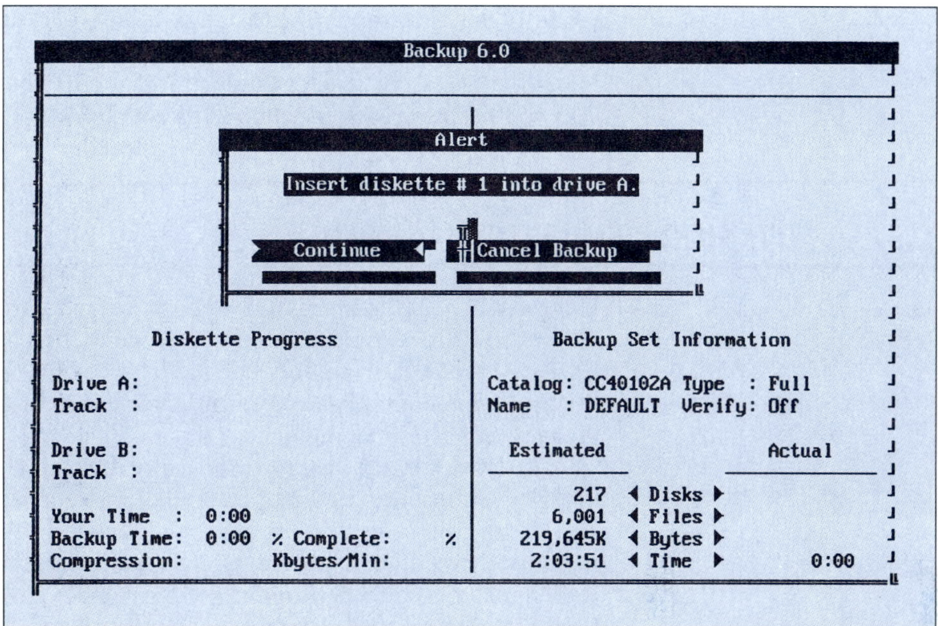

Figure 7–6
The Restore screen

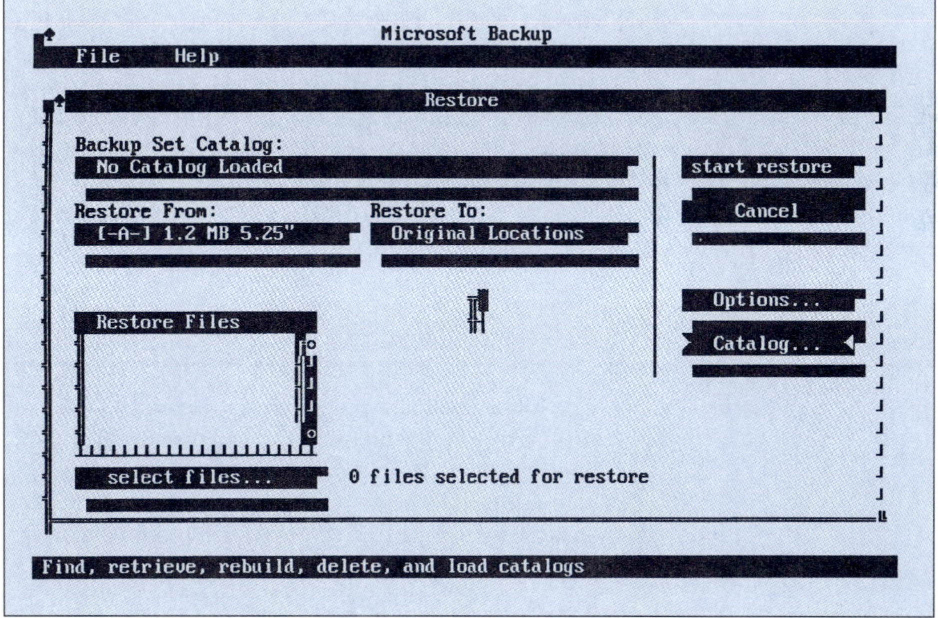

files, or an entire hard disk. When you select Restore, the MSBACKUP loads the most recent backup set catalog and displays the Restore screen similar to the one in Figure 7–6. The catalog's name appears in the Backup Set Catalog field. To select another backup set for restore, select Backup Set Catalog, and select one of the other files listed. If the file is not in the default catalog directory (C:\DOS), select the Catalog option (from Figure 7–6) and then select **Load.** Next, select the appropriate drive and directory from the list provided before selecting the catalog file.

If your hard disk does not contain any catalog for backup from which you want to restore, select **Catalog** and then **Retrieve.** At this time the MSBACKUP requests that you insert the last disk of the backup series in the diskette drive, and the MSBACKUP reads the catalog from the disk. If for any reason the catalog is not accessible, select **Catalog** and then **Rebuild.** At this time MSBACKUP asks you to insert each backup disk starting with disk number 1. The process will continue until the entire hard disk is restored.

7–6   ADVANCED MEMORY MANAGEMENT

How a user benefits from DOS 6.0's **memory management** depends on the type of PC he or she is using. PCs equipped with a 386, 486, or higher processor often have supplementary memory beyond 640 K. DOS 6.0 can use this memory, called the upper memory area (UMA), by loading part of DOS directly into it. This frees up some conventional memory.

DOS 6.0 can also load device drivers and TSR (terminate and stay resident) programs into the UMA instead of into conventional memory. For example, by placing Microsoft's mouse driver into the UMA, over 100 K of conventional memory is freed. TSR programs are various utilities that load into memory and then return to the DOS prompt. A typical TSR program might be a pop-up calculator or a pop-up calendar.

To utilize the memory management features of DOS 6.0, at the DOS prompt type *MEMMAKER* and press Enter. This command starts the MEMMAKER program, which optimizes your computer's memory by moving device drivers and memory-resident programs to upper memory.

To use MEMMAKER effectively, your computer must have an 80386 or higher processor and extended memory (see Chapter 1 for a definition of extended memory). Do not use MEMMAKER when you are running Windows.

To instruct MEMMAKER to undo its last changes, type *MEMMAKER UNDO* (followed by Enter).

According to Microsoft, memory management can free over 100 K of conventional memory over and above DOS 5.0.

7–7   DOS 6.0 SHELL

The **DOS Shell** is a powerful feature of DOS 5.0 and DOS 6.0 that brings a Windows-like environment to all PC users. This shell can be either mouse or keyboard driven. It changes the way the user interfaces with the computer from a command-line mode to a graphic mode. The graphic mode makes viewing files easier and simplifies the tasks of moving around in directories, running programs, and copying or moving files.

The shell program is easy to learn and use because it has pull-down menus. The online help facility is also available for the DOS Shell. In any given menu option, you can press F1 for online help. To use the DOS Shell, type *DOSSHELL* at the DOS prompt and press Enter. This starts the MS-DOS Shell. You will be presented with a screen similar to Figure 7–7. As you can see at the top of the screen, the title indicates that you are in the MS-DOS Shell. The second line is the menu options line. This menu includes five options:

```
File   Options   View   Tree   Help
```

The third line indicates which drive is in use; in our case we are in drive C. The next line indicates the drives in the computer, with the active drive highlighted.

Figure 7–7
MS-DOS Shell

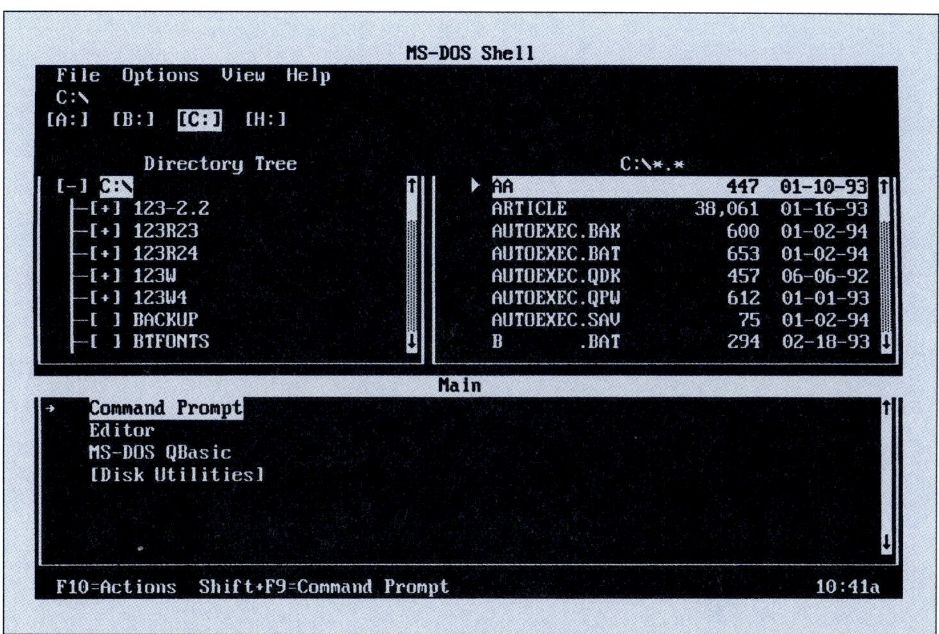

Notice the three windows, one on the right, one on the left, and one at the bottom. The window on the left displays the Directory Tree. The window on the right lists the files contained in the highlighted or specified directory that appears on the left. The window at the bottom shows the main menu of MS-DOS Shell.

Press the Tab key to move the cursor into the Directory Tree window on the left. If you move the highlight bar to one of the directories in the Directory Tree window and press Enter, files within that directory will appear on the right side of the screen. The bottom line on the screen (the third window) provides instructions on how to activate the menu options using the keyboard and how to return to the DOS prompt. For example, if you press the F10 key, the main menu will be activated. If you press Shift+F9, you will return to DOS prompt. If you do this, you type *EXIT,* following by pressing Enter, to return to the DOS Shell.

Press the Tab key to move the cursor back to the drives line at the top of the screen (if you are not already there). The right- and left-arrow keys can be used to change the default drive without activating any other features. For example, we are currently in drive C. If we use the left-arrow key we can change from drive C to drive B or A; and if we use the right-arrow key, we can change from drive C to drive D or H (if there are such drives). If you place a formatted diskette in the A drive, then highlight drive A and press Enter, DOS will read the information from the diskette in this drive and display it in the right window. This action is similar to using the DIR command.

As mentioned earlier, options from the menu at the top can be selected by pressing the F10 key and then using the arrow keys to highlight the File, Options, View, Tree, or Help option (followed by pressing Enter). A pull-down menu then appears with the available choices under the selected option of the main menu. The arrow keys can then be used to highlight the desired choice, followed by pressing Enter.

A faster and simpler way to activate and choose the menu options would be to use a mouse. If you have a mouse, move the mouse pointer to the item that you wish to choose and click the left button.

Let us now briefly explain the commands under the options of the main menu.

<table>
<tr><td>

7–7–1

</td><td>

The File Option of DOS Shell

As Figure 7–8 indicates, the File option includes several commands. Some of these commands are familiar to you, and each is explained next.

The OPEN command starts a selected program and an associated file (if there is one).

The RUN command displays a dialog box in which you type the name of a program (followed by pressing Enter) to start the program.

The PRINT command prints the selected text file or files. To start the print command, you must first type *PRINT* (press Enter) at the DOS prompt. Then you can issue the PRINT command from the DOS Shell.

The ASSOCIATE command is an interesting feature of DOS 6.0. Through **file association,** all files having the same extension are associated with a program or application software. The DOS Shell automatically starts an application and opens a file for you. When you choose a file with the specified extension, the software associated with that file's extension starts with the file loaded. For example, you would like to associate all .WK1 files with Lotus 1-2-3, all .DOC files with WordPerfect, and all .DBF files with dBASE. First, from the right side of the screen where you have your files listed under the chosen directory, highlight a chosen file. For example, if you frequently work with Lotus 1-2-3 Releases 2.3 or earlier, all your worksheet files are automatically saved with the .WK1 extension. You can highlight the CH10-1.WK1 file (as an example) in the files window, then select File from the main menu, then select Associate. A dialog box with the Associate File title will appear on the screen. See Figure 7–9.

You can then type in the drive and path to your Lotus program (e.g., *C:\123R23\LOTUS.EXE),* followed by pressing Enter, to associate all .WK1 files with 1-2-3. From this point on, every time you highlight a file with the .WK1 extension, LOTUS 1-2-3 will automatically be activated and the specified file will be loaded and ready to work on. You have eliminated the need to load the program. You simply choose which file you wish to work on and DOS does the rest by choosing the proper software and loading the file for you. If you are consistent with the extensions that you use for your files, you can greatly simplify your work by associating certain extensions with different software.

</td></tr>
</table>

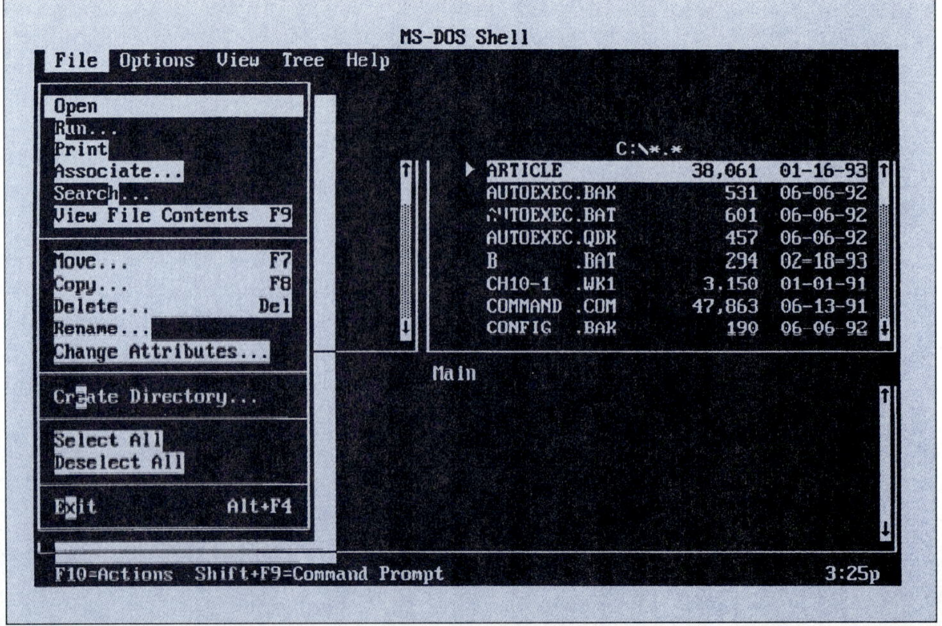

Here is another example of the usefulness of the ASSOCIATE command. Insert a disk in drive A; then through the DOS Shell you can display a directory of the disk. See Figure 7–10, which illustrates the directory listing of files on a disk. Now, highlight the file that you wish to work on and press Enter to load that file and the application that it has been associated with (if any association has been made).

The SEARCH command searches for and finds files on all or part of the current disk drive, depending on what you specify. As usual, you can use wildcards as well. For example, after issuing the SEARCH command, you can type *.WK1 (press Enter) to find all your Lotus 1-2-3 worksheet (WK1) files in the current directory.

Figure 7–9
Associate file dialog box

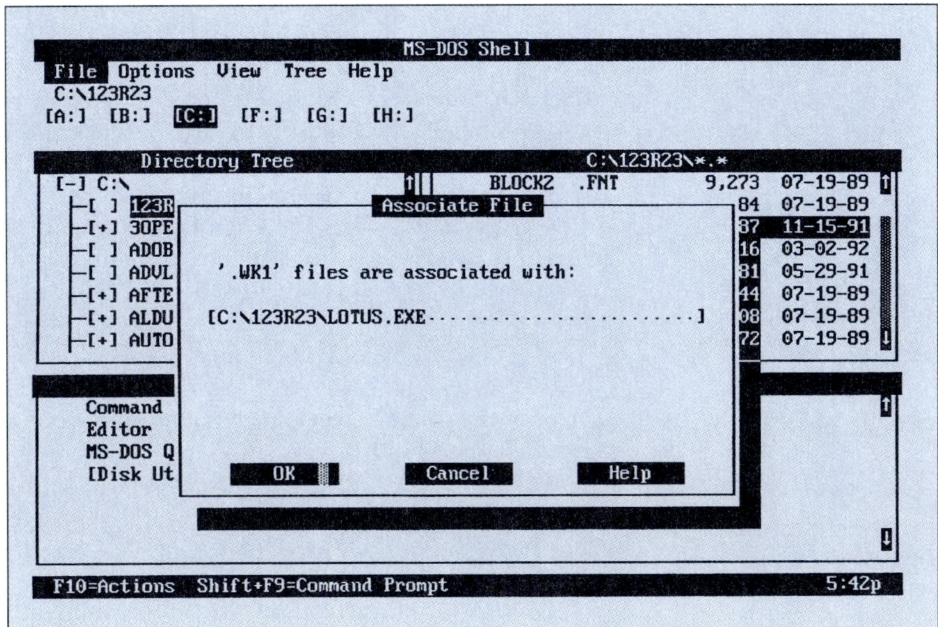

Figure 7–10
Directory listing of a disk

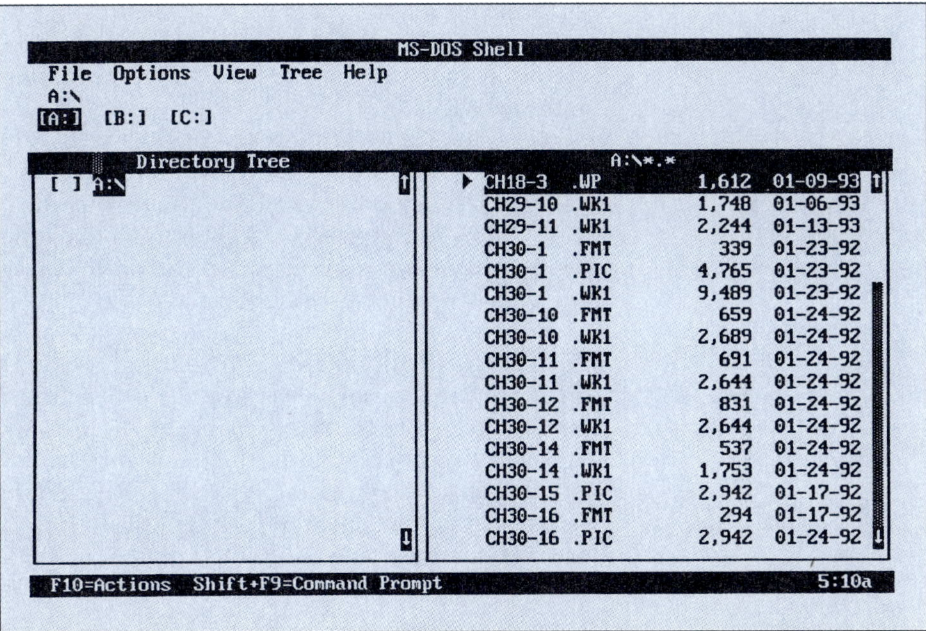

The VIEW FILE CONTENTS command displays the contents of the selected text or binary file on the screen. For a shortcut, you can press the F9 function key.

The MOVE command moves the selected file or files from one directory to another directory. After issuing the command, you must specify the exact path for the origin and destination of the selected file(s). For a shortcut, you can press the F7 function key.

The COPY command, as you have previously seen, copies one or several files from one directory to another directory. After issuing the command, you must specify the exact path for the origin and destination of the selected file(s). For a shortcut, you can press the F8 function key.

The DELETE command deletes the selected file(s) or directory. For a shortcut, you can press the Delete (Del) key.

The RENAME command changes a file name to a new name. Select the desired file then specify the new name.

The CHANGE ATTRIBUTES command displays the attributes assigned to a file. Attributes include Hidden, System, Archive, and Read-only. By using this command, you can assign or remove attributes.

The CREATE DIRECTORY command creates a new directory on the current drive. If you are already in a subdirectory, this command creates a subdirectory within that directory, that is, the new directory becomes a child of your current directory.

The SELECT ALL command selects all files in the current directory for further processing; for example, for deletion. The DESELECT ALL command is the opposite of the Select All command. It cancels all selections except one in the currently selected directory.

The Exit or Alt+F4 option allows you to leave the DOS Shell.

7–7–2   The Options Option of DOS Shell

As Figure 7–11 indicates, there are seven commands under the main menu called Options. Let us briefly explain each.

The CONFIRMATION command specifies whether the DOS Shell should prompt you for confirmation before deleting files and replacing files with duplicate names.

The FILE DISPLAY OPTIONS command lists files in sequence by name, extension, date, size, or order on the disk. It also controls the display of hidden and system files.

The SELECT ACROSS DIRECTORIES command controls whether or not you can select files in more than one directory. A mark next to the command name (Select Across Directories) indicates that the command is enabled.

The SHOW INFORMATION command displays information on the selected file(s), the directory, and the disk. This command is useful for finding out about the number of files in the current drive, the disk space available, and so forth.

The ENABLE TASK SWAPPER command turns on or off the task swapping facility and displays the Active Task List to the right of the program list. If the task swapping feature is enabled, you can run more than one program at a time and switch back and forth among programs. A mark next to the command indicates that task swapping is enabled. Because this is a very powerful feature, it deserves further explanation.

Task swapping is not the same as multitasking. In multitasking, the system performs more than one task at a time. This may include, for example, run-

Figure 7–11
Commands under the Options option

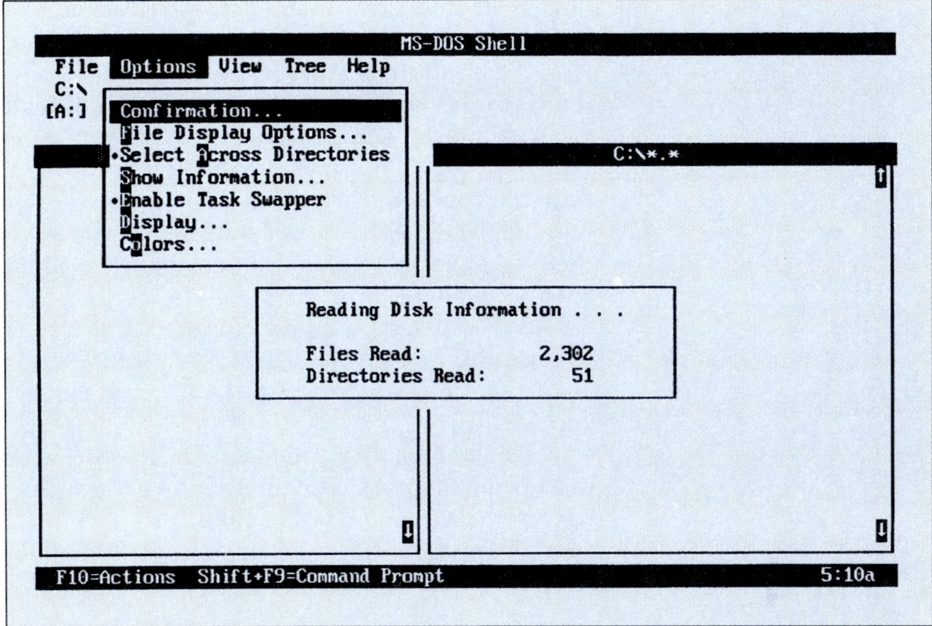

ning dBASE and Lotus 1-2-3 at the same time. In contrast, task swapping merely suspends what you are currently working on without you having to exit the first program to open and use the second. For example, suppose you are writing a report in WordPerfect and you need some information contained in a Lotus 1-2-3 spreadsheet. Normally, you would have to save your report and exit WordPerfect, load Lotus 1-2-3 and the spreadsheet to gather your information, exit Lotus 1-2-3, reload WordPerfect, retrieve your document and continue work. If the task swapping feature is enabled, you do not need to go through these steps.

Before you can use the task swapping capabilities of DOS 5 and 6, you must activate the task swapper. This is done by choosing the Enable Task Swapper option under the Options menu. To do this, activate the menu bar at the top of the screen with a mouse or by pressing the F10 key, select Options, and then highlight and select Enable Task Swapper by pressing Enter. You should now see a fourth window on your DOS shell screen at the lower right: the Active Task List window (refer to Figure 7–16). From this point, choose the WP51 directory from the Directory Tree window (assuming this directory option is available to you). The files in your WP51 directory will then be listed in the upper-right window of your screen. Press the Tab key to move to the files window, scroll down to and highlight WP.EXE, then double-click the left button of the mouse or simply press Enter. You are now in WordPerfect and can begin working with your document.

When you need to use information in another program, hold down the Alt key and press the Tab key. This will return you to the DOS Shell. In your Active Task List window, you should see WP.EXE. From this point, run the software that you need, say Lotus 1-2-3. To do this, press Shift+Tab to move the cursor back to the Directory Tree window. Use your arrow key to highlight the name of your Lotus subdirectory. Press the Tab key to move the cursor back into the upper-right files window. Use the down-arrow key to highlight the 123.EXE file. Press Enter to run 123. You should be in Lotus 1-2-3. You can now retrieve your Lotus spreadsheet and work with it. To switch back to WordPerfect, press Alt+Tab, then press your Tab key two times to move the cursor back into the Active Task List window. The window now displays 123.EXE and WP.EXE. Press your down-arrow key one time, then press Enter to switch to WordPerfect. By means of this method, you can switch back and forth between Lotus 1-2-3 and WordPerfect.

For now, exit WordPerfect by pressing these keys: F7,N,Y. Press any key to return to the MS-DOS shell. The cursor will highlight the 123.EXE file. Press Enter to switch back into Lotus 1-2-3. Then press /Q (quit) and Y (yes) to exit Lotus 1-2-3. Finally, press any key to return to MS-DOS shell. Now there are no active tasks in your Active Task List window. Remember, you must exit each software application (as we just did) before you will be allowed to leave the DOS shell, because the software will remain active and open but suspended while you are working in the other one.

To use task-swapping effectively, you may need more RAM. If the amount of RAM that you have available is not sufficient to handle the software programs among which you wish to switch, an error message of not enough memory will appear.

The DISPLAY command changes the screen mode and resolution used to display the MS-DOS shell. After you select this command, select your desired option from the pull-down menu.

The COLORS command changes the color scheme used for the MS-DOS shell.

7–7–3　　The View Option of DOS Shell

Using the commands under the View menu, you can display a single file list, dual file lists, or information on all files in the current directory. When you invoke the View menu, you will see a screen similar to Figure 7–12. As this figure indicates, there are seven choices in the menu.

If SINGLE FILE LIST is chosen, the screen will appear similar to Figure 7–13. As this figure indicates, one drive and the files that are associated with it are displayed.

When DUAL FILE LISTS is selected, then the screen is split horizontally into two sections, which allows the user to view two drives or directories at a time. See Figure 7–14.

Figure 7–12
Commands under the View option

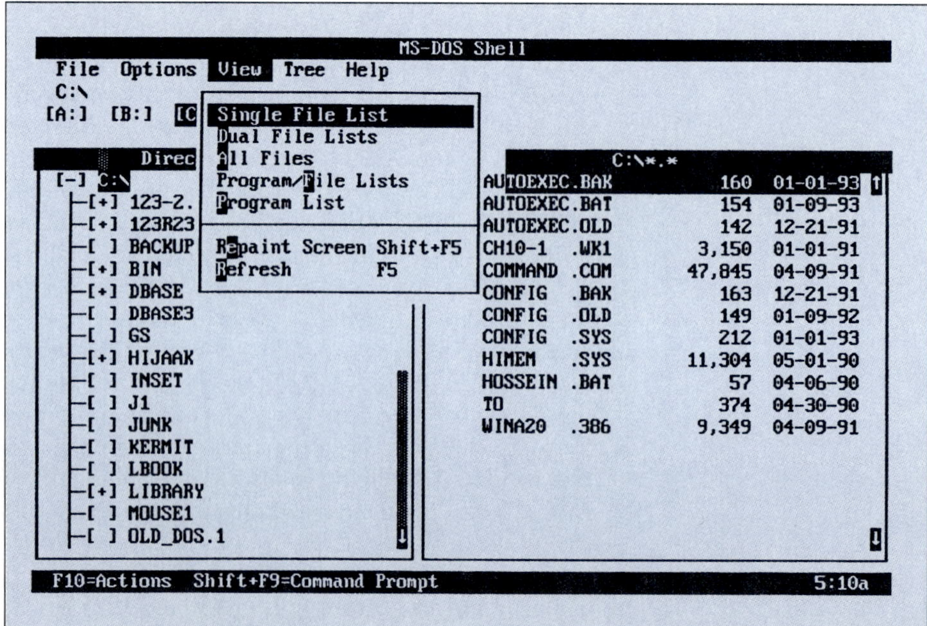

Figure 7–13
Directory listing under SINGLE
FILE LIST

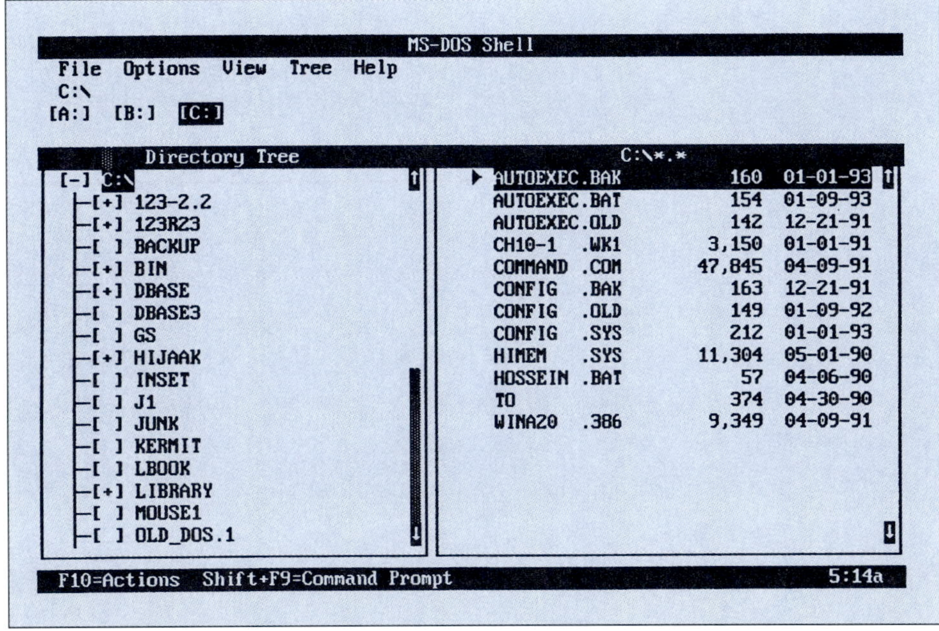

Figure 7–14
Directory listing under DUAL FILE
LISTS

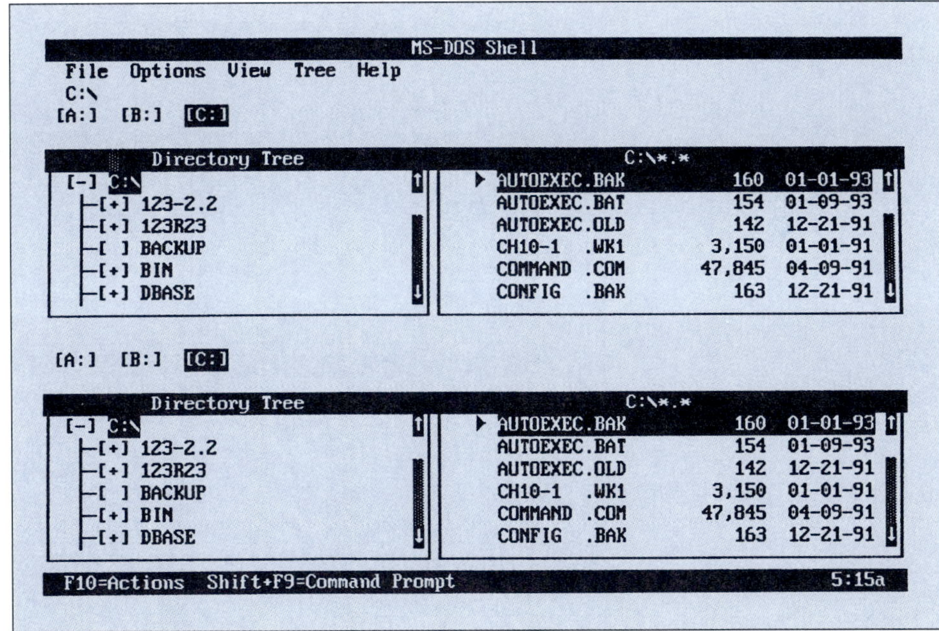

If ALL FILES is chosen, a screen similar to Figure 7–15 appears. It gives
information on all files for any given drive.

When PROGRAM/FILE LISTS is selected, the screen is split into two
again. The Directory Tree of the selected drive appears at the top and the program directory appears at the bottom as displayed in Figure 7–16.

If PROGRAM LIST is selected, then just programs will be displayed as
shown in Figure 7–17. The options in this screen are the same as the options
under the main menu in Figure 7–7. Also, your active task list (if you have one)
will be displayed in the right window.

Figure 7–15
Directory listing under ALL FILES

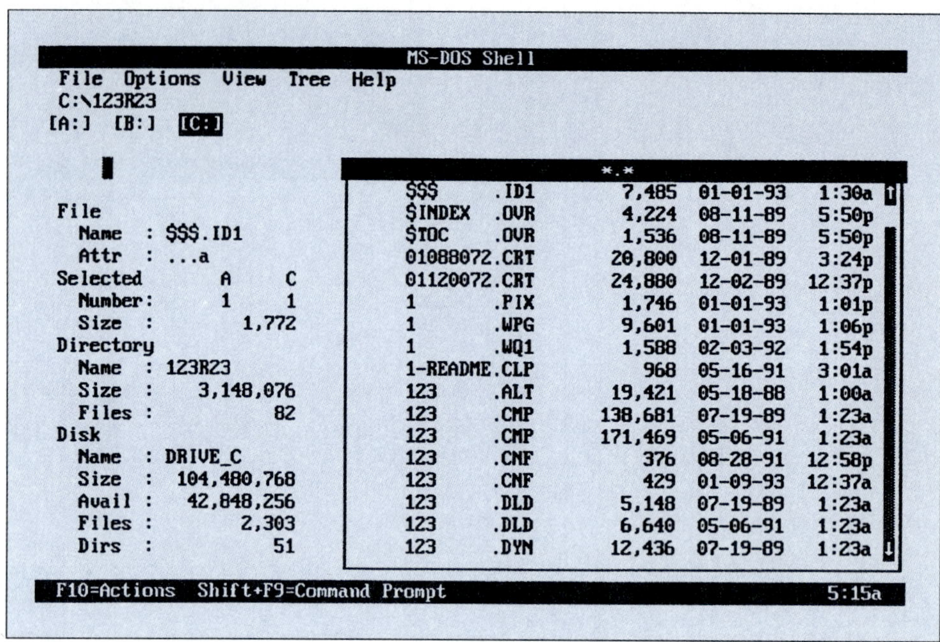

Figure 7–16
Directory listing under PRO-
GRAM/FILE LISTS

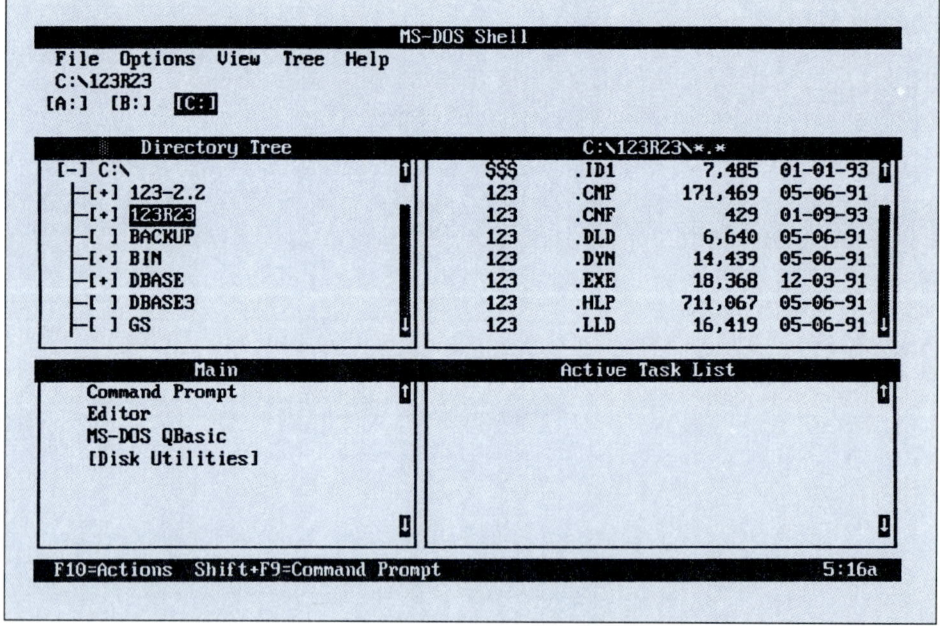

The REPAINT SCREEN command (Shift+F5), redraws the screen. The REFRESH command (F5), rereads the default drive and updates the lists to show changes such as deleted or restored files.

7–7–4   The Tree Option of DOS Shell

If you invoke the Tree option, you will be presented with a screen similar to Figure 7–18. As you can see in the figure, this menu option includes four commands. The commands allow you to display or hide subdirectories in the Directory Tree.

Figure 7–17
Directory listing under PROGRAM LIST

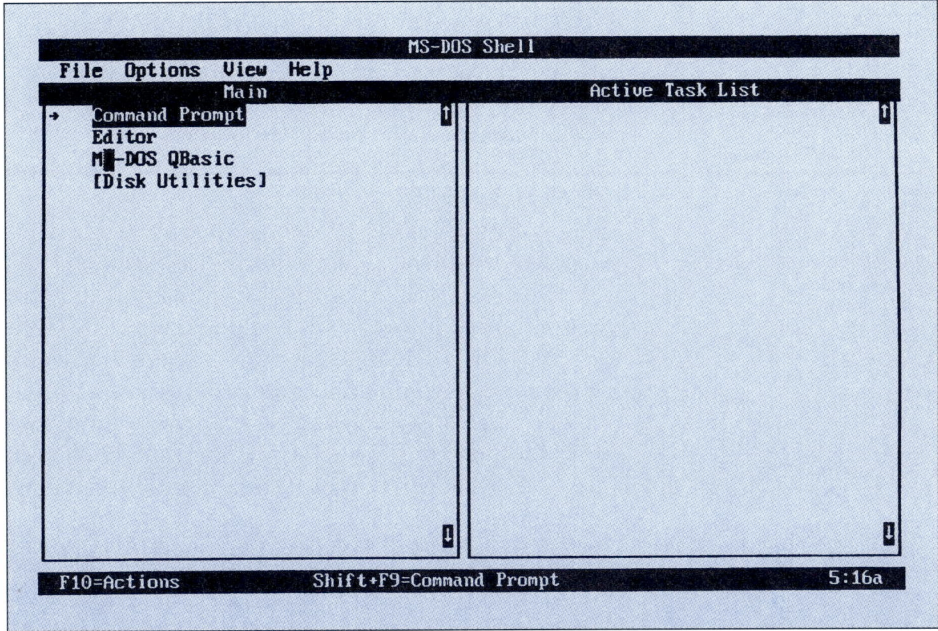

The EXPAND ONE LEVEL (+ for shortcut) command displays the next level of subdirectories for the selected directory in the Directory Tree.

The EXPAND BRANCH (* for shortcut) command displays all levels of subdirectories in the selected directory in the Directory Tree.

The EXPAND ALL (Ctrl +* for shortcut) command displays all subdirectories in all directories in the Directory Tree.

The COLLAPSE BRANCH (– for shortcut) command hides all currently displayed subdirectories in the selected directory in the Directory Tree.

Figure 7–18
Commands under the Tree option

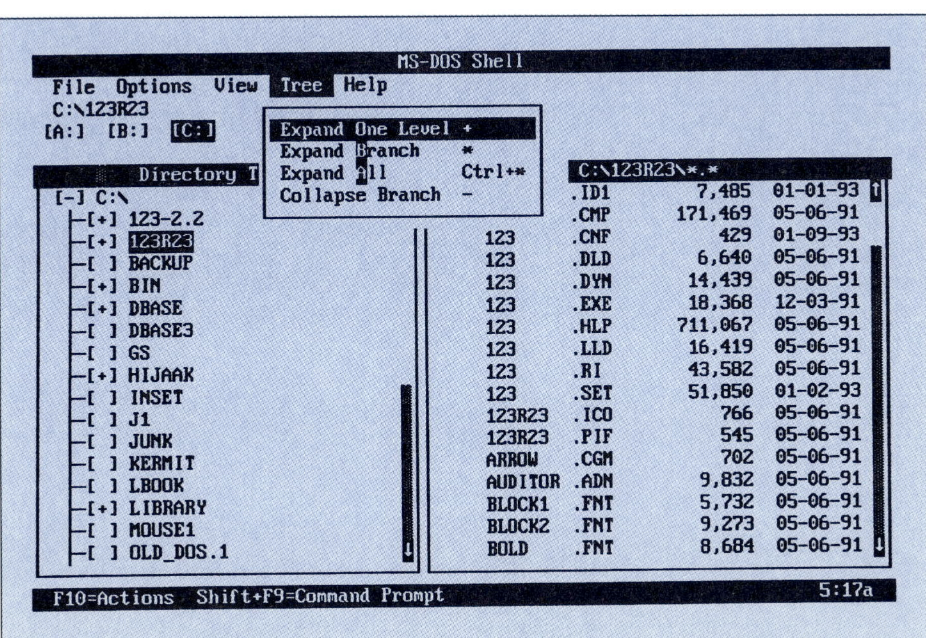

7–7–5   The Help Option of DOS Shell

If you invoke the Help option of the main menu, you will be presented with a screen similar to Figure 7–19. As the figure indicates, there are seven commands in this menu. Let us briefly explain each.

The INDEX command opens the Help window and displays the MS-DOS Shell Help Index.

The KEYBOARD command opens the Help window and displays a list of shortcut keys you can use with the DOS Shell.

The SHELL BASICS command opens the Help window and displays a list of topics for basic skills you need to work with the DOS Shell.

The COMMANDS option opens the Help window and displays a list of all DOS Shell commands, grouped by menu.

The PROCEDURES command opens the Help window and displays a list of topics you can see for help on DOS Shell tasks.

The USING HELP command opens the Help window and displays a list of topics that explain how to use DOS Shell help.

The ABOUT SHELL command displays copyright and version information about the DOS Shell program.

7–8   THE MAIN MENU OPTIONS OF DOS SHELL

As you see in Figure 7–20, the Main Menu option of MS-DOS Shell (the third window) includes the following options:

- Command Prompt
- Editor
- MS-DOS QBasic
- Disk Utilities

If you select the COMMAND PROMPT option, you will return to the DOS prompt. At the DOS prompt you can issue any DOS command.

Figure 7–19
Commands under the Help option

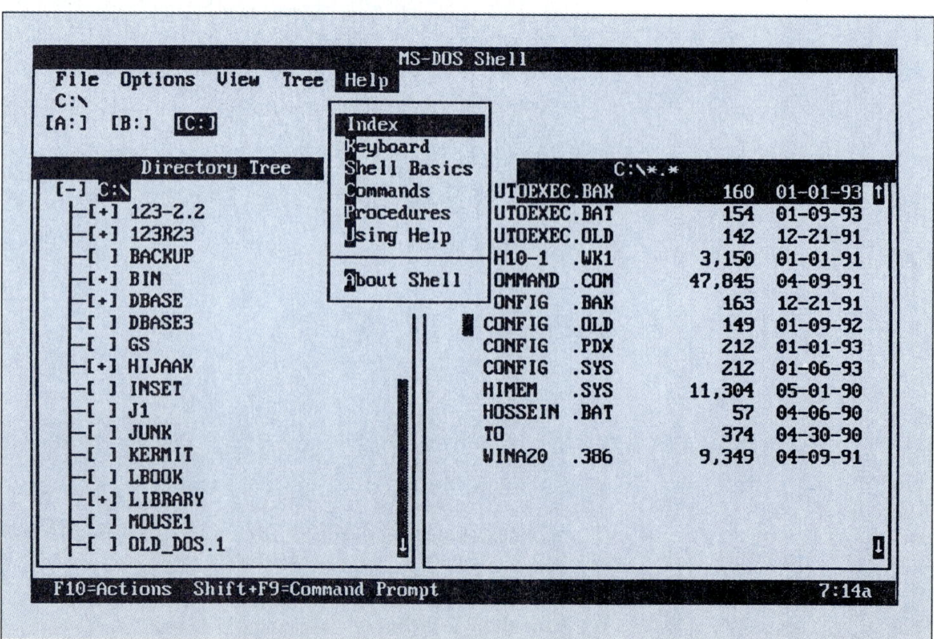

Figure 7–20
MS-DOS Shell

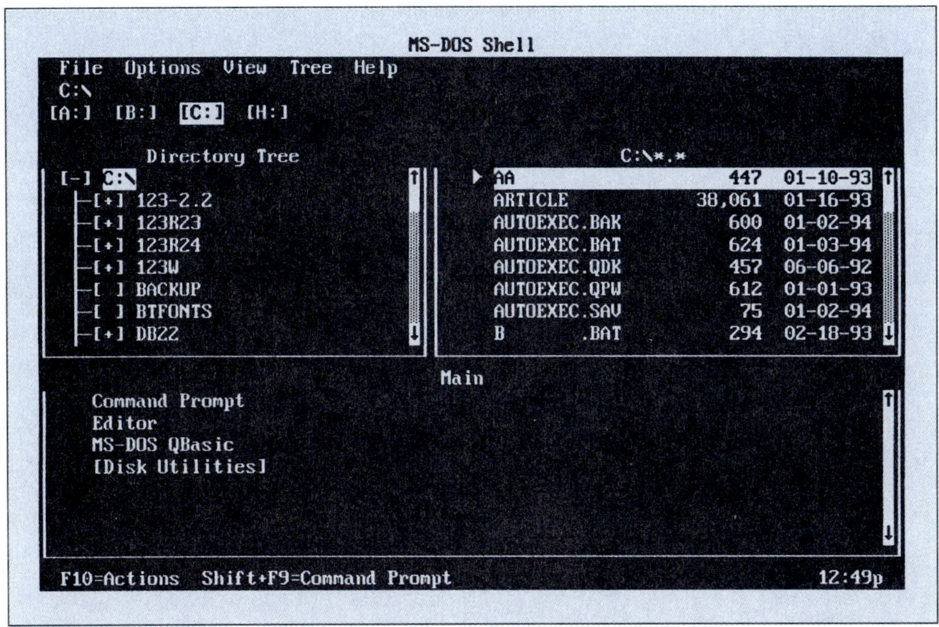

Figure 7–21
Disk Utilities options of MS-DOS Shell

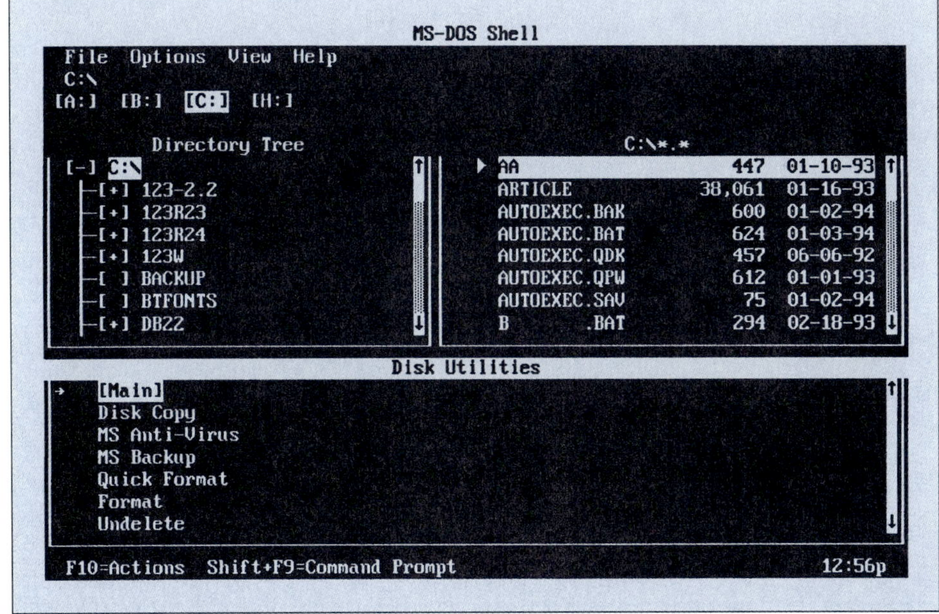

The EDITOR option returns you to the MS-DOS Editor (discussed in the next chapter). MS-DOS Editor is similar to a word processor; it allows you to generate different types of files and documents.

MS-DOS QBASIC returns you to QBasic, a programming language included in your DOS files.

The DISK UTILITIES option offers several utilities displayed in Figure 7–21. You can select any of these options and follow the prompt.

You have seen all these options before; however, using these options through the MS-DOS shell makes your job easier. Also, you do not need to remember the exact syntax of a command.

SUMMARY

This chapter provided an overview of DOS 6.0. The chapter covered the compression feature, anti-virus tools, Backup and Restore capabilities, memory management, and the DOS Shell in some detail. These features make DOS 6.0 easier to use than earlier versions. In the next chapter we will concentrate on macros and full-screen editing features.

REVIEW QUESTIONS

*These questions are answered in Appendix A.

1. What are three unique advantages of DOS 6.0 compared with its earlier versions?
*2. What new commands are included in DOS 6.0?
3. What is disk compression?
4. How do you start the anti-virus program?
5. Which function key is used to access help while working with the DOS Shell?
6. How and why does DOS 6.0 give you more RAM to use?
7. What is the DOS Shell?
8. How many options are available in the DOS Shell main menu?
9. What are some of the options under the File command?
10. What does the F10 key do while working with the DOS Shell?
*11. While you are in the DOS shell, how do you get back to the DOS prompt?
12. What is the function of the ASSOCIATE command? How do you associate DBF files with dBASE IV?
*13. To use the PRINT command in the DOS Shell you must first execute one other command. What command is that?
14. What are the commands under the Options menu?
15. What is task swapping? How do you task swap between Lotus 1-2-3 and WordPerfect?
16. Are task swapping and multitasking the same thing? Discuss.
17. What are the options under View? What is the purpose of each of these commands?
18. What are the commands under the Tree option?
19. What will happen when you use the Expand Branch option from the Tree menu?
20. What are the commands under the Help option?
*21. Which command under the Help option gives you all the keyboard shortcuts?
22. What are some of the advantages of using the DOS Shell?
23. How do you start the MSBACKUP program?
24. How do you restore a crashed hard disk?

HANDS-ON EXPERIENCE

1. Get DOS 6.0 started. From the DOS prompt, do the following:
    a. By typing *HELP,* invoke the help facility of DOS. After viewing the help facility, use CLS to clear the screen.
    b. Generate help for the DIR, VER, and FORMAT commands.
    c. Type *DOSSHELL,* then by using the F1 function key, invoke the help facility for the DOS Shell. What is available?
2. At the DOS prompt create a simple batch file named START.BAT in drive A. Your batch file should include the following three commands: DIR, DATE, and TIME. Using DOS Shell, do the following:

   a. Display the directory listing of drive A.
   b. By using the RUN command from the File menu, execute your batch file.
   c. By using the PRINT command, print the START.BAT file.
   d. Select two software applications, such as Lotus 1-2-3 and WordPerfect (if you have them!), in your system and perform task swapping between them.
   e. By means of the ASSOCIATE command, associate all your WordPerfect data files (letters, documents, etc.) with WordPerfect. (Hint: associate the files with the WP.EXE file in your WordPerfect directory.)
   f. Using the COPY command, make a copy of START.BAT and call it TRY.ABC.
   g. Using the DELETE command, erase START.TXT.

3. With your data disk in drive A, experiment with the various options of the VIEW command. What is the difference between SINGLE FILE LIST and DUAL FILE LISTS commands? What does the ALL FILES command do?

4. Use the CREATE DIRECTORY command to create the following directories in drive A: WEST and EAST. Under WEST, create two other subdirectories called CALIFOR-NIA and OREGON. Now by using the TREE command practice with all the options of this menu. What does the EXPAND ALL command do? The COLLAPSE BRANCH? The EXPAND ONE LEVEL?

5. Using the MSAV program, scan and remove any possible computer virus from drives C and A.

6. Using the MSBACKUP program, create a full backup of your hard disk.

KEY TERMS

Backup facility	File association	Task swapping
Disk compression	Help facility	Virus
DOS Shell	Memory management	

KEY COMMANDS

F10 (to activate the DOS Shell menu)	For the Help Menu, see Figure 7–19	For the Tree menu, see Figure 7–18
Shift+F9 (to return to the DOS prompt)	MEMMAKER (external)	For the View menu, see Figure 7–12
DBLSPACE (external)	MSAV (external)	
For the File menu, see Figure 7–8	MSBACKUP (external)	
	For the Options menu, see Figure 7–11	

ARE YOU READY TO MOVE ON?

Multiple Choice

1. All of the following are true about DOS 6.0 except
   a. it is relatively easier to use than its earlier versions
   b. it offers an online help facility
   c. it includes the UNDELETE and UNFORMAT commands
   d. it provides memory management
   e. they are all true

2. To be able to use DOS 6.0 in your computer, your computer must have at least
   a. a minimum of 256 K of RAM
   b. a minimum of 4.0 MB of free hard disk
   c. both A and B
   d. 4 MB of RAM
   e. none of the above

3. In DOS 6.0 you can receive help by
   a. typing *HELP* at the DOS prompt and pressing Enter
   b. typing *HELP* at the DOS prompt, followed by the command for which you need help, then pressing Enter
   c. doing both a or b
   d. using only the first 35 commands
   e. none of the above

4. The DOS Shell main menu includes all of the following commands except
   a. FILE
   b. OPTIONS
   c. VIEW
   d. TREE
   e. they are all included

5. If you are in DOS 6.0 Shell, Shift+F9
   a. returns you to DOS prompt
   b. returns you to drive C
   c. returns you to drive A
   d. returns you to online help
   e. none of the above

6. To activate the main menu of the DOS Shell, you must first press
   a. the F1 key
   b. the F10 key
   c. the F5 key
   d. the F6 key
   e. none of the above

7. The File option of the DOS Shell includes all of the following commands except
   a. RUN
   b. OPEN
   c. PRINT
   d. they are all included
   e. only A and B

8. To execute the PRINT command in the DOS Shell, you first must run
   a. the PRINT.COM command
   b. the COMMAND.COM command
   c. the FORMAT.COM command
   d. the DISKCOPY.COM command
   e. none of the above

9. Task Swapping allows you to
   a. activate only one software application at a time
   b. switch among several software applications at a time
   c. only use word processing software
   d. do multitasking
   e. only print text files

10. The Tree option of the DOS Shell includes all of the following commands except
   a. EXPAND ONE LEVEL
   b. EXPAND BRANCH
   c. EXPAND ALL

      d. they are all included
      e. only a and b

True/False

1. DOS 6.0 includes a disk compression program.
2. To start the anti-virus program, you must type MSAV and then press the Enter key.
3. A computer with 256 K of RAM and 4.0 MB of free hard disk can utilize DOS 6.0.
4. MEMMAKER is an internal command.
5. The Restore facility of DOS 6.0 is not included in the MSBACKUP program. It is a part of another utility.
6. DOS 6.0 utilizes computer memory more effectively than earlier versions of DOS.
7. DOS Shell *is not* a menu-driven program.
8. The File option is not included in the main menu of the DOS Shell.
9. If you are using the DOS Shell, you will be able to run a batch file.
10. The ASSOCIATE command in DOS 6.0 does not allow you to associate all WK1 files with Lotus 1-2-3.

ANSWERS

Multiple Choice		True/False	
1.	e	1.	T
2.	c	2.	T
3.	c	3.	T
4.	e	4.	F
5.	a	5.	F
6.	b	6.	T
7.	d	7.	F
8.	a	8.	F
9.	b	9.	T
10.	d	10.	F

8–1   INTRODUCTION

In this chapter we discuss more of the powerful features of DOS 6.0. In addition to understanding macros, you will learn how to create and modify a macro. The Edit component of DOS 6.0 as a full-screen editing program is highlighted. The chapter introduces a couple of new commands offered by DOS 6.0 and concludes with some of the enhancements to the existing commands.

8–2   DOS 6.0 MACROS

In earlier versions of MS-PC DOS, the repetitive and commonly used commands were inserted into a batch file for simplifying the DOS work. In DOS 6.0, similar to DOS 5.0, the supplementary **DOSKEY program** makes this task much easier. DOSKEY is a unique program that provides **macro capabilities** to the user. This feature allows the user to decide how DOS commands should work, create new commands, and keep a record of commands that have been used so that they can easily be reused.

DOSKEY is a separate program and not part of COMMAND.COM; therefore it must be manually loaded into memory before it can be used. If you want to take full advantage of DOSKEY, add it as a line to your AUTOEXEC.BAT file so that it is loaded into memory each time you turn on your computer.

A typical example of how DOSKEY can simplify DOS commands follows. Let us say you normally format a disk in drive A and add a few parameters to the FORMAT command, such as /Q for a quick format (one of the new switches that DOS 6.0 offers—it erases the file allocation table), or /4, which formats a 360-K floppy disk in a high-capacity drive. You can type the following:

DOSKEY FORMAT=FORMAT A:/4/Q

If you have not yet loaded DOSKEY into memory, DOS responds with this message as soon as you press Enter:

```
DOSKEY installed
```

Now you can type *FORMAT* and press Enter, then follow the prompt. This command changes the default FORMAT command to automatically include the A:/4/Q parameters.

Any other macros that you customize with DOSKEY can also be saved in batch files for future use. DOSKEY's optional parameters are summarized in Table 8–1.

One limitation is that the buffer size is 1 K of memory. When the buffer is full, the oldest command is eliminated to make room for the new command(s). Therefore, if the DOSKEY feature is used often, the DOSKEY/BUFSIZE command must be issued to allocate more space to the buffer.

8–3   THE HISTORY OPTION OF DOSKEY

DOSKEY enables the user to recall a history of DOS commands. You activate DOSKEY by typing *DOSKEY* and pressing Enter to bring it into memory. From this point on, the history of DOS commands is kept in memory and can be recalled easily by using the up arrow key. After you issue a few DOS commands

Table 8–1
DOSKEY optional parameters

Parameter	Function
/INSERT	Forces insert mode as default
/OVERSTRIKE	Forces overstrike mode as default
/REINSTALL	Installs a new copy of DOSKEY
/BUFSIZE	Specifies the size of the command buffer
/MACROS or /M	Displays all macros and enables you to direct them to a file
/HISTORY or /H	Displays all commands stored in memory
MACRO=TEXT	Creates a DOSKEY macro of up to 127 characters

such as TIME, DATE, DIR/W, A: (pressing Enter after each command), you can recall these commands by pressing the up-arrow key to display the commands in the order that they were entered at the DOS prompt. Similarly, if you type *DOSKEY/H* (press Enter), a list of all the commands in the DOSKEY History buffer will be displayed. Remember that the buffer size is limited to 1 K; therefore, if the commands you have issued exceed the 1-K buffer capacity, the oldest command(s) issued will be eliminated from the buffer to make room for the most recent commands.

When you use the up-arrow key, the most recent command in the history buffer will be displayed. When you use the down-arrow key, the following command in the history buffer will be displayed. Press the PgUp key and the first command in the history buffer will be displayed; press the PgDn key and the last command in the history buffer will be displayed.

You can use several keys and key combinations to edit a command on the command line in addition to the standard DOS editing keys. Table 8–2 provides a summary of these keys and key combinations.

Table 8–2
DOSKEY editing keys

Key(s)	Function
Alt+F7	Erases all the commands in the history
Alt+F10	Erases all macros in memory
Ctrl+left arrow ($\leftarrow$)	Moves the cursor one word to the left
Ctrl+right arrow ($\rightarrow$)	Moves the cursor one word to the right
End	Moves the cursor after the last character in the command line
Esc	Erases the current command line
F7	Lists all commands in the history, numbers each command, and indicates the current command
F9	Enables you to specify the number of the command that you want in the history to make a correction. You can press F7 to see the command numbers.
F10	Lists all macros in memory
Home	Moves the cursor to the first character in the command line

8–4   CUSTOMIZING MACROS USING DOSKEY

DOSKEY enables separate macros to be customized to the user's desires. This is done in a manner similar to the way batch files are created. By typing the name of the macro followed by Enter, several commands can be executed. A few characters of macros are created by using dollar sign equivalents. See Table 8–3.

When you create a macro, you can include any valid DOS command, including an embedded batch file. You can execute a batch file from within a macro, but you cannot execute a macro from within a batch file. This is so because when a command is entered, DOS first looks for AUTOEXEC.BAT, then any macro names, then all .COM, all .EXE, and finally all .BAT files.

8–4–1   Example 1—A Move Macro

To create a Move macro do the following:

■ Type *DOSKEY* and press Enter; this starts DOSKEY. You will see this response:

```
DOSKEY installed
```

■ Type *DOSKEY MOVE=COPY $1 $2 $T DEL $1.*

This macro tells DOS to copy the first file name to the second file name. The $T parameter tells DOS that another macro command is following, and the $1 following the DEL command indicates that the first file can now be deleted.

Let us use this Move macro in drive A, to copy SALES.WK1 to PROFIT.WK1 and then delete SALES.WK1. Our complete syntax to replace line 2 (from above) is

    Move SALES.WK1 PROFIT.WK1

Press Enter then type *MOVE* and press Enter. Checking the directory contents before and after execution of the macro verifies that SALES.WK1 no longer exists and that there is in fact a new file named PROFIT.WK1.

Table 8–3
Dollar sign equivalents

Character	Meaning
$g or $G	Same as >, used for redirecting output
$l or $L	Same as <, used for redirecting input
$b or $B	Same as ¦ (vertical split bar found on the backslash key), used for piping
$t or $T	Separates macro commands
$$	Used in the command line
$1 through $9	Replaceable parameters; same as %1 through %9 in a batch file
$*	A replaceable parameter that represents all information that you type on the command line following the macro name

| 8–4–2 | ### Example 2—Improving the Move Macro |

This new macro is similar to the first one. It copies one file to another file, deletes the first file, generates a wide directory of the current drive, and directs the output to the printer.

    DOSKEY MOVEPRNT=COPY $1 $2 $T DEL $1 $T DIR/W >PRN

If you replace $1 and $2 with WORKING.TXT and RESTING.TXT, then the macro will copy WORKING.TXT to RESTING.TXT, delete WORKING.TXT, generate a wide directory listing of the default drive, and send the output to the printer.

| 8–4–3 | ### Example 3—Simplifying the DIR Command |

To simplify the DIR command, type

    DOSKEY DIRW=DIR $1/W

Now every time the macro DIRW is executed, a wide directory listing of the default drive is displayed.

| 8–4–4 | ### Example 4—Improving the DIR Macro |

To further simplify the DIR macro, type

    DOSKEY DIRC=CLS $T DIR $1/W

This macro, called DIRC, first clears the screen and then displays a wide directory listing of the default drive.

| 8–4–5 | ### Example 5—Improving the DEL Command |

To enhance the DEL command, type

    DOSKEY DEL=DEL $1/P

With this macro, DEL is modified to ask for verification before deleting the specified file. For example, after creating the macro, if you type DEL PROFIT.WK1, after pressing Enter, DOS responds

```
PROFIT.WK1, Delete (Y/N)?
```

Now, it is up to you to press N.

| 8–4–6 | ### Example 6—Hard Disk Cleaning Macro |

To create a useful macro for detecting lost clusters on your hard disk, type

    DOSKEY CLUSTER=CHKDSK C:/F

This macro can be used periodically to clean up your hard disk (drive C) and repair any lost clusters.

8–4–7

Example 7—Locating Directory Macro

If you use a particular directory more often than others, you can create a macro to move you to that directory quickly. Type

DOSKEY GOTO=C: $T CD\WORDPERFECT\SALES

This macro moves you from whichever drive you are in to drive C, then it takes you directly to the SALES subdirectory in your WORDPERFECT directory.

8–4–8

Example 8—Backing Up A Hard Disk Macro

Another useful DOS 6.0 macro is one that performs a backup of the drive C for you. The following command would create a macro to execute a full backup of the C drive to a diskette in drive A:

DOSKEY BACKUP-C=BACKUP C:\ A:/S

To run this macro, type *BACKUP-C* and press Enter. The system will prompt you to enter backup diskette 01. You can abort the backup command by pressing Ctrl+Break.

8–4–9

Example 9—Restoring a Hard Disk Macro

A related macro is one that executes a command for a system restore. The following command would create a macro to restore all of the data on your backup disks (in drive A) to the C drive:

DOSKEY RESTOR-C=RESTORE A: C:\/S

To run this macro, type *RESTOR-C* and press Enter. The system will prompt you to enter backup diskette 01. You can abort the restore command by pressing Ctrl+Break.

8–4–10

Example 10—Subdirectory Macro

Suppose you would like a macro to print all of the subdirectory names of drive C, in alphabetical order, on the printer. The following command would create this macro:

DOSKEY SUBDIR-C=DIR C:*./S/O > PRN

To run this macro, type *SUBDIR-C* and press Enter. When you specify PRN as the destination output port, the output is automatically sent to the LPT1 port. If your printer output port is different, then replace the PRN with the correct output port name. The result of this command is an alphabetical list, hard copy, of all subdirectories contained on drive C. (The O parameter is used for the order, e.g., alphabetical order.) The *. indicates all files that do not include an extension. It usually refers to directories, since directory names do not have an extension.

8–5   FULL-SCREEN EDITING

The full-screen editing feature brings the word processing environment with Windows support to the DOS environment. It is used for creating ASCII files such as batch files that you would like to update, correct, or simply view with the option of changing if you so desire. To start the Edit program, type *EDIT* and press Enter. This brings up the windows environment of the Edit program contained in DOS. It is similar to the DOS shell. A dialog box will be displayed in the middle of the screen as shown in Figure 8–1. All of the options can be used through the mouse as well as the keyboard.

Press Enter to see the Survival Guide; see Figure 8–2. The Survival Guide is a help feature offered in the Edit program. It states that to activate the MS-DOS Editor menu bar, you can press Alt; to activate menus and commands, you can press the highlighted letter; to move between menus and commands, you can

Figure 8–1
Starting menu of MS-DOS editor

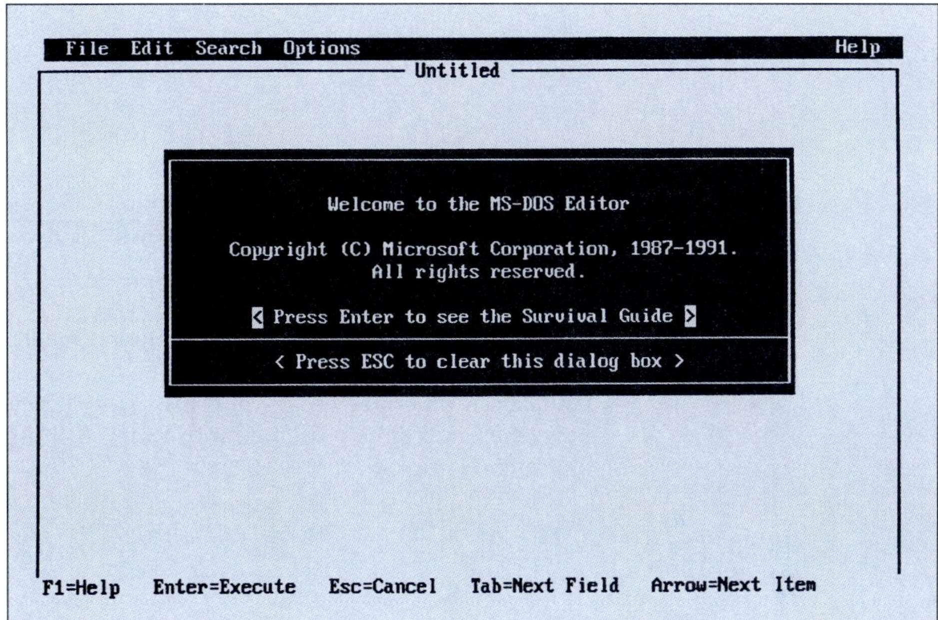

Figure 8–2
Survival guide of the Edit program

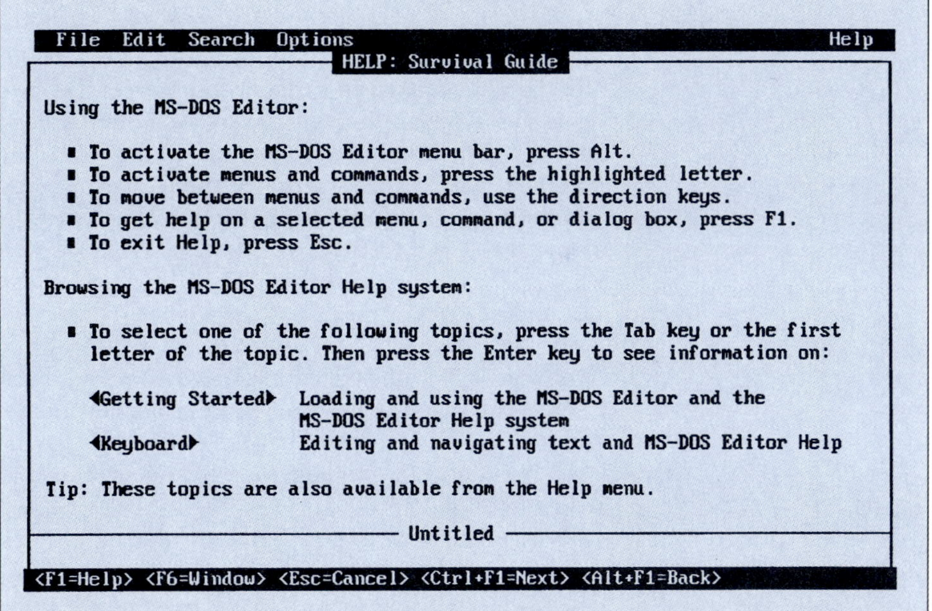

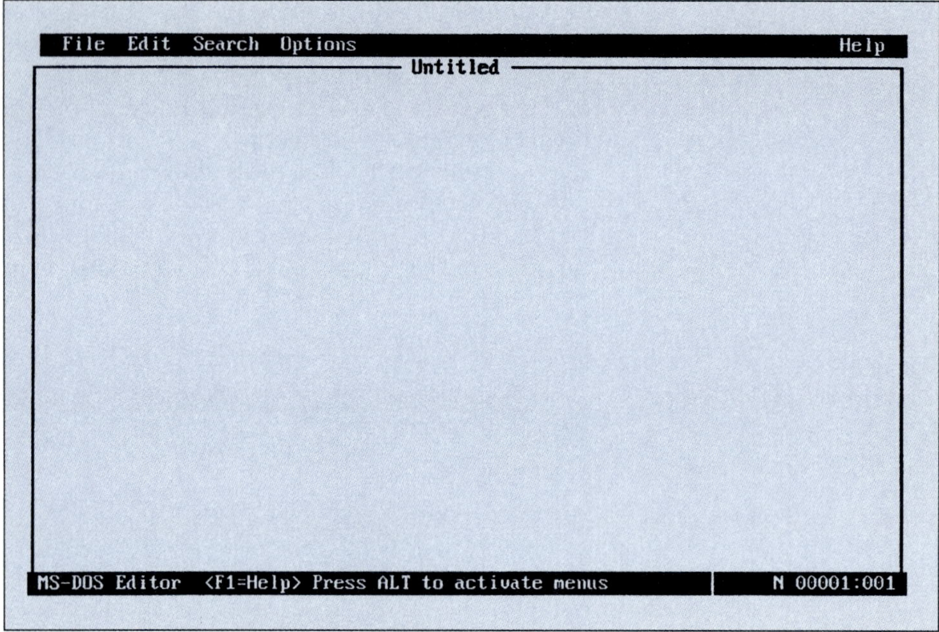

use the arrow keys; to get help on a selected menu, command, or dialog box, you can use the F1 key; and finally to exit Help, you can press ESC. If you are already familiar with the Edit program, press Esc to clear the dialog box. As soon as you press Esc, you will be presented with Figure 8–3. As this figure indicates, there are four menu options:

```
File     Edit     Search     Options
```

In the middle of the top of the screen note the word "Untitled." This indicates you have not started any file yet. At the bottom of the screen, note the following message:

```
MS-DOS Editor <F1=Help> Press ALT to activate menus
```

Also please notice in the lower right corner: N 00001:001. This number keeps track of the row number and column number of the current cursor position. As soon as you start typing or moving the cursor around, this number starts changing.

The setup of the screen is similar to that of the DOS Shell. The menu bar at the top can be accessed with the mouse or by pressing Alt, then moving to the desired option and pressing Enter. Let us briefly explain each of the main menu options.

8–5–1 Options Under File

As Figure 8–4 illustrates, there are six commands under the File option. The NEW command is used to create a new document. If you already have a document open (a document that has not been saved at all or has not been saved since the last changes), a dialog box will appear. You can do one of the following:

- Select Yes to save the existing document.
- Select No to close the existing document without saving it.
- Select Cancel to cancel the New command and return to the existing document.

Figure 8–4
Commands under the File option

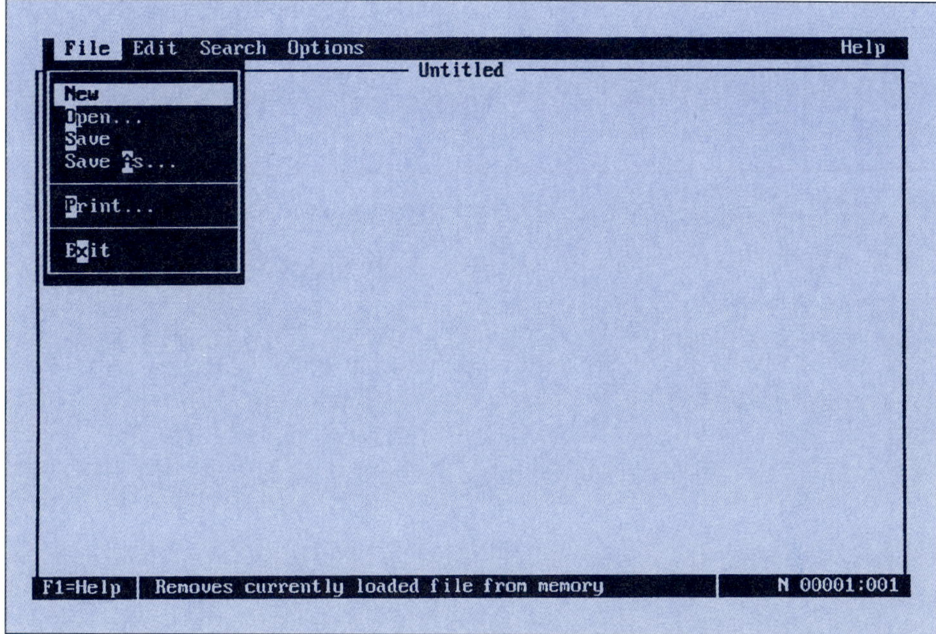

The OPEN command allows you to open an existing document so you can edit or print it.

The SAVE command is used to save the current version of your document. When you issue this command, the Editor asks you for a file name if you haven't saved the document previously. If an existing document has the same name as the document being saved, a dialog box will appear. You can do one of the following:

- Select Yes to save the document, overwriting the file on disk.
- Select No to enter another file name.
- Select Cancel to cancel the New command and return to the existing document.
- Select Help to display the Help: Overwrite existing file dialog box.

To move the cursor in the dialog box from one option to another option, you must use the Tab key.

The SAVE AS command is used to save your document under a new name. This allows you to preserve the previous version of your document by typing a new name in the Save As dialog box.

The PRINT command allows you to print all or part of a document. By means of the Print command, you can print selected text, the contents of the Help window, or the entire current document.

The EXIT command is used to leave the MS-DOS Editor. If your document has been modified since you last saved it, the Editor displays a dialog box.

- Select Yes to save your document including changes.
- Select No to discard your changes.
- Select Cancel to cancel the Exit command and return to your document.
- Select Help to display Help: Overwrite existing file dialog box.

Let's walk through one example. Once the Edit program is started, we can create, retrieve, or view any file we choose. We will create a batch file called

SIMPLE.BAT. We want the file to display two messages and execute four commands as follows:

    DOS 6 IS A POWERFUL OPERATING SYSTEM
    TIME
    DATE
    DIR/W
    CLS
    THIS IS A GREAT WAY TO HAVE FUN!

Get the Editor started and in a blank screen type the following (remember to press Enter after each line):

    ECHO   DOS 6 IS A POWERFUL OPERATING SYSTEM
    TIME
    DATE
    DIR/W
    CLS
    ECHO   THIS IS A GREAT WAY TO HAVE FUN!

After typing these lines, activate the File option by pressing Alt+F. From the File pull-down menu, choose Save As. In response to the prompt, type *SIMPLE.BAT* and press Enter. The file name SIMPLE.BAT now appears at the top of the screen as the title instead of the word "Untitled."

If you leave the Edit program, you can execute the batch file as you would any other batch file. Now if you wish to go back and edit the file, simply type *EDIT* and press Enter; then choose the File option followed by the Open option. Another dialog box will be displayed in the middle of the screen; see Figure 8–5. The dialog box will prompt you for which file you wish to open. You can change the default *.TXT file mask by backspacing over the TXT and replacing it with BAT extension, followed by pressing Enter. All the .BAT files are then displayed in the Files box. You can then use the mouse to highlight and click the

Figure 8–5
Dialog box for the OPEN command

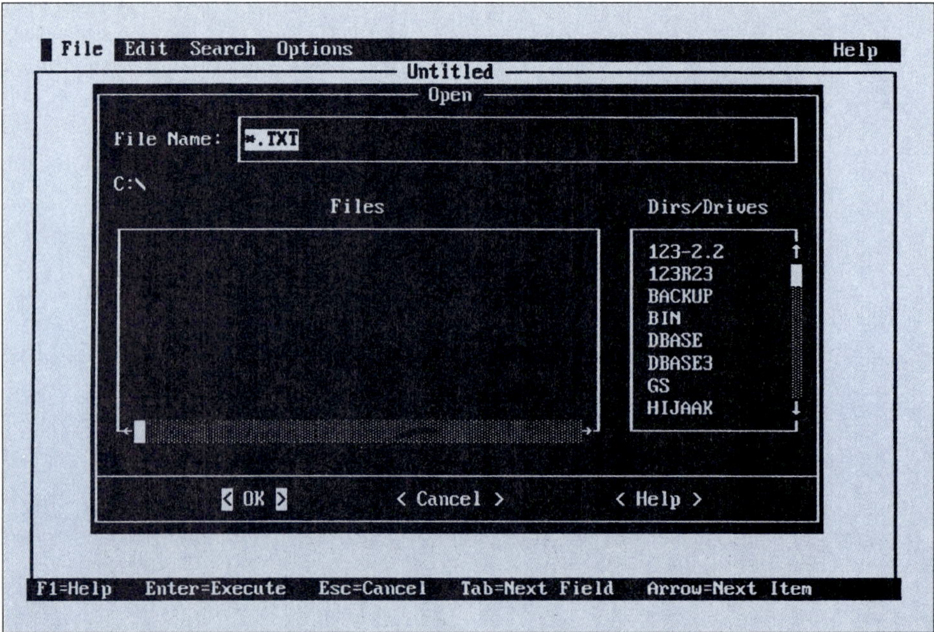

one you want, or you can press Tab to move the cursor to the Files box, then use the arrow keys to move to your desired selection and press Enter. This will retrieve the file to the screen for viewing or editing.

8–5–2   Options Under Edit

As Figure 8–6 illustrates, there are four commands under the Edit option. The CUT command, or Shift+Del, is used to remove selected text and put it into a temporary holding area (clipboard). The PASTE command (Shift+Ins) allows you to insert the text to a new position. You can also open a new or existing document and insert the text. The removed text stays in the clipboard until you use the Cut command again. The new text replaces any text already in the clipboard. To cut text, place the cursor at the beginning of the text to be cut and press the Shift+arrow keys. For example, to cut the word "TEXT" on your screen (if you have such a word) put the cursor on the first T and then press and hold down the Shift key; then press the right arrow key four times. Once the text is highlighted, select Cut from the Edit menu. To remove selected text without copying it to the clipboard, while the text is being highlighted, press the Del key.

The COPY command, or Ctrl+Ins, is used to copy selected text to the clipboard. The COPY command does not alter the original text. After copying the text, you can later use the PASTE command (Shift+Ins) to insert the text to a new position. You can also open a new or existing document and insert the text. To copy text, position the cursor at the beginning of the text to be copied and press the Shift+arrow keys (just as you did with the CUT command). After the text to be copied is highlighted, select Copy from the Edit menu.

The PASTE, or Shift+Ins, command is used to insert a block of text from the clipboard to any position in a document. To insert text, position the cursor where you want the text to be inserted and then select Paste from the Edit menu.

The CLEAR, or Del, command is used to delete selected text without copying it to the clipboard. Remember, the CLEAR command does not change the contents of the clipboard. To use the CLEAR command, first highlight the desired text by using the Shift and arrow keys, then issue the CLEAR command.

Figure 8–6

Commands under the Edit option

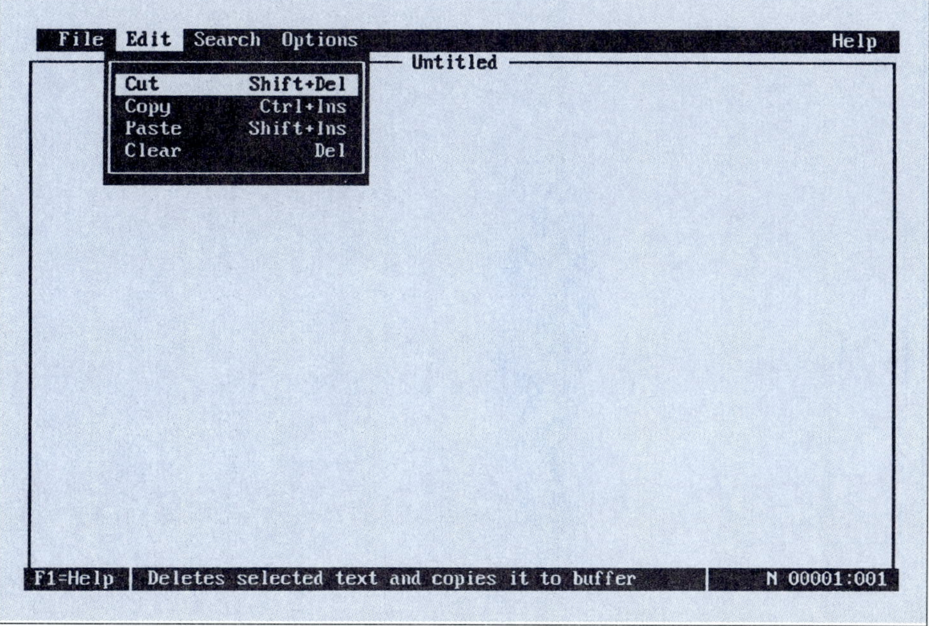

Let us walk through one example. Say that in the SIMPLE.BAT batch file you also want to echo DOS 6 IS A POWERFUL OPERATING SYSTEM at the end. Instead of typing the command line a second time, move the cursor to the beginning of the line that says ECHO DOS 6 IS A POWERFUL OPERATING SYSTEM and while holding down the left button of the mouse, highlight the entire line by sliding the mouse to the right. Then release the button and the line will remain highlighted (this is called dragging the mouse cursor). Then activate the Edit option, choose Copy, and move the cursor by using the arrow key or clicking the mouse button to move the cursor to the beginning of the line at the end of the batch file. Next select the Edit option again and then the Paste option. The first line of your batch file is now repeated at the bottom of the file.

8–5–3

Options Under Search

Figure 8–7 illustrates that there are three commands under the search option. The FIND command is used to search for a text string. You can request a case-sensitive match or whole-word match. When you invoke this command, the Editor responds with

```
Find What:
```

Type in the desired text string then press Enter. After pressing the Enter key, the cursor will be positioned to the first occurrence of the text that you just specified.

The REPEAT LAST FIND command, or F3 key, is used to repeat the search performed by the most recent Find or Change command. If no FIND or CHANGE command has been executed since you started the MS-DOS Editor, REPEAT LAST FIND will search for the next occurrence of (1) the word the cursor is on or (2) the word to the cursor's left, if the cursor is not on a word.

The CHANGE command is used to replace one text string with another. Using this command you can do one of the following:

■ Use a case-sensitive or whole-word search.

Figure 8–7
Commands under the Search option

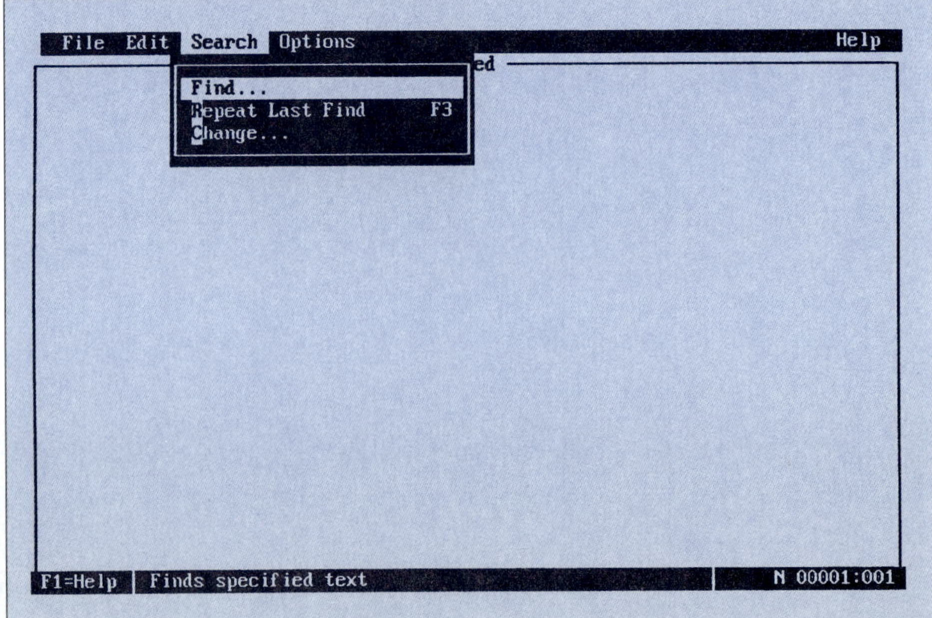

- Check each replacement before the change is made.
- Make all replacements without checking them.

Let us walk through an example. Start with a clear screen and type the following two lines:

WE WOULD LIKE TO GO TO THE PARTY TONIGHT. (press Enter)
WE WOULD LIKE TO STUDY DOS TOMORROW. (press Enter)

Let's say you would like to change the two occurrences of the word "WE" to "SAM." Do the following:

- Move the cursor to the W in the first WE.
- Press Alt to activate the menu.
- Move the cursor to Search and press Enter.
- Move the cursor to Change and press Enter.
- The change dialog box will be displayed. In the Find What: box type *WE*.
- Press Tab to move to the Change To: box and type *SAM*.
- Now select Match Upper/Lowercase or Whole Word by pressing Tab or press the Tab key four times to move to Change All.
- While the cursor is on Change All, press Enter.
- As soon as you press Enter, the two occurrences of *WE* are changed to *SAM*. Press Enter again to exit the dialog box.

8–5–4   Options Under Options

As Figure 8–8 illustrates, there are two commands under Options. The DISPLAY command is used to control screen colors, scroll bars in windows, and the number

Figure 8–8
Commands under the Options option

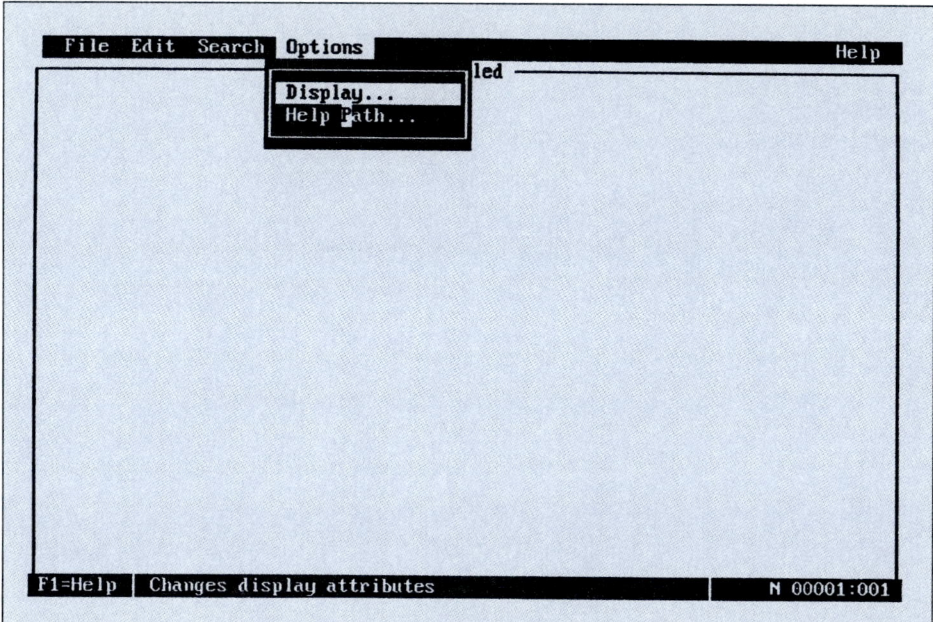

of spaces the Tab key advances the cursor. If you select the Display option, any changes you make to the display settings are saved and remain in effect until the next time you start the MS-DOS Editor. By using the Display option you can change the color of foreground (text) and background of your monitor.

The HELP PATH command is used to change the directories that the MS-DOS Editor searches to find the MS-DOS Editor Help file, EDIT.HLP.

8–6   MIRROR, UNDELETE, AND UNFORMAT COMMANDS

DOS 6.0, similar to DOS 5.0, has three commands that the previous versions of DOS did not have: MIRROR, UNDELETE, and UNFORMAT. The MIRROR command creates an image of the file allocation table, thereby serving as a backup. DOS doesn't actually erase files when the DEL command is used. They are merely marked as erased in the directory listing and the FAT entries are released so that the space they occupy on the disk can be reused. The Mirror program creates either two or three files on a disk. The read-only, hidden, system file called MIRORSAV.FIL and the read-only file called MIRROR.FIL (and possibly the MIR-ROR.BAK if the MIRROR command is run twice) are created. These files contain a record of the disk's root directory and the FAT when the program was run.

The UNDELETE and UNFORMAT commands both use the information created by the MIRROR command to retrieve any information that might have been accidentally lost through the inadvertent use of the DEL or FORMAT commands.

If the QUICK FORMAT command was used on a previously formatted disk, the files aren't actually erased. The FAT is marked as empty even though the disk still contains the data that was in the files. The UNFORMAT command could be issued and the program would search for the MIRROR.FIL file to find the information that was contained on the disk. It then will rewrite and reconstruct the FAT to its previous state before the undesired FORMAT command was issued.

The same applies to the UNDELETE command. Files aren't actually erased from the disk when they are deleted. Their space is just marked unusable in the FAT. Therefore, if nothing has been added to disk since the file was accidentally deleted, the file can be "undeleted" rather easily by using the UNDELETE command. Remember that UNDELETE can be used even if the user has forgotten to use the MIRROR command. Figure 8–9 is an example of

Figure 8–9

Example of the UNDELETE command

```
C>DEL A:HELLO.BAT

C>UNDELETE A:HELLO.BAT

Directory: A:\
File Specifications: HELLO.BAT

    Deletion-tracking file not found.

    MS-DOS directory contains     1 deleted files.
    Of those,     1 files may be recovered.

Using the MS-DOS directory.

      ?ELLO     BAT         6  1-08-93 12:04p  ...A  Undelete (Y/N)?Y
      Please type the first character for ?ELLO    .BAT: H

File successfully undeleted.



C>
```

what would be displayed after the user accidentally deleted HELLO.BAT. The responses to the UNDELETE command are also displayed in Figure 8–9.

8–7   ADDITIONAL SWITCHES FOR COMMONLY USED COMMANDS

Some of the commands that you have previously seen include additional switches. Let us introduce these commands and switches. (See Table 8–4.)

8–8   CLEAN BOOT AND INTERACTIVE EXECUTION OF CONFIG.SYS FILE

Two other interesting features of MS-DOS 6.0 are the clean boot and an interactive execution of the CONFIG.SYS file. While booting up, you can perform a clean boot by pressing the F5 function key. That is, MS-DOS 6.0 bypasses your CONFIG.SYS and AUTOEXEC.BAT files. This is helpful when you want to test a new feature on your system or want to bypass commands available in either CONFIG.SYS or AUTOEXEC.BAT files.

If you press the F8 function key while booting up, the system prompts for permission to execute each line of your CONFIG.SYS file. This feature is useful when you want to debug your CONFIG.SYS file for detecting possible problems.

When you press F8, one of the messages that you might receive is:

```
MS-DOS will prompt you to confirm each CONFIG.SYS command.
DOS = UBM [Y,N]?
```

You can respond with Y to accept this line or N to reject it and then the process will continue until you have fully processed each command in the CON-FIG.SYS file.

SUMMARY

This chapter highlighted DOS 6.0 macro commands. The process of macro creation and modification were discussed. We considered the Edit component of DOS 6.0 as a full-screen editing program. The three new commands in DOS 6.0—MIRROR, UNDELETE, and UNFORMAT—were described. The chapter introduced a summary of the new enhancements of some commands in earlier versions of DOS. It concluded with a discussion of clean boot and an interactive execution of the CONFIG.SYS file.

REVIEW QUESTIONS

*These questions are answered in Appendix A.

  1. What is a DOS macro?

  2. What are the differences between a macro and a batch file?

  3. What are some of the applications of macros?

*4. What is DOSKEY?

  5. What are some of the optional parameters of DOSKEY?

  6. What is the History option of DOSKEY?

*7. How do you retrieve previously used DOS commands through DOSKEY?

  8. How do you enter into the MS-DOS Editor? How do you exit from it?

  9. What are the options under the FILE command?

Command	Switch	Description
ATTRIB	+	Sets an attribute
	−	Clears an attribute
	R	Read-only file attribute
	A	Archive file attribute
	S	System file attribute
	H	Hidden file attribute
	/S	Processes files in all directories in the specified path
BACKUP	/S	Backs up contents of subdirectories
	/M	Backs up only files that have changed since the last backup
	/A	Adds backup files to an existing backup disk
	/F:[size]	Specifies the size of the disk to be formatted
	/D:date	Backs up only files changed on or after the specified date
	/T:time	Backs up only files changed at or after the specified time
	/L[:[drive:][path]logfile]	Creates a log file and entry to record the backup operation
COPY	/A	Indicates an ASCII text file
	/B	Indicates a binary file
	/V	Verifies that new files are written correctly
DEL	/P	Asks for verification before deletion is done
DISKCOMP	/1	Compares only the first side of the disks
	/8	Compares only the first eight sectors of each track
DISKCOPY	/1	Copies only the first side of the disk
	/V	Verifies that the information is copied correctly
ERASE	/P	Asks for verification before deletion
FIND	/V	Displays all lines NOT containing the specified string
	/C	Displays only the count of lines containing the string
	/N	Displays the line numbers with the displayed lines
	/I	Ignores the case of characters when searching for the string
	"string"	Specifies the text string to find
TREE	/F	Displays the names of the files in each directory
	/A	Uses ASCII instead of extended characters
UNDELETE	/LIST	Just lists the deleted files available for recovery
	/ALL	Undeletes all specified files without prompting
	/DT	Uses only the deletion-tracking file
	/DOS	Uses only the MS-DOS directory
UNFORMAT	/J	Verifies that the MIRROR files agree with the system information
	/U	Unformats without using MIRROR files
	/L	Lists all file and directory names found, or, when used with the /PARTN switch, displays current partition tables
	/TEST	Displays information but does not write changes to disk
	/P	Sends output information to printer connected to LPT1
	/PARTN	Restores disk partition tables
PROMPT	$Q	= (equals sign)
	$$	$ (dollar sign)

	$T	Current time
	$D	Current date
	$P	Current drive and path
	$V	MS-DOS version number
	$N	Current drive
	$G	> (greater-than sign)
	$L	< (less-than sign)
	$B	¦ (pipe)
	$H	Backspace (erases previous character)
	$E	Escape Code (ASCII code 27)
	$	Carriage return and linefeed
		Type PROMPT without parameters to reset the prompt to the default setting.
MIRROR	/1	Saves only the latest disk information
	/Tdrive	Loads the deletion-tracking program for the specified drive
	/U	Unloads the deletion-tracking program
	/PARTN	Saves hard disk partition information to a floppy diskette

*10. What is the difference between the SAVE and SAVE AS commands?

11. What command do you use to print a file created with the MS-DOS Editor?

12. What are the applications of the CUT command? What is the shortcut equivalent to this command?

13. What is the difference between the COPY and CUT commands?

14. When you "paste" the contents of the clipboard, are the contents permanently gone? Can you paste the same text more than once?

15. How do you highlight a block of text for cutting or copying? How do you change your mind if you decide not to cut or copy?

16. What are the applications of the SEARCH command?

17. What does the REPEAT LAST FIND command do?

*18. What command is used to replace one text string with another?

19. Can you search with a case-sensitive option? If yes, how?

20. What commands are available under Options? What are the applications of these commands?

21. What are two of the new commands offered by DOS 6.0? What are the applications of these commands?

22. What are some of the enhancements of commands in earlier versions of DOS?

23. What is clean boot? How do you execute the CONFIG.SYS file in an interactive manner?

HANDS-ON EXPERIENCE

1. Using DOSKEY create a macro that formats a disk in drive A with the following sizes:
   a. 360 K
   b. 720 K
   c. 1.2 MB
   d. 1.44 MB

2. Create a macro that copies file 1 to file 2, erases file 1, displays the default directory, asks for a new time, asks for a new date, and finally erases the screen.

3. Create a macro that displays the current subdirectory then transfers you to a subdirectory called WORDPERFECT\SALES\SOUTHERN\SAN DIEGO.

4. Using the MS-DOS Editor, start with a clear screen and type the following 4 lines:

> I AM LEARNING A POWERFUL EDITOR.
> I WILL GO TO A MOVIE TONIGHT.
> I WILL STUDY FOR THE TEST TOMORROW.
> IT HAS BEEN FUN LEARNING DOS.

Do the following:

   a. Save the file under TEST.TXT in your default drive.
   b. Move the first two lines to the end of line 4.
   c. Replace all occurrences of the word I with *We*.
   d. Erase the first line.
   e. Save the final document under TEST.TXT.

5. Practice with the UNDELETE and UNFORMAT commands. Create a sample file in
drive A and erase it. By using the UNDELETE command, try to rescue it.

6. Practice with the new switches of commands from earlier versions of DOS. How helpful are these enhancements?

7. By using the F5 function key, perform a clean boot. Practice with the F8 function key.
What does it do during the bootup?

KEY TERMS

Clean boot	History option
DOSKEY program	Macro capabilities
Full-screen editing	

KEY COMMANDS

DOSKEY editing keys, see
Table 8–2

Commands for new
switches, see Table 8–4

Commands under Edit,
see Figure 8–6

Commands under File, see
Figure 8–4

Commands under
Options, see Figure 8–8

Commands under Search,
see Figure 8–7

DOSKEY (starts the
DOSKEY program)
(external)

DOSKEY/H (generates a
listing of the DOSKEY
buffer) (external)

F5 (external)

F8 (external)

Undelete and Unformat
(rescues the information
lost by accidental use of
the DEL or FORMAT
commands) (external)

ARE YOU READY TO MOVE ON?

Multiple Choice

1. To get DOSKEY started, you must

   a. type *DOSKEY* and press Enter
   b. include the DOSKEY command as a line in your AUTOEXEC.BAT file
   c. do a or b
   d. type *KEY* and press Enter.
   e. do none of the above

2. Which one of the following is *not* one of the optional parameters of DOSKEY?

   a. INSERT
   b. OVERSTRIKE
   c. BUFSIZE
   d. MACROS
   e. they all are

3. The size of the history buffer by default is

   a. 1 K
   b. 2 K
   c. 3 K
   d. 4 K
   e. none of the above

4. To display the History option of DOSKEY type

   a. *DOSKEY/H* and press Enter
   b. *DOSKEY/M* and press Enter
   c. *DOSKEY/N* and press Enter
   d. *DOSKEY/W* and press Enter
   e. none of the above

5. While you are working with DOSKEY, all of the following keys can be used except

   a. up arrow
   b. down arrow
   c. PgUp
   d. PgDn
   e. they all can be used

6. The character that separates two commands in a macro is

   a. $A
   b. $B
   c. $T
   d. $G
   e. none of the above

7. Using the Edit program, you can do all of the following except

   a. do search operation
   b. do replace operation
   c. do cut and paste
   d. do spell checking
   e. they all can be done

8. The main menu of the Edit program includes all the following commands except

   a. FILE
   b. EDIT
   c. SEARCH
   d. SPELL
   e. OPTIONS

9. Using the Edit program, to move from one field to another while the dialog box is displayed you use

   a. the arrow key
   b. the Tab key
   c. the PgUp key
   d. the PgDn key
   e. none of the above

10. The file option in the Edit program includes all the following options except

   a. New
   b. Graph
   c. Open
   d. Save
   e. Save As

True/False

1. When you get the Edit program started, on the top of the screen you see the word "Untitled."

2. To activate the Edit menu you use the Alt key.

3. You cannot use the mouse with Edit.

4. There is no difference between the CUT and COPY commands.

5. Shift+Del and CUT do not perform the same task.

6. COPY and Ctrl+Ins perform the same task.

7. You can paste a removed text several times.

8. With the search operation you can specify uppercase and lowercase to be considered differently.

9. The clean boot (F5) command is not new in DOS 6.0; it has been always available.

10. The F8 function key is used for an interactive execution of the CONFIG.SYS file.

ANSWERS

Multiple Choice		**True/False**	
1.	c	1.	T
2.	e	2.	T
3.	a	3.	F
4.	a	4.	F
5.	e	5.	F
6.	c	6.	T
7.	d	7.	T
8.	d	8.	T
9.	b	9.	F
10.	b	10.	T

Appendix A
Disk Operating System (DOS)

A–1   DOS COMMAND SUMMARY

A:, B:, C: Changes the present disk drive to the one specified.

ATTRIB   Protects a file from being deleted accidentally.

BACKSPACE   Moves the cursor back one position, erasing the character just typed.

BACKUP   Backs up a hard disk.

CHDIR (CD)   Changes a subdirectory or makes a subdirectory the current directory.

CHKDSK   Determines the memory status of a disk and/or a computer. It tells the total amount of disk space in bytes, the number of bytes available on the disk, the amount of memory available on the computer and the amount of memory in use.

CLS   Erases the screen.

COMP   Verifies whether a particular file has been copied correctly.

COPY   Copies one or several files from a disk to the same disk or to another disk. There are several versions of the COPY command.

COPY CON   Generates a batch file.

Ctrl+Alt+Del   This key combination restarts the computer with a warm boot equivalent to turning the computer on without checking the memory status.

Ctrl+C   Cancels a command while it is being executed.

Ctrl+PrtSc (Ctrl+P)   Sends a copy of each line on the screen to the printer as it is being displayed. It toggles the printer on. To disengage these keys, press them again.

Ctrl+S (Ctrl+NumLock)   Pauses the directory listing for viewing.

Ctrl+Z (F6)   Terminates the creation of a batch file.

DATE   Enters the date. Allows you to enter the current date or allows you to change the current date.

DBLSPACE   Used to maximize the hard disk capacity.

DELETE   Erases a file or the entire disk.

DIR   Generates a listing of the current directory. Provides the name of each file, the file extension, the size of the file in bytes, and the date and time the file was created.

DIR/P   Lists the disk directory one screen at a time.

DIR/W   Provides a wide directory. Lists the directory horizontally. Only file names and extensions will be displayed.

DISKCOMP   Verifies if the copy generated by the DISKCOPY command is 100 percent correct.

DISKCOPY   Generates an exact duplicate of a disk. Formats the target disk while it is copying.

ECHO   Displays a given message in a batch file.

ERASE   Erases a file or the entire disk.

Esc   Erases the command or statement typed.

F1   Displays one character of the previous command with each press.

F3   Displays the previous command.

F6   Marks the end of a file while creating a batch file. It also stops an autoexec file. This is the equivalent of Ctrl+Z.

FASTHELP   Generate an alphabetical listing of DOS commands.

FDISK   Partitions a hard disk.

FILES   Allows specification of the maximum number of files that can be open concurrently.

FIND   Searches and finds a specific string or character in a directory or a file.

FORMAT   Formats a disk. There are several variations of this command.

GOTO   Transfers control to the line following the one containing the given label. The line must be preceded by a colon (:). It is used in batch files.

HELP   Accesses the online help.

LABEL   Labels a disk internally. Helps to identify a disk if the external label is missing. Also used to change an existing volume label.

MKDIR (MD)   Creates a subdirectory.

MODE   Sets up the width of the printer. Switches monitor display mode. Sets protocol for a serial port. Redirects parallel port output to a serial port.

MEMMAKER   Increases the size of conventional memory.

MORE   Generates one screen of a directory or a file at a time.

MSAV   Scans and removes known viruses.

PATH   Establishes a search path.

PAUSE   Halts the execution of a batch file until any key is pressed.

PRINT   Instructs the computer to print a file in the background while the computer is being used for other purposes.

RECOVER   Rescues a file or a series of files from a damaged disk.

REM   Allows documentation in a batch file.

RENAME   Changes the name of a file or several files.

RESTORE   Restores the hard disk if the disk has crashed.

RMDIR (RD)   Removes a subdirectory.

Shift+PrtSc   Sends a copy of the screen to the printer. It does not toggle the printer. In enhanced keyboards, use Print Screen key (one key).

SORT   Organizes the directory of a disk or a file in either ascending or descending order.

SYS   Copies the DOS hidden files from the DOS disk to another disk.

TIME   Enters the time. Allows you to type the current time or change the current time.

TREE   Displays the tree structure of a directory.

TYPE   Displays the listing of a program or file on screen or on the printer.

VER   Reveals the versions of DOS currently in use.

VERIFY   Verifies that the data written onto a disk has been properly recorded.

A–2   EDLIN COMMAND SUMMARY

C (Copy)   Copies from one location to another.

D (Delete)   Deletes the current line.

E (Save)   Ends the EDLIN session and saves the file on the disk.

I (Insert)   Inserts after the current line. It is also used to create a new file.

L (List)   Displays the entire file.

M (Move)   Moves lines from one place to another.

P (Display)   Displays 23 lines of the current file beginning with the current line.

Q (Abort)   Allows ending the editing session without saving the changes.

R (Replace)   Replaces the old string with the new string, then displays the line with the change when specified.

S (Search)   Searches lines for specific strings.

T (Transfer)   Transfers a file from one place to another.

W (Write)   Writes the lines specified to a disk.

A–3   AN EXAMPLE OF A TYPICAL AUTOEXEC.BAT FILE

When you turn on (boot-up) your computer, DOS searches the root directory of the booted drive for a file called AUTOEXEC.BAT. If DOS finds this batch file, the statements and instructions contained within it are executed automatically hence the name AUTOEXEC. If, however, DOS does not find AUTOEXEC.BAT at the time of boot-up, the computer prompts you to enter the date and time.

The AUTOEXEC.BAT file is useful for processing instructions that you want executed every time you start your computer. The following example shows the contents of a typical AUTOEXEC.BAT file:

```
ECHO OFF
CLS
PROMPT $P$G
PATH C:\ ;C:\DOS
CD MENU
MENU
```

The six instructions contained within this file will be executed every time the computer is started. An explanation of each instruction follows:

ECHO OFF
:   This instruction tells DOS to suppress the display of the commands contained within AUTOEXEC.BAT as the batch file is executed.

CLS
:   This instruction clears the screen.

PROMPT PG
:   This instruction alters the display of the DOS system prompt to include the name of the current directory followed by a greater than (>) symbol. For example, if you change your directory to \LOTUS\FORECAST, your DOS prompt will be C>LOTUS>FORECAST. This instruction is especially helpful if you work with multilayer directories.

PATH C:\;C:\DOS
:   This instruction sets a path to the root directory (C) and to the DOS subdirectory of drive C. It allows you to execute instructions contained within these two directories regardless of your current subdirectory location.

CD MENU
:   This instruction changes the current directory to the subdirectory named MENU in preparation for the last instruction.

MENU
:   This instruction executes the MENU program, thereby providing easy access to the application program options contained within MENU.

AUTOEXEC.BAT is nothing more than a DOS batch file that is executed automatically every time your computer is started, provided that DOS finds the file name in the root directory of your booted disk drive. AUTOEXEC.BAT takes all of the work out of getting your computer started and ready to go! As explained in Chapter 5, you can use the DOS COPY CON, EDLIN, or EDIT commands or a word processing program such as WordPerfect, to create the AUTOEXEC.BAT file.

A–4   AN EXAMPLE OF A TYPICAL CONFIG.SYS FILE

At boot-up time, DOS searches the root directory of the booted drive for another file: CONFIG.SYS. If DOS finds the file, its contents are processed automatically. CONFIG.SYS is a DOS batch file just like AUTOEXEC.BAT; however, its function and purpose is very different. Whereas AUTOEXEC.BAT executes initial instructions at boot-up time, CONFIG.SYS establishes certain system parameters within which your system will operate. The following example contains some typical CONFIG.SYS instructions:

```
FILES=40
BUFFERS=25
DEVICE=C:MOUSEMOUSE.SYS
```

The three instructions contained within this file will be executed every time the computer is started. An explanation of each instruction follows:

FILES=40	This parameter defines how many files can be open at any one time, in this case 40. The number of files that should be specified on your computer depends on the type of applications you are using. In an environment other than Windows, 25 files would probably be sufficient. Windows, however, operates by opening, running, and using many small files and programs simultaneously. It requires a larger number of files to be specified in this parameter in order to operate smoothly and allow multitasking of application programs.
BUFFERS=25	Buffers are small amounts of memory used by DOS to hold data that is being transferred during disk read and write operations. Each buffer is 528 bytes in size. The number of buffers specified depends on the applications that you are using, but in most cases, 25 is sufficient.
DEVICE=C: \MOUSE \MOUSE.SYS	Device drivers, like the one indicated in this statement, are used to tell DOS how to communicate with the device itself. Other types of device drivers include PRINTER.SYS and CLOCK.SYS. The device driver in this CONFIG.SYS file simply informs DOS that a mouse is connected to the computer and tells DOS where to look for instructions on how to communicate with the mouse (C:\MOUSE).

The same procedure for creating AUTOEXEC.BAT files applies to creation of CONFIG.SYS files.

A–5   IMPORTANT DOS ERROR MESSAGES AND WHAT THEY MEAN

Abort, Ignore, Retry, Fail?

A disk error has occurred. Select *A* to abort the process that requested the disk read or write operation. Select *R* to retry the operation. Select *F* to end the operation but continue the process that requested the disk read or write. Select *I* to ignore the disk error and perform the requested read or write operation anyway. Avoid selecting *I*, the Ignore option, because choosing it can result in a loss of data. Earlier versions of DOS do not include the Fail option.

Abort, Retry, Fail?

An error involving the floppy disk drive has occurred. In most cases you can select *R* to try again after correcting the problem, usually by closing the latch on the drive or by reinserting the disk. In some cases you may have inserted the disk incorrectly. If your second attempt fails, enter *A* to terminate the process.

Bad command or filename

The command that you entered is not a valid DOS command, or DOS cannot find the specified file name. Often the correct path is not provided for DOS to locate the specified file.

Bad or missing Command Interpreter

COMMAND.COM is not on the root directory of the booted disk, or COMMAND.COM has become corrupted in some way. Copy the COMMAND.COM file back into the root directory of your booted disk to resolve the problem.

Disk error reading (writing) drive X

The disk in the specified drive has a bad sector. (Drive *X* is the drive being read from or written to.) If entering *R* (Retry) does not resolve the problem, enter *A* (Abort) to end the process.

Disk unsuitable for system disk

FORMAT detected a bad track on the disk where system files reside. The disk can only be formatted for data, not as a system disk.

File cannot be copied onto itself

The source file name is the same as the target file name. If you are copying to the same directory, make sure that the source file name is different from the target file name. If you are copying from or to another drive and/or subdirectory, make sure that the respective drive, path, and file names are specified correctly.

File creation error

You tried to create a file using a file name that already exists in the directory, or there was not enough space for the file. Either change the file name or save the file to another drive and/or subdirectory.

Format failure

A disk error prevented DOS from formatting the disk. Your diskette might be damaged. Make sure that you have correctly specified the format parameters for the type and capacity diskette you are attempting to format. You might also try another diskette to determine whether the problem is with your command parameters or with a possible physical defect on the diskette.

Incorrect DOS version

You attempted to execute a DOS command from a version of DOS that is different from the version used to boot the system. Reenter the DOS command using the corresponding file from the DOS version used to boot the system.

Insufficient disk space

The disk does not contain enough room (unallocated disk space) to perform the operation.

Invalid number of parameters

The command line you entered did not contain the correct number of parameters for the command you invoked. This error is common when you work with subdirectories.

Invalid parameter(s)

One of the command options is wrong or does not exist. For example, you might have typed *DIR/V* instead *DIR/W*.

Invalid path, not directory, or directory not empty

You could not remove a directory for one of the specified reasons. Correct the problem and reenter the command.

Non-System disk or disk error

Not a bootable DOS disk. This happens when you accidentally leave your data disk in drive A and then try to reboot the computer from drive A.

Not ready error reading drive X: Abort, Retry, Fail?

DOS cannot read or write to the specified drive. Make sure the drive latch is closed and that the drive contains a diskette, that the diskette is properly formatted, and that the diskette is properly inserted into the drive. If the problem is with a diskette, and if these suggestions fail to resolve the problem, try formatting the diskette again using the same disk drive that is giving you problems. Reformatting the diskette almost always corrects the problem. If the problem is with a hard drive, attempt to execute a full system backup immediately. The error could indicate that your hard drive is about to fail. After the backup is complete, proceed with attempting to diagnose and correct the problem on the hard drive.

Program too big to fit in memory

DOS cannot load an executable program because of insufficient RAM. Remove or disable any unnecessary TSR programs, then try loading the program again.

Write-protect error writing drive *X*

You tried to write data to a disk with a write-protect tab covering the notch, or the disk does not have a write-protect notch.

A–6   ANSWERS TO SELECTED REVIEW QUESTIONS

Chapter 1

2. Disk drive and keyboard.

6. Floppy and hard disks.

13. It varies. It starts at 1 MB, 4 MB, or higher.

17. Keep it in a dust-free environment. Protect it against excessive heat and humidity. Provide a constant electrical current.

22. Every application program provides an editing feature so you can edit your mistakes. Or, in the worst case, you can retype your mistakes.

27. Priority of operations, or precedence of operations, refers to the order in which a computer handles calculations. The order is as follows:

    - Expressions inside parentheses have the highest priority.
    - Exponentiation (raising to power) has the next highest priority.
    - Multiplication and division have the third highest priority.
    - Addition and subtraction have the fourth highest priority.
    - When there are two or more operations with the same priority, operations proceed from left to right.

Chapter 2

4. You should always enter the correct date and time at the boot-up time. If you do so, whenever you save a file it will be timed and dated correctly. Later, you can easily find out which version of the file is the most or the least recent. To bypass the date and time, press Enter twice.

8. The DIR/W command generates a wide directory in a horizontal format. You see only the file names and their extensions. The DIR/P command generates a directory in a vertical format, which you see one screen at a time. To see the next screen press any key.

11. Press Ctrl+C or Ctrl+Break.

17. Type *VER* and press Enter.

Chapter 3

2. FORMAT A:/S.

5. To generate an exact duplicate of a disk use the DISKCOPY command. The target disk does not need to be formatted because the DISKCOPY command formats and copies at the same time.

10. The SYS command copies the DOS hidden files from the DOS disk to another disk.

13. COPY FileA.ABC + FileB.ABC FileC.ABC.

16. DISKCOPY erases the target disk. COPY *.* does not. With DISKCOPY the target disk does not need to be formatted. With COPY *.* the target disk must be formatted. DISKCOPY transfers the hidden files. COPY *.* does not.

Chapter 4

3. Subdirectories significantly improve the efficiency and effectiveness of secondary storage devices. With subdirectories, you are able to store different files in certain folders for easy retrieval. Subdirectories are even more important in a hard disk environment because a hard disk possesses much more storage space than a floppy disk.

8. To move up one directory level, type

   CD ..

   To move up two directory levels, type

   CD ..\..

12. To erase a directory, first you must erase all the files and subsequent directories in that directory by using the DEL command. Then you can erase the empty directory by typing the RD command followed by the directory name.

15. You must run the FDISK program.

20. You must use the A parameter. For example:

   C>BACKUP C:*.* A:/S/A/D 10/10/94

   backs up all the files created since 10/10/94 and adds them to the disk in drive A without erasing any of the files in drive A.

Chapter 5

4. With the COPY CON command, you cannot edit the created file.

8. ECHO, REM, PAUSE, and GOTO are some examples.

11. EDLIN is a limited line editor available on your DOS disk. It is helpful for batch file creation.

13. Put the DOS disk, which includes the EDLIN program, in drive A. Insert a formatted disk in drive B and type EDLIN B:SAMPLE.BAT. Or, at C> prompt, type EDLIN A: SAMPLE.BAT. EDLIN creates a file called SAMPLE with BAT as its extension.

19. For the new file, the message is New file. For an existing file, the message is End of input file.

Chapter 6

3. Type *DIR>PRN.*

6. Filters are used to exercise control over DOS commands. The filters are SORT, FIND, and MORE.

11. DIR/P can be used only with directory listings. The MORE filter can be used with directory listings as well as with specific files.

13. Piping is used to connect two or more DOS commands.

19. The FILES command is used to extend the number of open files. The default is 8 and the maximum is 255.

Chapter 7

2. UNFORMAT and UNDELETE are two examples.

11. Press Shift+F9.

13. At the DOS prompt you must type *PRINT* and then press Enter. Then you can use the PRINT command from the menu.

21. The KEYBOARD command.

Chapter 8

4. The DOSKEY command provides macro capability in DOS 6.0

7. You can press the up-arrow key or you can type *DOSKEY/H* then press Enter.

10. The SAVE command saves the current document under its present name. The SAVE AS command allows you to select a new name for your document.

18. The CHANGE command in the Search menu.

B–1   INTRODUCTION

This appendix presents guidelines for importing and exporting files to and from selected software, thereby enabling you to utilize the best features of each software package. By importing files from other software you also save time and frustration because you do not duplicate the same data file. The guidelines cover file transfer among DOS, WordPerfect 5.1 and 6.0, Lotus 1-2-3, dBASE III Plus/dBASE IV, Quattro Pro, Paradox, and BASICA.

Some software applications such as Quattro Pro and Paradox provide extensive support for file transfer. Other packages such as Lotus 1-2-3 provide a translate utility that enables you to translate one file format to another. The guidelines in this appendix involve exporting and importing ASCII files. For extensive information about the availability and use of the built-in file transfer facilities of each software application, consult the package's documentation.

B–2   WHY USE FILE TRANSFER?

File transfer allows the movement of a file generated by one software application program to another. There are three good reasons for performing such a task:

1. Utilizing a capability of one software package that is not available in another. For example, you might transfer a Lotus 1-2-3 spreadsheet to a report generated by a word processing program thereby creating a factual and comprehensive report. You may also want to import dBASE data into 1-2-3 for graphing—a feature that is not available in dBASE.

2. Utilizing the enhanced power in one package for the same basic tasks that can be performed by two software applications. For example, database operations performed by 1-2-3 are much faster than those performed by dBASE; therefore, you might want to translate a dBASE file into a 1-2-3 spreadsheet for faster processing.

3. Converting data files from earlier software application programs to more recent versions. This is a common practice. Consider converting VisiCalc (the most popular spreadsheet program before 1-2-3) files into 1-2-3 files. Without data transfer facilities, you would have to enter all the data again, a very time-consuming, error-prone, and tedious task.

B–3   WHAT IS AN ASCII FILE?

Probably the easiest and most straightforward method for file transfer is to use ASCII files. ASCII (American Standard Code for Information Interchange) is a data format generated and accepted by most software application packages.

An ASCII file, or simply a "print image" file (sometimes called a DOS text file), is a file composed of standard keyboard characters. To verify whether a file is in ASCII format or not is a simple task. At the DOS prompt type *TYPE file name.extension* and press Enter, for example, *TYPE SAMPLE.TXT* (press Enter). If the file is displayed on the screen in standard keyboard characters, it is in ASCII format; otherwise it is not. In other words, you should be able to read an ASCII file. For example, 1-2-3 files generated by the /Print File command (files with the PRN extension) are ASCII files.

As mentioned earlier, different software packages include specific capabilities for file transfer. For example, 1-2-3 includes the translate utility, which is able to translate from and to several different file formats. The next few sections provide specific guidelines for file transfer among selected software applications.

B–4   FILE TRANSFER AND DOS

Files created by the COPY CON, EDLIN, and EDIT (in DOS 5 and 6) commands are automatically in ASCII format. If you are using EDLIN, enter the following command to load and edit an ASCII file:

EDLIN SAMPLE.BAT (press Enter)

In this case both EDLIN and SAMPLE.BAT are assumed to be in your default directory and drive. If they are not, you must include the drive identifier and/or the exact path. SAMPLE is the name of the file and BAT is its extension. After you have loaded the file, it is available for editing. When you save a file in EDLIN or EDIT, the file is automatically saved in ASCII file format.

B–5   FILE TRANSFER AND WORDPERFECT 5.1

B–5–1   Creating ASCII Files

To generate an ASCII file in WordPerfect press Ctrl+F5 (Text In/Out). You are presented with the following menu:

```
1 DOS Text;  2 Password;  3 Save As;  4 Comment;  5 Spreadsheet: 0
```

From this menu select option 1 (DOS Text). You are presented with the following menu:

```
1 Save;  2 Retrieve (CR/LF to [HRt]);  3 Retrieve (CR/LF to [SRt] in HZone): 0
```

From this menu select option 1 (Save). At this point WordPerfect responds with

```
Document to be saved (DOS Text):
```

Type in a name (for example, SAMPLE) and press Enter. The file extension is optional. You must also specify the drive identifier and/or the correct path if you are not saving into the default drive and directory.

It is a good idea to save your file in WordPerfect format as well. To do this use either F10 or F7. If you do save your file in WordPerfect format, be sure to use a different name; otherwise, the file created in ASCII format will be overwritten by the file with the same name in WordPerfect format!

B–5–2   Importing ASCII Files

To import an ASCII file into WordPerfect press Ctrl+F5 (Text In/Out). From this menu select option 1 (DOS Text). From this menu select either option 2, Retrieve (CR/LF to [HRt]) or option 3, Retrieve (CR/LF to [SRt] in HZone). Type the name of the file and press Enter. The file will be imported into the WordPerfect document at the cursor position.

The "CR/LF" refers to the carriage return/line feed codes in the ASCII file. These codes are used to end one line and move the cursor to the next line.

Using the CR/LF to [SRt] option enables the imported file to closely match the WordPerfect format. If you use this option, you should set the margin width of your WordPerfect document to closely match that used by the ASCII file. If you use the CR/LF [HRt] option, set the WordPerfect document margin wider than the margin of the ASCII file that is being imported.

B–6   IMPORTING FILES INTO WORDPERFECT: A SECOND METHOD

Another method of importing ASCII format files into WordPerfect is through the F5 (List Files) key. To use this method, press F5. WordPerfect responds by displaying the name of the default directory in the lower left corner of the screen. If this drive/directory path is correct, press the Enter key; otherwise, type the desired drive and directory path and press Enter. WordPerfect displays the listing of files contained in the displayed directory. To import an ASCII file from this screen, you have two options.

1. You can highlight the file that you want to import and select 1 or R (Retrieve) from the List Files menu. WordPerfect briefly displays

```
Document Conversion in Progress
```

in the lower-left corner of the screen as the file is being imported. The imported file is converted into standard WordPerfect format and displayed on the screen.

2. Highlight the file that you want to import, then press Ctrl+F5 (Text In/Out). WordPerfect responds by displaying

```
(DOS) Retrieve [drive:\path\file name.extension]? No (Yes)
```

If you press Y, WordPerfect retrieves the specified file without further prompting.

Note that using this method does not trigger the "Document Conversion in Progress" message that a normal retrieve request generates. This is so because WordPerfect does not need to convert the document into WordPerfect file format. The file is imported in its simple ASCII format with no additional format codes.

B–7   FILE TRANSFER AND WORDPERFECT 6.0

WordPerfect version 6.0 provides a powerful tool for file transfer. To convert a WordPerfect 6.0 file to another file format, follow these steps:

1. Create or retrieve your WordPerfect 6.0 file.
2. From the File menu select the Save As option.
3. Type the desired name (up to eight characters) and then choose the Format option. You can choose from a list of more than 30 file formats.

4. After highlighting the desired format, choose the OK option. At this time the WordPerfect 6.0 file is converted to the selected file format.

To import a file to WordPerfect 6.0 format, do the following steps:

1. Choose the Open option from the File menu or press the Shift+F10 key-combination.
2. Type the filename of the file you want to convert, or select it from the File Manager or QuickList, then choose OK.
3. From the provided list, highlight the current format of the file you want to open.
4. Choose the Select option.
5. Choose the Save As option from the File menu.
6. Type a filename (up to eight characters) for the converted file.

If you use the original filename, the converted file will be replaced with the file in WordPerfect 6.0 format.

You should remember the converted documents are saved in WordPerfect 6.0 format unless they are converted as ASCII files. WordPerfect 6.0 saves converted ASCII files as ASCII files by default.

B–8   FILE TRANSFER AND LOTUS 1-2-3

B–8–1   Creating ASCII Files

To create ASCII files in 1-2-3, use the /Print File command. After selecting /Print File, you must specify the desired range (press Enter), then select Align, Go, and Quit. When you print to a file, the file is saved with a PRN extension. Remember that when you generate an ASCII file from your spreadsheet, the converted file is no longer a true worksheet. To maintain this spreadsheet in its original form, you must use the /File Save command before conversion and save your file in WK1 format. However, if you forget to save in standard format first, 1-2-3 offers the /Data Parse command which enables you to convert this ASCII file back to its original form. After issuing the /Print File command you must specify the Range, then choose Align, then Go, and finally Quit. The Quit command closes the file and finalizes the file creation process.

B–8–2   Importing ASCII Files

To import an ASCII file into 1-2-3, use the /File Import command. After issuing this command specify the file name and then press Enter. You are prompted to select Formulas or Values. Select Values. The file is imported into the spreadsheet at the position of the cellpointer, and as many rows down and columns to the right as necessary are used to accommodate the entire file.

B–9   FILE TRANSFER AND dBASE

B–9–1   Creating ASCII Files

In dBASE, to create an ASCII file you use the COPY command. The syntax of this command is:

> COPY TO {file name}/{scope}/FIELDS {field list}/FOR
> {condition}/WHILE {condition}/TYPE {file type}

The scope, FIELDS, FOR, and WHILE entries are optional. These options provide more control over the final results. The TYPE option indicates the type of file to be created. Three file types are most commonly generated by dBASE:

1. WKS (worksheet): This file extension generates spreadsheet files accepted by 1-2-3. For example, to generate a 1-2-3 WK1 file in dBASE, at the dot prompt type *COPY TO SAMPLE.WK1/TYPE WKS*. Now in 1-2-3, by using the /File Retrieve command, you can bring this file into 1-2-3 and perform any operations on it.

2. SDF (system data format ASCII file): This file type copies database fields using the same format as the fields in the database file structure. It does not contain field separators; therefore, there is no space between fields. An example is *COPY TO SAMPLE/TYPE SDF*.

3. DIF (VisiCalc worksheet): This format was originally used by VisiCalc—the first commercial spreadsheet. It now can be read by 1-2-3 also. An example is *COPY TO SAMPLE.TXT/TYPE DIF*.

B–9–2   Importing ASCII Files

To import an ASCII file into dBASE, at the dot prompt issue the APPEND FROM command. For example,

> APPEND FROM SAMPLE.TXT

As usual you can use the FOR condition to append selected records. In this example, the SAMPLE.TXT file will be appended to your current file.

Export and import facilities are also available through the dBASE III Plus assist menu and dBASE IV Control Center.

B–10   FILE TRANSFER AND 1-2-3 PIC FILES

1-2-3 generates PIC files when you issue the /Graph Save command. By integrating graphs into your reports, you can significantly improve the quality of your documents. In the past, graphs were manually cut and pasted into reports. By using the procedure described below, you can electronically include any of your 1-2-3 graphs in WordPerfect 5.1 documents. Follow these steps:

1. Start with 1-2-3 and create the graph of your choice.
2. By using the /Graph Save command, save your graph. This procedure generates a file with a PIC extension.
3. Exit 1-2-3 and start WordPerfect 5.1. Press Alt+F9. This invokes the graphics menu:

```
1 Figure;  2 Table Box;  3 Text Box;  4 User Box;  5 Line;  6 Equation: 0
```

4. Press 1 or F for Figure. The following menu is displayed:

```
Figure: 1 Create;  2 Edit;  3 New Number;  4 Options: 0
```

5. Options 2, 3, and 4 are used when the graph has already been imported into the document. In our case, select 1 or C for Create. The following menu is displayed:

```
Definition: Figure
1 - Filename
2 - Contents                  Empty
3 - Caption
4 - Anchor Type               Paragraph
5 - Vertical Position         0"
6 - Horizontal Position       Right
7 - Size                      3.25" wide x 3.25" (high)
8 - Wrap Text Around Box      Yes
9 - Edit
```

The Filename option indicates the name of the graphics file to be imported into your WordPerfect document.

The Contents option will be modified after a file has been retrieved into the memory of the computer through the use of option 1. In our case, after loading a PIC file, Contents will be set to "Graphic."

The Caption option allows you to enter a caption to appear with your graph.

The Anchor Type option allows you to specify how the graph should appear in relation to the text that surrounds it. If you select option 4 (Anchor Type), you receive the following menu:

```
Anchor Type: 1 Paragraph;  2 Page;  Character: 0
```

If you select the Paragraph option, the graph stays with the text that surrounds it even if the surrounding text is moved to a new position in the document. If you select Page, the graphics box stays at a fixed location on the page even if the surrounding text is moved to a new position in the document. If you select the Character option, the graph is treated as part of the text.

The Vertical Position and Horizontal Position options allow you to specify where the graph will appear on the page. If you select option 5 (Vertical Position), WordPerfect responds:

```
Offset from top of paragraph: 0"
```

If you select option 6 (Horizontal Position), WordPerfect displays the following menu:

```
Horizontal Position: 1 Left;  2 Right;  3 Center;  4 Full: 0
```

It is up to you to decide the exact position of your graph.

The Size option allows you to specify the exact height and width of the graph on the page.

The Wrap Text Around Box option allows Yes or No alternatives. If you select Yes, the text wraps around the graphics box. If you select No, the text is allowed to print over the top of the graph. Usually, you should select the Yes option.

The Edit option brings the graph to the screen.

6. After selecting the Create option, select F (for File name). Enter the drive, path, name, and extension of your file (if the file is not on the default drive) and press Enter.

7. Exit this menu by pressing the space bar; then press Shift+F7 and select option 6 (View Document). Your graph is displayed on the screen. To print the graph, press the space bar and select option 1 (Full Document).

B–11   FILE TRANSFER AND QUATTRO PRO

B–11–1   Creating ASCII Files

Follow the steps outlined next to create an ASCII file using Quattro Pro. For this exercise we assume that the spreadsheet you are saving occupies the range of cells A1 through F5 (A1..F5).

1. Press the / (forward slash) key to access the main menu.
2. Press P (Print).
3. Press B (Block). Assuming that your cellpointer is located in cell A1, Quattro Pro responds with the following prompt:

```
[Enter] [Esc] The block of the spreadsheet to print: A1
```

4. Type *A1..F5* and press Enter.
5. Press D (Destination). Quattro Pro displays the Destination menu.
6. Press F (File). Quattro Pro prompts you with the following message:

```
Enter print file name:
```

7. Type a name for your file (up to eight characters) and press Enter. We typed *SALES* and pressed Enter. Quattro Pro now returns you to the main Print menu.

Quattro Pro saves the spreadsheet data, using the file name you specified, with the extension PRN.

To verify that the ASCII file was created successfully, use the left-arrow key to display the File menu, then select the Utilities option, then select the DOS Shell option. Quattro Pro responds with the following message:

```
Enter DOS Command, Press Enter for full DOS Shell
```

Press the Enter key; you will be presented with a DOS prompt. Type the following command to view the ASCII file:

```
TYPE SALES.PRN (press Enter)
```

(Note: If you entered a different file name, replace the word "SALES" with the name you specified.) The data from cells A1..F5 will be displayed on screen. Type the DOS command EXIT and press Enter to return to Quattro Pro.

B–11–2   Importing ASCII Files

Make sure you have a blank spreadsheet, then follow the steps outlined to import an ASCII file into Quattro Pro. We assume that you have generated an ASCII file using another application, in this case, 1-2-3.

1. Press the / (forward slash) key to access the main menu.
2. Press T (Tools).
3. Press I (Import).
4. Press A (ASCII Text File). Quattro Pro responds with the following prompt:

```
Enter name of file to import:
```

A listing of all files in the default directory with the extension PRN is displayed for you. You may highlight the desired file name and press Enter, or you may type the drive, path, and file name of the desired file and then press Enter. Quattro Pro imports the specified ASCII file and displays its contents on screen for you.

B–12   FILE TRANSFER AND PARADOX

B–12–1   Creating ASCII Files

Follow these steps to create an ASCII file using Paradox. We assume that you have already created a table consisting of 10 records.

1. If necessary, press the F10 key to display the main menu.
2. Press T (Tools) to select the Tools option from the main menu.
3. Press E (ExportImport) to select the ExportImport option.
4. Press E (Export) to select the Export option. Paradox responds by displaying the various output file formats that are available to you.
5. Press A (ASCII) to select the ASCII option.
6. Press D (Delimited) to select the Delimited option. Paradox prompts you to enter the name of the table that will be used to create the ASCII file.
7. Press the Enter key and Paradox responds by displaying the names of tables that are available to be selected.
8. Highlight the desired table name and press Enter, or type the name of the table from which you want to create an ASCII file and press Enter. We high-lighted the table name CUSTOMER and pressed Enter. Paradox responds with a prompt requesting the name of the converted file.
9. Type a name for your output ASCII file, then press Enter. We typed CUSTLIST then pressed Enter. Paradox responds in the lower right corner with the message

```
Converting Customer to custlist.TXT . . .
```

The ASCII file is created on the default drive, in the default directory, under the file name that was specified during the ASCII file creation process.

When the message in the lower right corner of the screen stops flashing, ASCII file creation is finished.

Follow these steps to verify that the ASCII file has been successfully created:

1. If necessary, press the F10 key to display the main menu.
2. Press T (Tools).
3. Press M (More).
4. Press T (ToDOS). Paradox will clear the screen and display a DOS prompt for you.
5. Type the following command to send the contents of the ASCII file to the printer:

    TYPE CUSTLIST.TXT > LPT1

    (Note: If you used a name other than CUSTLIST for your ASCII file, specify that name instead of CUSTLIST. Also, if LPT1 is not the port you are using for printed output, specify the correct output port instead of LPT1.)

Your output will be sent to the printer. Each record in the file will be printed on a separate line with commas separating each field and quotation marks surrounding the contents of each field. View the ASCII data output to make sure that it is correct, then type *EXIT* and press Enter to return to Paradox.

B–12–2   Importing ASCII Files

Follow the steps outlined next to import an ASCII file into Paradox. We assume that you have already created a comma delimited ASCII file using another application program.

1. If necessary, press the F10 key to display the main menu.
2. Press T (Tools) to select the Tools option.
3. Press E (ExportImport) to select the ExportImport option.
4. Press I (Import) to select the Import option. Paradox responds by displaying various application program file formats that are available to you.
5. Press A (ASCII) to select the ASCII option.
6. Press D (Delimited) to select the Delimited option. Paradox prompts you to enter the name of the file to be imported.
7. Press Enter to view the names of available ASCII files from which you can select.
8. You may highlight the desired import file and press Enter, or type the name of the desired import file and press Enter. We typed SALESMAN.TXT and pressed Enter. Paradox responds by prompting you for the name of the new Paradox table that will be created as a result of the import operation.
9. Type the name of the new Paradox table that will be used to hold the incoming ASCII data and press Enter. We typed TEST and pressed Enter. Paradox imports the ASCII file data; it displays the imported data from left to right on the screen with the name of the new table in the upper left corner and Field-1, Field-2, and so forth displayed at the top of each column of data.

B–13   FILE TRANSFER AND BASICA

BASICA can generate ASCII files in several ways. The following program is one that can be used to generate a sequential ASCII file. The resulting file can easily be imported to any software that accepts ASCII files.

```
10      REM TO CREATE ASCII FILE CALLED STUREC
20      OPEN "STUREC" FOR OUTPUT AS #1
30      FOR I=1 TO 3
40              READ A$,B$,C
50              WRITE #1,A$,B$,C
60      NEXT I
70      CLOSE
80      DATA SUSAN SHAY, BUSINESS, 3.85
90      DATA KIM BROWN, COMPUTER, 2.60
100     DATA ED STRONG, MATH, 4.00
110     END
```

To see the contents of the ASCII file STUREC, type these instructions:

RUN (press Enter)   (program will run)
SYSTEM (press Enter)   (exit from BASICA to DOS prompt)
A > TYPE STUREC (press Enter)
"SUSAN SHAY","BUSINESS",3.85
"KIM BROWN","COMPUTER",2.60
"ED STRONG","MATH",4.00

Also, if a file is saved using the SAVE "File name",A command, the file is saved in ASCII format with the BAS extension automatically supplied.

BASICA can read an ASCII file by using the LINE INPUT #1 command. For example, you can read an ASCII file line by line into a one-dimensional array in a BASICA program. The following routine reads a 1-2-3 ASCII file (PRN file) called MYFILE.PRN into array X$(100):

```
10      DIM X$(100)
20      OPEN "MYFILE.PRN" FOR INPUT AS #1
30      J=1
40      WHILE NOT EOF(1)
50              LINE INPUT #1,X$(J)
60          J=J+1
70      WEND
80      END
```

The following routine prints the contents of array X$:

```
10          FOR I=1 TO J
20              PRINT "X$(I)=",X$(I)
30          NEXT I
40          END
```

SUMMARY

This appendix reviewed ASCII files and the advantages of file transfer among different software. Specific guidelines for file transfer using DOS, WordPerfect, Lotus 1-2-3, dBASE, Quattro Pro, Paradox, and BASICA were presented. To become familiar with this important topic, you have to practice by creating a sample file in one software package and exporting or importing it into the other packages.

REVIEW QUESTIONS

1. What is file transfer? Why should it be done in some cases?
2. What is an ASCII file?
3. How do you know if a file is in ASCII format?
4. How do you create an ASCII file using DOS?
5. How do you create an ASCII file using WordPerfect?
6. How is an ASCII file imported into WordPerfect?
7. How do you import a PIC file into WordPerfect?
8. What are the advantages of importing a PIC file into a WordPerfect document?
9. How do you create an ASCII file using 1-2-3?
10. How is an ASCII file imported into 1-2-3?
11. How do you create an ASCII file using dBASE?
12. How is an ASCII file imported into dBASE?
13. What are some of the file transfer features of Quattro Pro?
14. How is an ASCII file imported into Quattro Pro?
15. How do you create an ASCII file using Paradox?
16. How is an ASCII file imported into Paradox?
17. How do you read the contents of an ASCII file into a BASICA array?
18. How do you create an ASCII file using BASICA?

Appendix C
A Quick Trip Through Microsoft Windows

C–1   INTRODUCTION

This appendix presents some of the unique advantages of Microsoft Windows[1] as a graphics-based environment compared with a character-based environment such as DOS. After discussing how to get in and how to get out of Windows, we will look at the procedures for using a mouse and the keyboard in the Windows environment. Next, the help and tutorial facilities of Windows will be introduced. The appendix concludes with discussions of the different parts of a Windows screen, running applications in Windows, quitting an application, working with the Clipboard, and working with a Windows group.

C–2   WINDOWS 3.1: AN OVERVIEW

Windows 3.1 is based on a graphical user interface (GUI) environment (pronounced "gooey") that runs on top of DOS (i.e., you must have DOS to run Windows). This graphical environment has several advantages not found in the DOS character-based environment. Let us summarize some of these advantages:

1. Windows is easier to use than DOS because with Windows you do not need to memorize the strict DOS command syntax. In Windows you can perform all DOS functions and more through a series of pull-down menus.

2. All Windows applications share the same principles. When you learn one Windows application, you can easily transfer some or all of what you have learned to other Windows applications.

3. The user can work with Windows applications using a mouse, the keyboard, or shortcut keys for speed (described later in this appendix). All these options enable you to become more efficient using Windows programs.

4. Windows presents a multitasking environment. This means that using Windows you can run more than one program at the same time. Imagine that you are typing a report using WordPerfect and decide you need a spreadsheet created in Lotus 1-2-3. If you are using Windows you can easily switch to Lotus 1-2-3 and incorporate the desired spreadsheet into your report. You can even integrate a graph into your report. Perhaps you decide that you need a telephone number out of your online telephone directory. You can easily run your telephone directory software, access the correct phone number, then exit the telephone directory software without ever exiting WordPerfect.

5. Windows applications and DOS applications can be run simultaneously. You can even run multiple DOS programs and multiple Windows programs at the same time.

6. Several programs can be linked together. If you change data in one program, the same data in the other program will be changed automatically.

7. Windows allows better memory management. You are not restricted by 640 K, the traditional DOS barrier. Using Windows, you can use memory well beyond 640 K. Windows makes your hard disk an extension of your RAM. If a program does not fit into your RAM, it will simply spill over to your hard disk.

8. Accessory programs are free of charge. Windows comes with a group of accessories that are readily available to you free of charge:

---

[1]   For a detailed discussion of Microsoft Windows, consult *Information Systems Literacy: Windows 3.1* by Hossein Bidgoli, published by Macmillan Publishing Company, 1993.

<table>
<tr>
<td>

Table C–1
Unique Advantages of Windows

</td>
<td>

Ease of use.

Shared principles among Windows programs.

Use of mouse, keyboard, and shortcut keys.

Multitasking.

Ability to run Windows and DOS applications at the same time.

Linkage of several programs.

Better memory management.

Free accessories.

True WYSIWYG.

</td>
</tr>
</table>

- Windows Write—a simple word processor
- Windows Paintbrush—a drawing program
- Windows Terminal—a communications program
- Windows Print Manager—a program that allows you to work and print at the same time
- Many more useful programs such as the Calculator, Calendar, Notepad, Cardfile, and the Clock
- True WYSIWYG Windows allows you to display on the screen exactly what will appear on the printed output. This is called What-You-See-Is-What-You-Get (WYSIWYG). Using this feature, you will have a pretty good idea of the output of an application before printing it.

The unique advantages of Windows are listed in Table C–1.

C–3   GETTING IN AND OUT OF WINDOWS

The first step is to install Windows on a hard disk system. Windows will not run on a floppy system. After installing Windows, switch to the drive and directory containing your Windows files by using the DOS CD command (e.g., type *CD WIN31* then press Enter); then type *WIN* and press Enter. You will be presented with a screen similar to the one shown in Figure C–1.

There are three methods that you can use to get out of Windows. The first is to move the mouse pointer to the File option at the upper left of the screen and click the left button of the mouse. You will be presented with a screen similar to the one shown in Figure C–2. Move the mouse pointer to the Exit Windows option and click the left button. The second method is to move the mouse pointer to the control-menu box at the extreme upper left of the screen and double-click the left button of the mouse. The third method is to move the mouse pointer to the control-menu box and click the left button once. You will be presented with a screen similar to the one shown in Figure C–3. Move the mouse pointer to the Close option and click the left button.

Regardless of which of these three methods you use, you will be presented with a screen similar to the one shown in Figure C–4. Move to OK and click the left button of the mouse to leave Windows. If you click while on Cancel, this indicates that you have changed your mind and you wish to stay in Windows. When you exit Windows you exit either to DOS or to your starting menu, depending on how you started Windows in the first place.

Figure C–1
Windows starting screen.

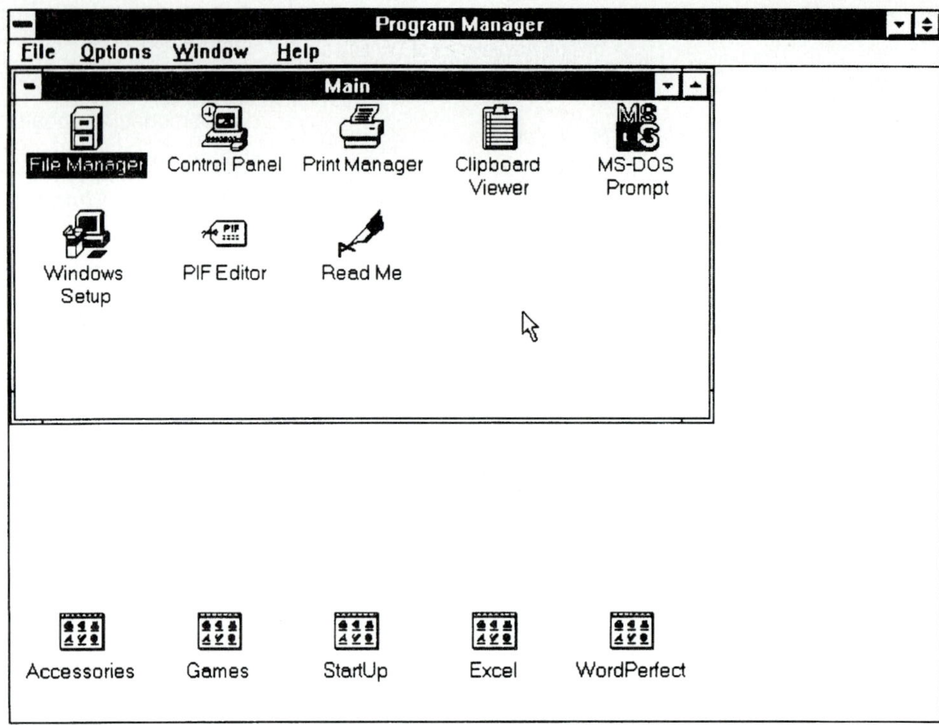

Figure C–2
File pull-down menu.

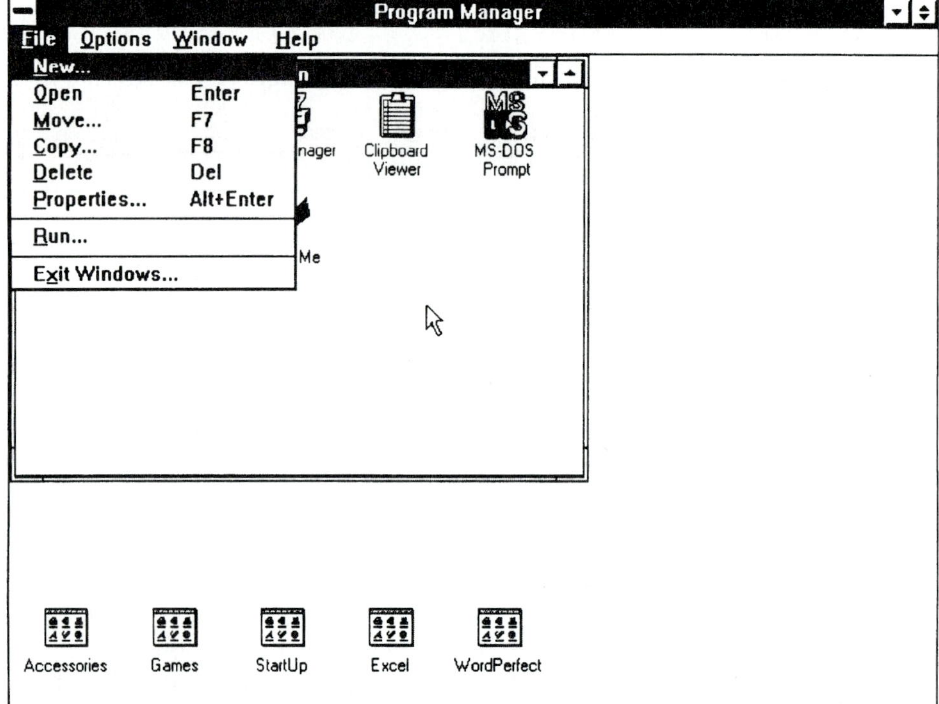

Figure C–3
Control-menu box options.

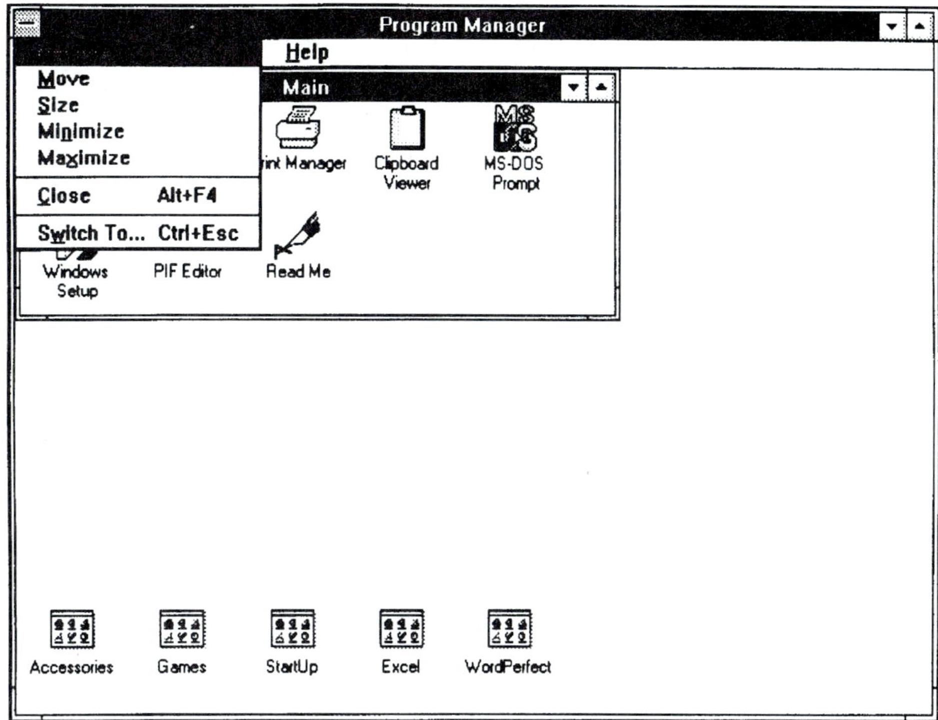

Figure C–4
Windows exit dialog box.

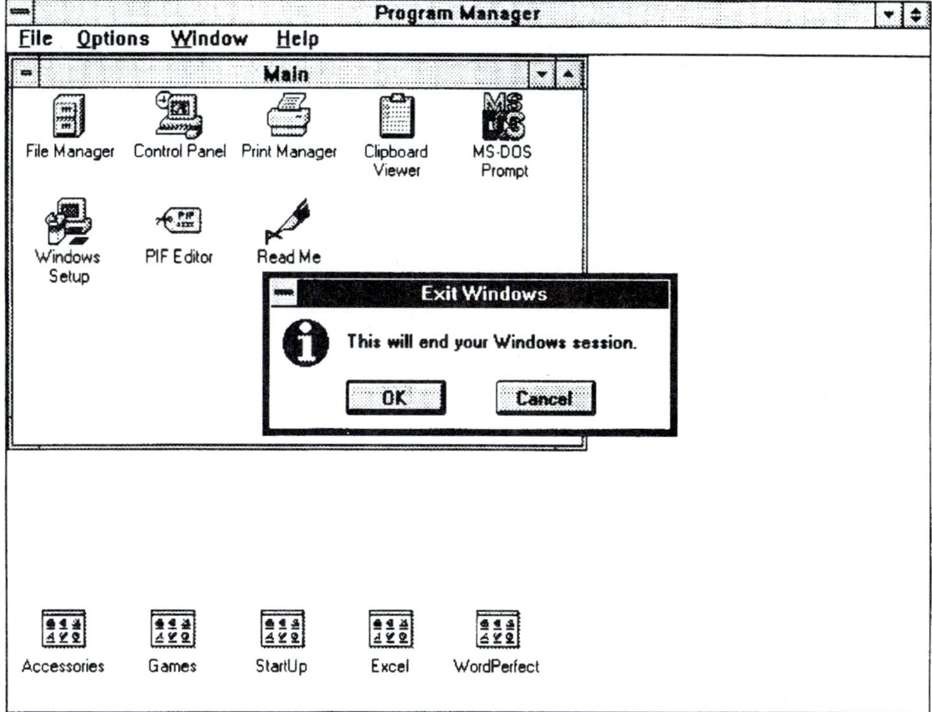

You can also use the keyboard to exit Windows. To do so, press Alt+F to open the File menu then either press the letter X or move the cursor to Exit Windows and press Enter. Press Enter again to exit Windows.

C–4   UNDERSTANDING WINDOWS TERMINOLOGY

Windows, just like other software, has its own terminology. Among the important terms are desktop, icon, and mouse. Let us briefly explain each.

Desktop in Windows is similar to the surface of a desk. All your Windows work takes place in the desktop. When you start Windows you start at the desktop. You can do a number of tasks from the desktop; among the most common tasks are the following:

- Fast application switching—going from one application software to another
- Icon spacing change—moving around the existing icons, deleting the unwanted ones, and so forth
- Displaying your document
- Changing colors

An icon is a graphic representation of an application or a document. You can move the mouse pointer to the desired application icon and double-click the left button of the mouse to start the application or open a document.

The mouse will be explained in detail in the next section. It is the main interface between you and Windows and Windows applications. Although you can use the keyboard or the shortcut keys, using the mouse is probably the most efficient way to accomplish most Windows tasks.

C–5   USING A MOUSE IN THE WINDOWS ENVIRONMENT

Windows offers three user interface options: keyboard, mouse, and shortcut keys. Most users agree that a mouse is preferable to a keyboard in graphical environments such as Windows because of its speed, accuracy, ease of use, and other special functions that it can provide. Using a mouse you can easily select pull-down menu options, quickly execute application programs, move and/or resize group windows, relocate icons to new locations on the screen, and much more.

If you are right handed, hold the mouse in your right hand, and if you are left handed, hold the mouse in your left hand. Place the mouse on a flat surface (preferably on the mouse pad) and rest your hand on top of it. Place your thumb on one side of the mouse and the two fingers on the opposite end of your hand on the other side. This will leave your index finger and middle finger positioned over the mouse buttons. Lightly rest your fingers on these buttons. To see how the mouse works, move the mouse in a circular motion and look on the screen for the mouse pointer. You will see that it is also moving in a circular pattern, matching the movements of the mouse. If you move the mouse to the left, the mouse pointer moves to the left side of the screen; if you move the mouse away from you, the mouse pointer moves to the top of the screen.

Now let's try selecting some menu items using the mouse. Move the mouse so that the mouse pointer is pointing to the File option at the upper left of the screen, click the left button of the mouse. If you have done this correctly, the File pull-down menu will be displayed (see Figure C–2). Move the mouse pointer

Figure C–5
Window pull-down menu.

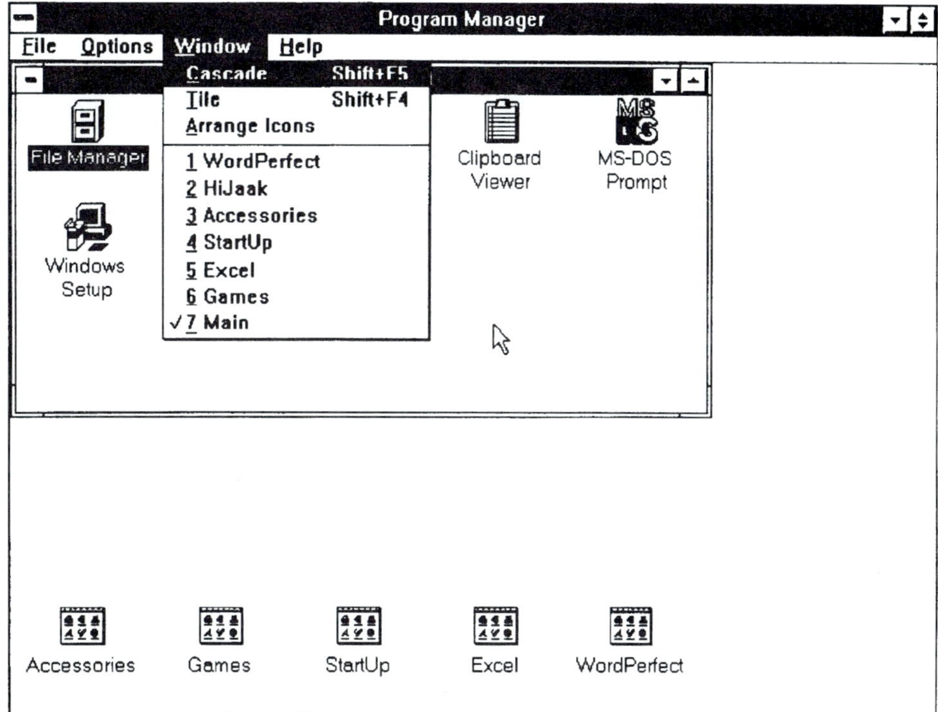

to the Window option and click the left button again to display the Window pull-down menu (Figure C–5). Notice that positioning the mouse pointer and clicking the left button selects the desired menu item automatically. For now, move the mouse pointer back into the middle of the screen and click the left button to "deselect" any currently highlighted menu items.

Rapid double-clicking of the left button while pointing the mouse pointer onto an icon automatically executes the application that the icon represents. To see how this works, move the mouse pointer to the Accessories icon and double-click the left button. This automatically opens the Accessories window (Figure C–6). Now you can double-click on any of these options.

Let's try another example. Move the mouse pointer to the MS-DOS Prompt option in the Main group (see Figure C–1) and double-click the left button. Windows responds by displaying a DOS prompt. Type the command *EXIT* (press Enter) to return to the Windows main screen.

Finally, you can move windows, group icons, application icons, and so forth to other locations on the screen using a method called "click and drag." To try this, point the mouse pointer onto the title bar of the Main group window (see Figure C–1). Click the left button; then, while holding the button down, drag the mouse pointer to a new location on the screen. You will notice that an outline form of the Main group moves with the mouse pointer. Your window will be relocated to the position of the mouse pointer when you release the left button.

Let's try changing the size of the Main group window. Move the mouse pointer to the right edge of the Main group window. Notice that at a certain position over the edge of the window the mouse pointer becomes a double-pointing arrow. When you see this, click and drag a small distance to the right. Again notice the outline form; when you release the mouse button, your window will conform to the size you just constructed by dragging the mouse. If you change your mind before releasing the left button of the mouse, press the Esc key.

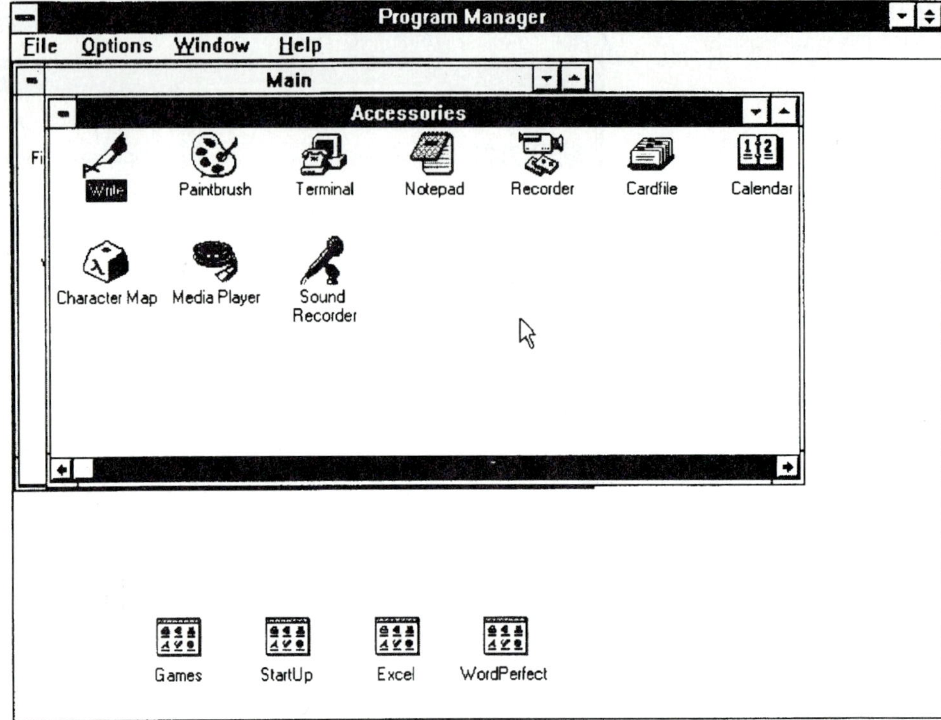

Figure C–6
Applications in the Accessories group.

As a final example of moving screen items to new locations, move the mouse pointer onto the MS-DOS Prompt option inside the Main group window. Click and drag the icon to a new location outside of the window, then release the left button of the mouse. The icon will obediently follow your command to position itself in a new location. For now, drag the icon back into the Main group window.

C–6   USING THE KEYBOARD IN A WINDOWS ENVIRONMENT

As mentioned, Windows and Windows programs allow use of the keyboard in addition to the mouse. Keyboards are comfortable for good typists, and since keyboards have been around for years, people are more familiar with them than with the mouse.

If you are working with Windows and want to use a keyboard, you may use one of the following areas of a keyboard:

- The typing keys located in the center of the keyboard. These keys are similar to the keys of a typewriter.
- The numeric and cursor movement keys located on the right side of the keyboard. Enhanced keyboards have a dedicated cursor movement pad. For standard keyboards, if you press the Num Lock key, the numeric pad serves as a 10-key machine for entering numbers. Cursor keys are used to move the cursor around.
- The function keys: F1 through F12 located across the top of the enhanced keyboard or F1 through F10 on the left side of the standard keyboard. All these keys perform different functions depending on the application program you are using.

Windows and Windows applications can also be accessed through the combination of keys called shortcut keys. The key-combination method always involves one of the following special keys—Shift, Alt, Ctrl—combined with another key. For example, Alt+F invokes the File menu. To use a key combination, first press either the Shift, Alt, or Ctrl key and hold it down; then press another key. In this appendix, the mouse is emphasized as the major Windows interface.

C–7   HELP FACILITIES OF WINDOWS

As you can see in Figure C–1, one of the options in the Program Manager is Help. The Program Manager, which is the heart of Windows, is used to start other applications and organize applications and files into groups. If you move the mouse pointer to the Help option and click the left button, you will see a screen similar to the one presented in Figure C–7. You can move the mouse pointer to any of these options and click the left button to execute the desired option. For example, if you click left on the Contents option, you will receive a screen similar to Figure C–8. As you can see in this figure, the Search option is available; it enables you to search for a particular topic. You can also select the Glossary option to generate an alphabetized listing of all the topics in Windows.

C–7–1   Tutorial Facility of Windows

If you select the Windows Tutorial option from the Help pull-down menu, you will be presented with a screen similar to Figure C–9. The tutorial provides an overview of Windows and mouse operations. If you have not used a mouse before, this tutorial is very helpful.

Figure C–7
Starting screen of the Help option.

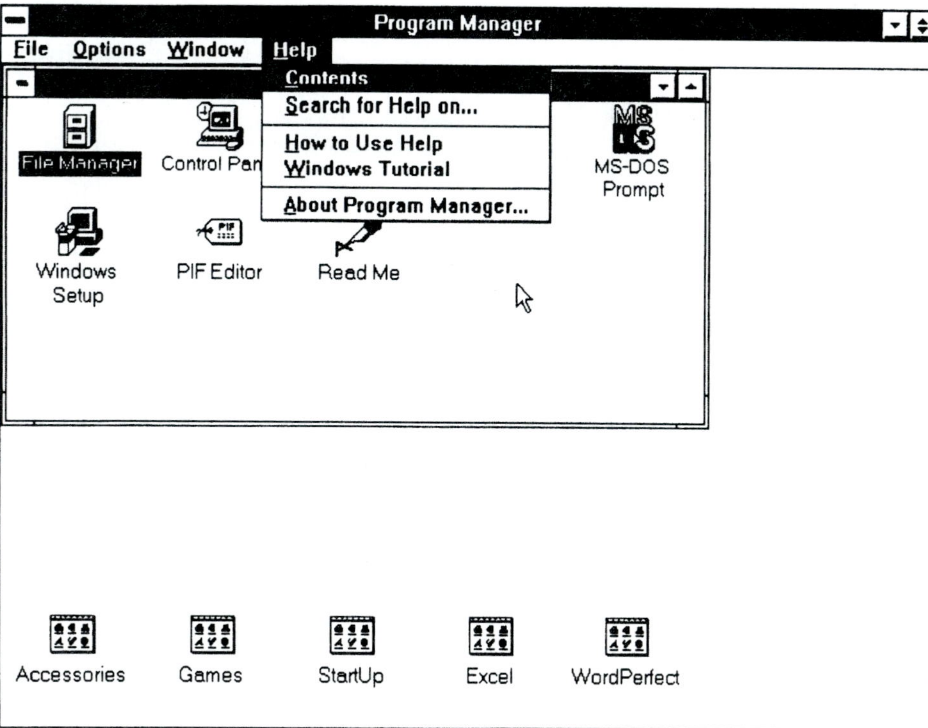

Figure C–8
Information under the Contents option of the Help menu.

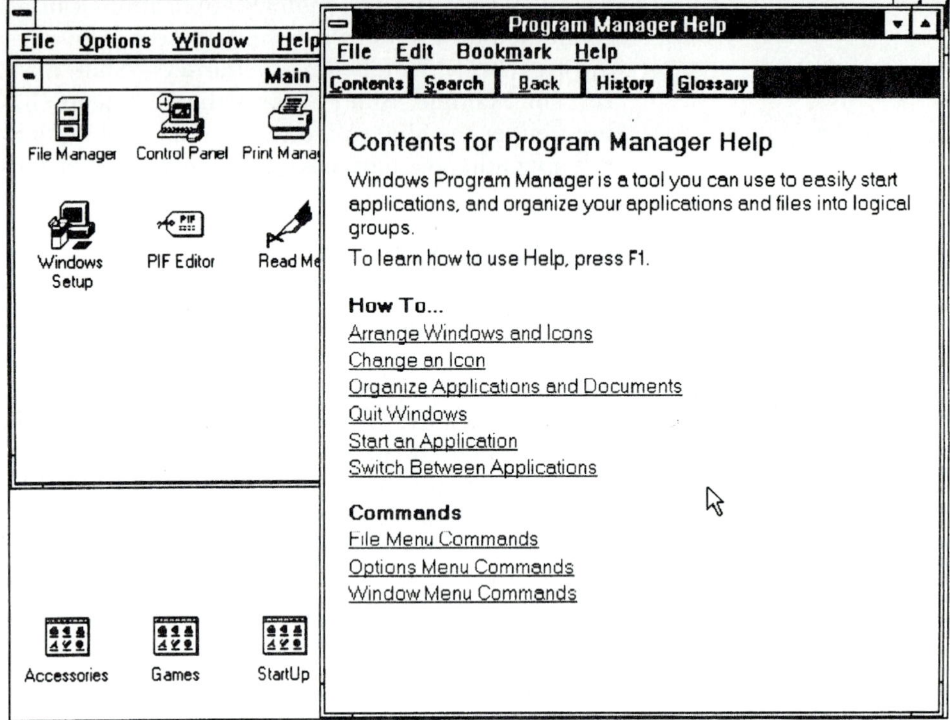

Figure C–9
Starting screen of the Windows tutorial.

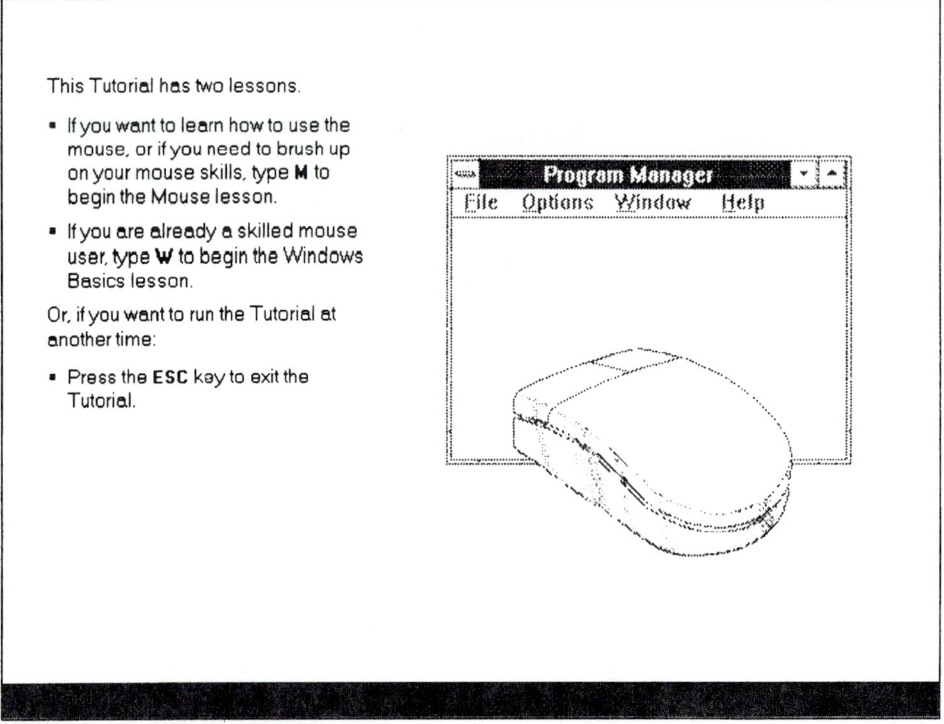

C–8   DIFFERENT PARTS OF A WINDOWS SCREEN

Most Windows screens include the elements illustrated in Figure C–10. Refer to the figure as you read the following descriptions:

- The Window title (in the Title bar) is usually the name of the application, name of a document, or name of a file. In Figure C–1, the window title is Program Manager. In Figure C–10 the title is Notepad—[Untitled] because no document has been opened yet.

- The Control-menu box is at the upper left of each window. The control-menu box is very helpful if you are using the keyboard to work with Windows. By using control-menu commands, you can resize, move, maximize, minimize, close Windows, and switch to applications. If you use a mouse, you can perform all of the tasks just mentioned by clicking and dragging.

- Insertion point indicates the current position of the cursor at any given time in your document. Text and graphs will be inserted at this point. (Not shown in our figure.)

- The Menu bar lists available menu options. For example, in Figure C–1 the menu bar includes File, Options, Window, and Help. In Figure C–10, the menu bar includes File, Edit, Search, and Help.

- The Minimize button can reduce the window to an icon.

- The Maximize button can enlarge the active application window so that it fills the entire desktop. After you enlarge a window, the maximize button is

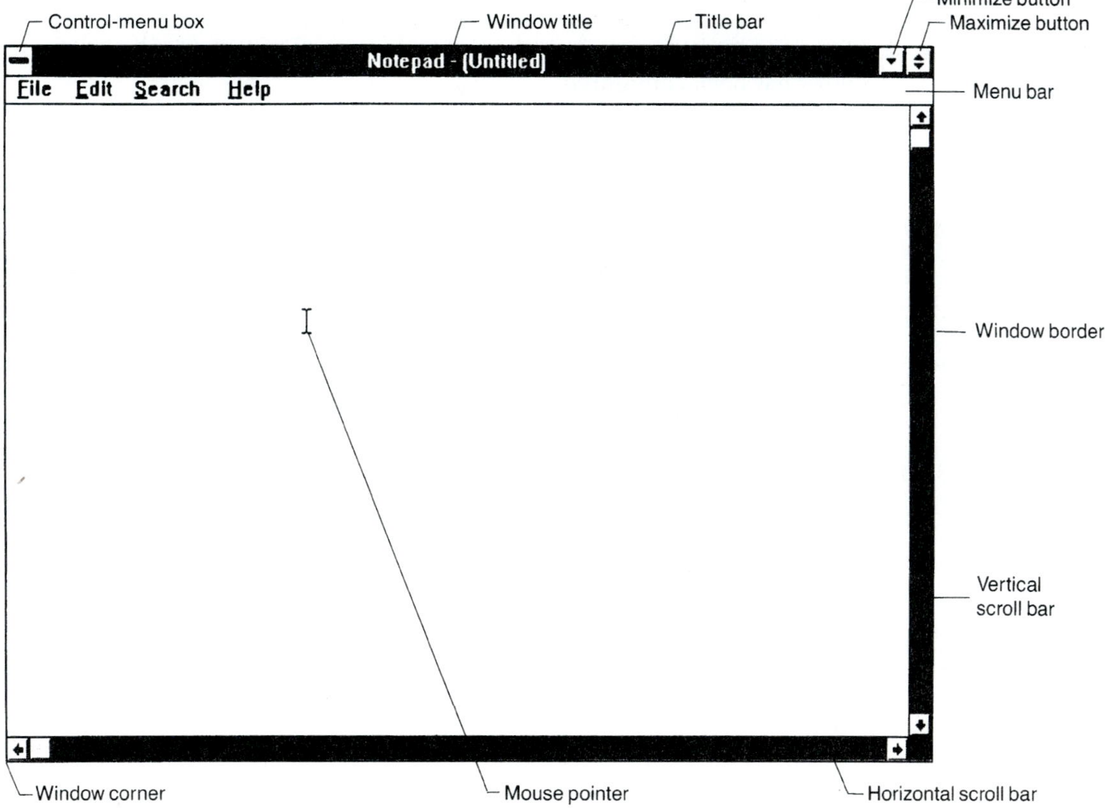

Figure C–10
Elements of the Windows screen.

replaced by the restore button. (This is the case in Figure C–10.) You can click the restore button to return a window to its previous size.

- The Window border is the outside edge of a window. You can lengthen or shorten the border on each side of a window.
- The Vertical and Horizontal scroll bars are used to view parts of a document that do not fit on the current screen.
- The Mouse pointer is a small arrow that moves on the screen corresponding to the movement of the mouse on your desktop. The mouse pointer changes to a double-pointed arrow when it is moved to the edge of a window.

C–8–1   Control Menu Commands

Table C–2 summarizes the control menu commands. Some applications do not have all of these commands. For example, Figure C–11 does not include all the commands outlined in Table C–2.

C–9   WHAT IS THE PROGRAM MANAGER?

As soon as you start Windows you start the Program Manager. The Program Manager always runs during a Windows session. As you will see later in this appendix, a variety of tasks can be performed through the Program Manager. When you run other applications, the Program Manager runs either in the background or as an icon on your desktop.

When you first start Windows the Program Manager opens on your desktop with the Main group window open inside the Program Manager window (see Figure C–12). This may be different from your system, depending upon how Windows has been configured.

Table C–2
Control Menu Commands

Command	Function
Restore	Restores the window to its former size after you have enlarged it (by using the Maximize command) or reduced it to an icon (by using the Minimize command).
Move	Uses the keyboard to move a window to another location.
Size	Uses the keyboard to change the size of a window.
Minimize	Reduces a window to an icon.
Maximize	Enlarges a window to its maximum size.
Close	Closes a window or a dialog box. You can also use this command to quit an application from an application window.
Switch To	Opens the task list. This features enables you to switch between running applications. It also arranges windows and icons on your desktop.
Next	Switches you between open document windows and icons. This is available for document windows only.
Edit	Displays a cascading menu with additional commands.

Figure C–11
Control menu options.

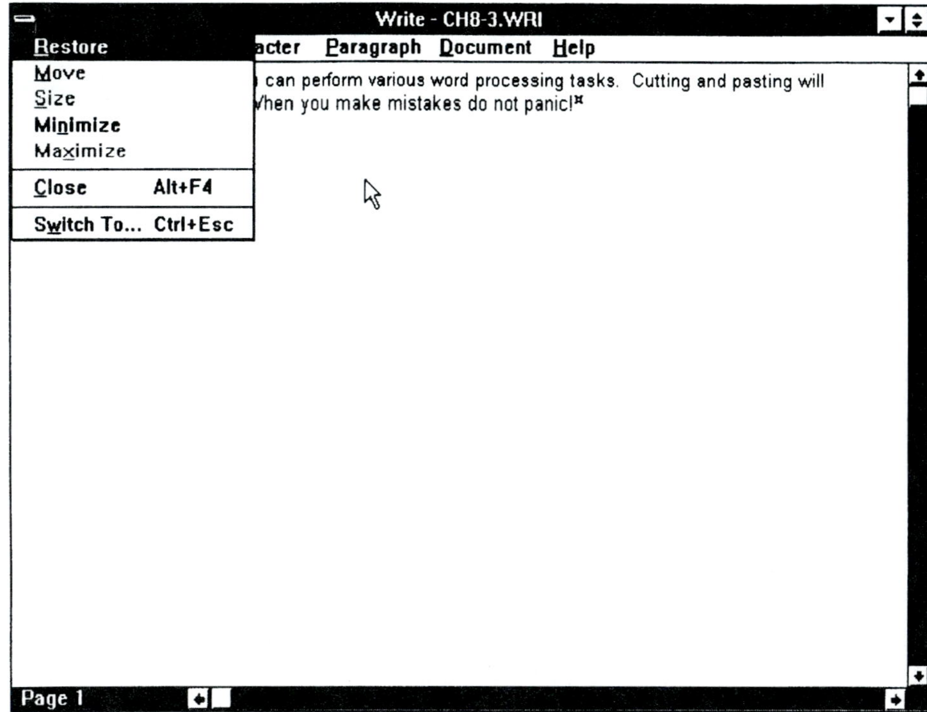

The Accessories group, the Games group, the StartUp group, and applications groups are represented as group icons along the lower border of the Program Manager window (see Figure C–12). Your screen might be slightly different from what is presented in Figure C–12.

Figure C–12
Program Manager window.

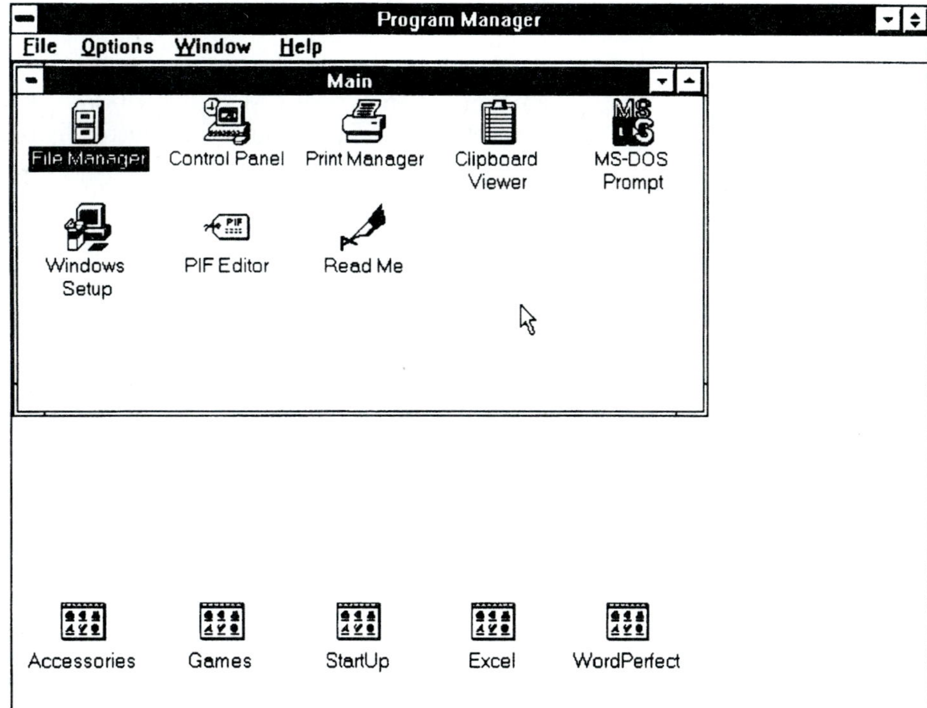

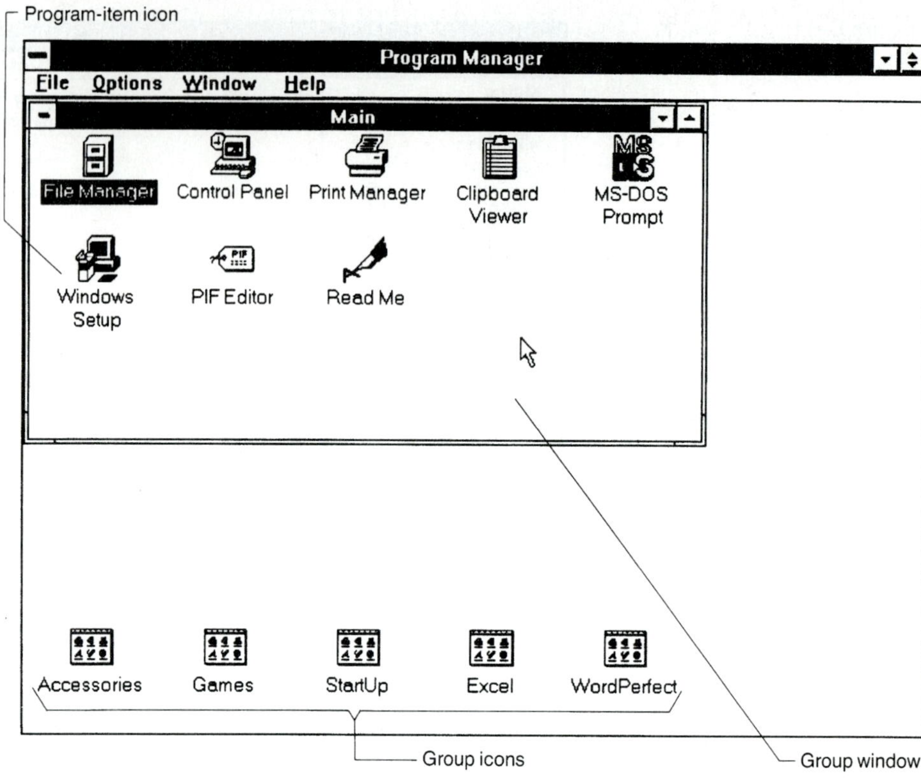

C–9–1

Different Parts of the Program Manager Window

Refer to Figure C–13 as you read the following descriptions of the different parts of the Program Manager window:

- Group window is a separate window inside the Program Manager window. As you can see in Figure C–13, this window includes icons that start different applications. Group windows are affected by the commands from the Program Manager menu bar: File, Options, Window, and Help.

- Program-item icons are displayed inside a group window and represent applications, documents, accessories, and so forth. You can select program item icons to start particular applications. For example, you can double-click the File Manager icon to start it.

- Group icon is a minimized group window. These icons are displayed in the lower border of the Program Manager window. Figure C–13 shows five of these icons.

C–9–2

Starting an Application from the Program Manager

Use the mouse and follow these steps to start an application:

1. Open the Program Manager Window (if it is not already open).
2. Open the group window (if it is not already open) that includes your desired application by double-clicking the group icon.
3. Double-click the icon for your desired application.

C–10   RUNNING TWO OR MORE APPLICATIONS AT THE SAME TIME

Windows allows you to run more than one application at one time. When you run multiple applications at the same time, the processing speed may be slower than normal. Processing speed also depends on the type of computer that you are using. To start several applications, start them in the desired sequence using the method that we just discussed.

C–11   SWITCHING BETWEEN APPLICATIONS

When you are running more than one application at a time, the window in which you are currently working is called the active window. The active window appears in the foreground. It might overlap or completely block other application windows that are also running on your system. To make another application active, you must select its window.

To switch between applications, you can choose one of the following methods:

1. If the application is visible, click the mouse anywhere in the application's window. If the application is running as an icon, click left on its icon, then click left on the Restore option.

2. Press Alt+Esc repeatedly to navigate through all the open application windows and icons. When you see the desired one, press Enter.

3. Display Task List by pressing the Ctrl+Esc keys. You will be presented with a screen similar to the one displayed in Figure C–14. In the Task List window, double-click the name of the desired application or highlight the name of the desired application and then select Switch To from the options available in the dialog box.

Figure C–14
Task List dialog box.

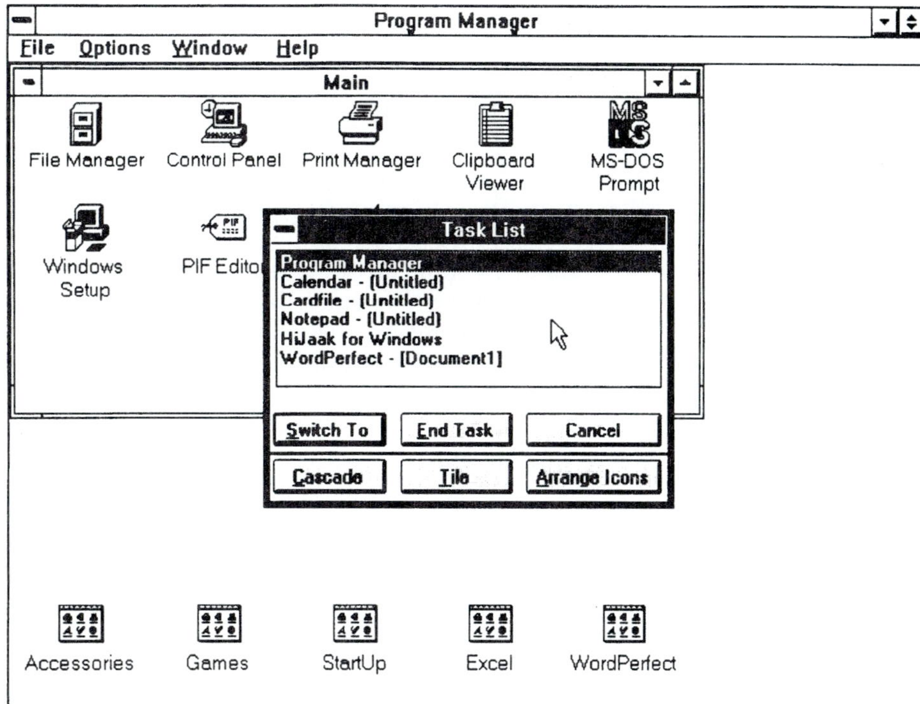

To return to the application that you last used, press Alt+Tab.

C–12   TRANSFERRING INFORMATION USING THE CLIPBOARD

The Windows Clipboard serves as a temporary location that stores information. Using the Clipboard, you can copy or move information from one application and then copy ("paste") it in another application. The information that you copy to the Clipboard stays there until you clear the contents of the Clipboard or copy other information to it.

The Clipboard can also serve as a buffer for exchanging information among several applications.

C–12–1   Moving or Copying Information to the Clipboard

How information is moved or copied to the Clipboard depends on the type of application that you are running—a Windows application or a non-Windows application. It also depends on whether your application is running as a window or a full screen.

A Windows application allows you to easily move or copy information to the Clipboard. You can also move or copy an image to the Clipboard. To copy or move information to the Clipboard, follow these steps:

1. Highlight or select the text or the information that you want to move or copy. (For highlighting text, see the next section.) You can copy or move text, graphics, or both.
2. From the application's Edit menu (e.g., the Edit menu of Lotus 1-2-3), select Cut or Copy. Cut removes the selected text from its current position to the Clipboard. Copy only takes a snapshot for the Clipboard; the existing information remains intact.

You can copy the contents of an entire screen to the Clipboard by displaying the information then pressing the Print Screen key or Shift+PrtSc or Alt+PrtSc. This process puts a snapshot (also called a bitmap) of the screen onto the Clipboard.

C–12–2   Selecting Text or Graphs

Editing commands can be performed on a block of text instead of on a single character. First you must select (highlight or block) the text. Then you can select various commands such as Cut, Copy, Bold, and so forth from the Edit menu of the application software.

To select text using the mouse, follow these steps:

1. Point to the first character of the desired text.
2. Drag the insertion point to the end of the desired text.
3. Release the mouse button.

To cancel the selection, click the mouse button again anywhere in the document. Some applications allow you to select a word by double-clicking it, a sentence by triple-clicking, an entire paragraph by quadruple-clicking, and so on.

To select a graph in the majority of Windows applications, you can click left on it.

C–12–3   ## Transferring Information from the Clipboard

To transfer the contents of the Clipboard to another application, follow these steps:

1. Start the desired application.
2. Position the insertion point at the place that you want the information from the Clipboard to appear.
3. From the Edit menu of the application (e.g., the Edit menu of Lotus 1-2-3), select Paste.

C–13   QUITTING AN APPLICATION

When you are done working with an application, you should exit from it. Use one of the following methods to exit a Windows application:

- Select Exit from the application's File menu.
- Select Close from the Control menu.
- Double-click the control-menu box.
- Press Alt+F4.

To quit a non-Windows application, select the application's Exit or Quit command.

C–14   WORKING WITH GROUPS

Figure C–15 shows groups containing program-item icons that represent applications, accessories, or documents. To start an application from a group, you have to select the application's icon. As you can see in Figure C–15, Windows includes several predefined groups as follows:

1. The Main group contains Windows system applications:
   - File Manager—manages your files and disk drives
   - Control Panel—allows you to change the configuration of your system
   - Print Manager—allows you to install and configure printers
   - Clipboard Viewer—allows you to view, edit, and save the contents of the Clipboard
   - MS-DOS Prompt—allows you to exit to the DOS prompt
   - Windows Setup—displays the system configuration
   - PIF Editor—is a tool for editing program information files
   - Read Me—includes basic information about Windows
2. The Accessories group includes several interesting applications such as word processing, drawing, painting, communications, and so forth.
3. The Games group includes several games that you can use for learning the basics of Windows or for fun.
4. The StartUp group contains applications that start when you start Windows. This group is empty until you add applications to it. You can add any application to the group.

Figure C–15
Example of groups.

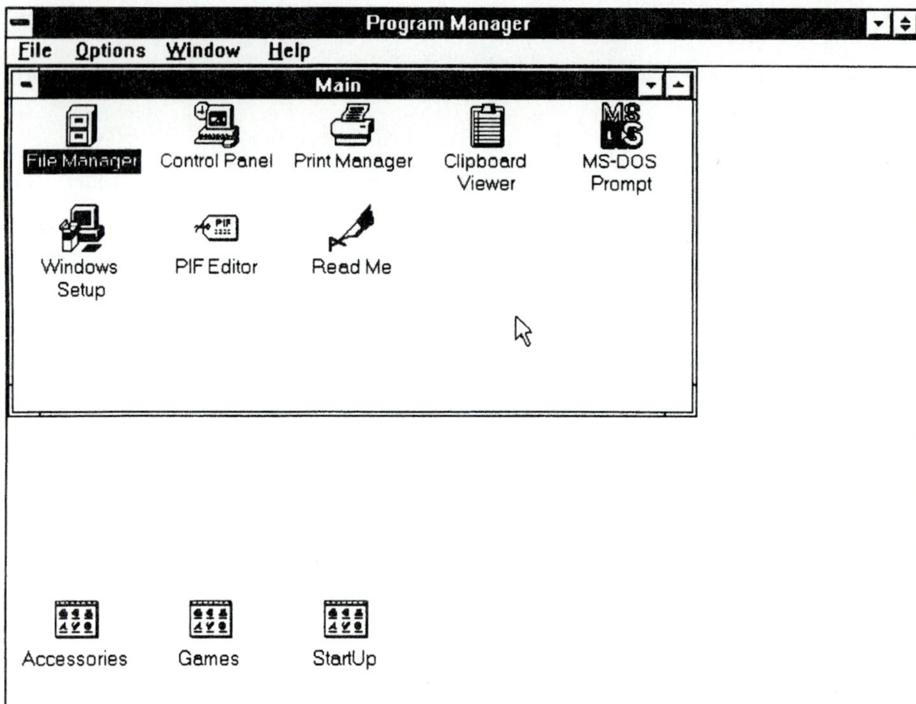

5. The Applications group contains applications found on the hard disk during setup. If you select the custom setup, and select not to have Windows set up applications from your hard disk, your Program Manager window will not contain an Applications group. This is the case in our example.

C–14–1   Opening a Group Window

To start an application you must first open its window then select the appropriate program-item icon. To open a group window double-click the group icon.

SUMMARY

This appendix provided an overview of Windows operating system. The advantages of Windows as a graphics-based environment were highlighted. After the process of getting in and getting out of Windows was explained, some of the basic features of Windows were discussed: using the mouse, selecting from the Windows screen, using the Program Manager, running an application, working with the Clipboard, and working with a group.

REVIEW QUESTIONS

1. What are some of the advantages of Windows?

2. How do you start Windows? How do you exit from it?

3. What is a desktop? What is an icon?

4. How do you use the mouse in Windows environment? How do you use the keyboard? Which one is easier to use?

5. How do you receive online help in Windows?

6. How do you get the tutorial facility of Windows started?

7. What is the control menu? How do you activate it?
8. What are some of the commands in the control menu?
9. What is the Program Manager?
10. How do you start an application from the Program Manager?
11. How can you run more than one application in Windows at the same time?
12. How do you switch between applications?
13. What is the Clipboard?
14. How do you transfer information from an application to the Clipboard?
15. How do you quit an application?
16. What is a group? How do you start a group?

Index